TRINITY CHRISTIAN SCHOOL
2170 Itabashi Way
Burlington ON L7M 5B3
T-905-634-3052 F-905-634-9382

D1532577

ADDISON WESLEY

Math
Makes Sense

3

Author Team

Peggy Morrow

Steve Thomas

Don Jones

Linden Gray

Sharon Jeroski

Trevor Brown

Ralph Connelly

Susan Gordon

Michael Davis

Ken Harper

Angie Harding

Maggie Martin Connell

Jeananne Thomas

PEARSON

Addison
Wesley

Publishing Team
Lesley Haynes
Enid Haley
Mei Lin Cheung
Lynne Gulliver
Marg Bukta
Susan Lishman
Kathleen ffolliott
Stephanie Cox
Denise Wake
Judy Wilson

Publisher
Claire Burnett

Product Manager
Anne-Marie Scullion

Photo Research
Karen Hunter

Design
Word & Image Design Studio Inc.

The information and activities presented in this
book have been carefully edited and reviewed.
However, the publisher shall not be liable for any
damages resulting, in whole or in part, from the
reader's use of this material.

Brand names that appear in photographs of
products in this textbook are intended to provide
students with a sense of the real-world applications
of mathematics and are in no way intended to
endorse specific products.

The publisher has taken every care to meet or
exceed industry specifications for the
manufacturing of textbooks. The spine and the
endpapers of this sewn book have been reinforced
with special fabric for extra binding strength. The
cover is a premium, polymer-reinforced material
designed to provide long life and withstand rugged
use. Mylar gloss lamination has been applied for
further durability.

PEARSON

Addison
Wesley

Program Consultants and Advisers

Program Consultants

Craig Featherstone
Maggie Martin Connell
Trevor Brown

Assessment Consultant
Sharon Jeroski

Elementary Mathematics Adviser
John A. Van de Walle

Program Advisers

Pearson Education thanks its Program Advisers, who helped shape the vision for *Addison Wesley Mathematics Makes Sense* through discussions and reviews of prototype materials and manuscript.

Anthony Azzopardi	Peggy Hill
Sandra Ball	Auriana Kowalchuk
Bob Belcher	Gordon Li
Judy Blake	Werner Liedtke
Steve Cairns	Jodi Mackie
Daryl Chichak	Lois Marchand
Lynda Colgan	Cathy Molinski
Marg Craig	Bill Nimigon
Ruth Dawson	Eileen Phillips
Jennifer Gardner	Evelyn Sawicki
Lorelei Gibeau	Leyton Schnellert
Florence Glanfield	Shannon Sharp
Pamela Hagen	Martha Stewart
Dennis Hamaguchi	Lynn Strangway
Angie Harding	Mignonne Wood

Program Reviewers

Field Testers

Pearson Education would like to thank the teachers and students who field-tested *Addison Wesley Math Makes Sense 3* prior to publication. Their feedback and constructive recommendations have been most valuable in helping us to develop a quality mathematics program.

Aboriginal Content Reviewers

Early Childhood and School Services Division,
Department of Education, Culture, and Employment
Government of Northwest Territories:

Steven Daniel, Coordinator, Mathematics, Science, and Secondary Education
Liz Fowler, Coordinator, Culture Based Education
Margaret Erasmus, Coordinator, Aboriginal Languages

Grade 3 Reviewers

Ray Appel
Abbotsford School District,
BC

Peggy Bredin
Durham District School Board #13,
ON

Donna Cox
Renfrew County District School
Board, ON

Cilla Dale
Nipissing-Parry Sound Catholic
District School Board, ON

Georgette Davis
Kawartha Pine Ridge District
School Board, ON

Linda Edwards
Toronto District School Board, ON

Bev Ferner
Moose Jaw School Division No. 1, SK

Maureen Jones
Toronto Catholic District
School Board, ON

Susan LeFebvre
School District 57 (Prince George),
BC

Ann LeSage
Nipissing University, ON

Maria Makuch
Ottawa-Carleton District School
Board, ON

Mona Massad
Windsor-Essex Catholic District
School Board, ON

Carolyn May
Algonquin & Lakeshore Catholic
District School Board, ON

Frank McComb
Rainy River District School Board,
ON

Suzanne Mole
Winnipeg School Division No. 1, MB

Jeanne Moy
New Westminster School District,
BC

Anne Muldoon
Upper Canada District School
Board, ON

Ann Nottingham
School District No. 40 (New
Westminster), BC

MaryAdelle Patterson
Durham Catholic District School
Board, ON

Cheryl Potvin
Ottawa-Carleton District School
Board, ON

Donna Preston
School District No. 57 (Prince
George), BC

Heather Richards
Halton District School Board, ON

Jennifer A. Robinson
Peel District School Board, ON

Walter Rogoza
Rainy River District School Board,
ON

Bonnie Roynon
Near North District School Board, ON

Shannon Sharp
School District No. 44 (North
Vancouver), BC

David Sobolewski
Edmonton Public School Board, AB

Gay Sul
Frontier School Division, MB

Andrea Thio
Winnipeg School Division No. 1, MB

Wendy Wignal
School District No. 63 (Saanich), BC

Vicky Wingate
Rainbow District School Board, ON

Lynne Michelle Wright
Sudbury Catholic District School
Board, ON

Table of Contents

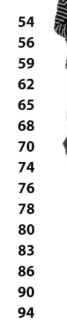

Geometry

Multiplication and Division

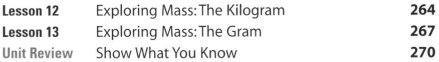

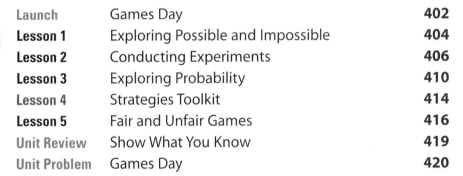

Welcome to
Addison Wesley Math Makes Sense 3

Math helps you understand what you see and do every day.

You will use this book to learn about the math around you. Here's how.

In each Unit:

- A scene from the world around you reminds you of some of the math you already know.

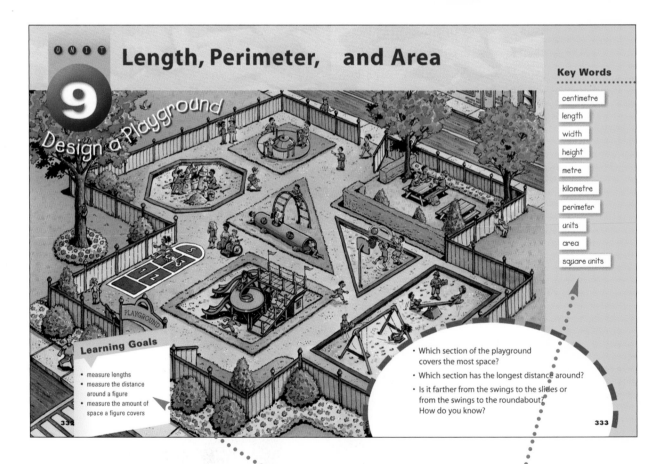

UNIT 9
Design a Playground

Length, Perimeter, and Area

Key Words

- centimetre
- length
- width
- height
- metre
- kilometre
- perimeter
- units
- area
- square units

Learning Goals

- measure lengths
- measure the distance around a figure
- measure the amount of space a figure covers

- Which section of the playground covers the most space?
- Which section has the longest distance around?
- Is it farther from the swings to the slides or from the swings to the roundabout? How do you know?

332

333

Find out what you will learn in the **Learning Goals** and important **Key Words**.

In each Lesson:

You **Explore** an idea or problem, usually with a partner. You often use materials.

Then you **Show and Share** your results with other students.

Practice questions help you to use and remember the math.

reminds you to use pictures, words, or numbers in your answers.

LESSON

8

Using Mental Math to Subtract

Explore

There were 43 people skating.
Twenty-seven people left to get hot chocolate.
How many people were still skating?

Use mental math to find out.

Show and Share

Show how you used mental math to solve the problem.

Connect

There were 52 frogs in a pond.
Twenty-four frogs hopped away.
How many frogs were still in the pond?

Here are some mental math strategies to find 52 − 24.

➤ Take away tens, then take away ones.
  Think: 52 − 20 = 32
  Count back: 32 − 4 = 28

➤ Add to match the ones, then subtract.
  Think: Add 2 to 52 to make 54.
  54 − 24 = 30
  Take away the 2 you added.
  30 − 2 = 28

There were 28 frogs still in the pond.

2-digit numbers.

Numbers Every Day

Mental Math
Add.

8 + 20 = ☐
5 + 40 = ☐
6 + 30 = ☐
2 + 50 = ☐
7 + 60 = ☐

Practice

Use mental math.

1. Subtract. Record each list of facts.
   a) 59 − 10   b) 67 − 10   c) 88 − 10
      59 − 20   77 − 10   78 − 20
      59 − 30   87 − 10   68 − 30
      59 − 40   97 − 10   58 − 40
   Look at each list of facts. What patterns do you see?

2. Subtract. What patterns do you see?
   a) 63 − 41   b) 79 − 31   c) 83 − 21   d) 93 − 11

3. Subtract.
   a)   60   b)   50   c)   40   d)   30
      − 28   − 28   − 28   − 28

4. Subtract.
   a)   74   b)   92   c)   67   d)   85
      − 56   − 18   − 38   − 47

5. How many different ways can you find 81 − 58?
   Use words, pictures, or numbers to show each way.

6. There were 32 geese on a beach.
   More geese flew in, and then there were 61 geese.
   How many geese flew in?

7. The answer is 43.
   What could the subtraction problem be?
   Show your work.

Reflect

Explain how you can use mental math to subtract.

ASSESSMENT FOCUS Question 8   77

Connect summarizes the math.

Stay sharp with **Numbers Every Day**.

Think about the big ideas of the lesson in **Reflect**.

- Learn about strategies to help you solve problems in each **Strategies Toolkit** lesson.

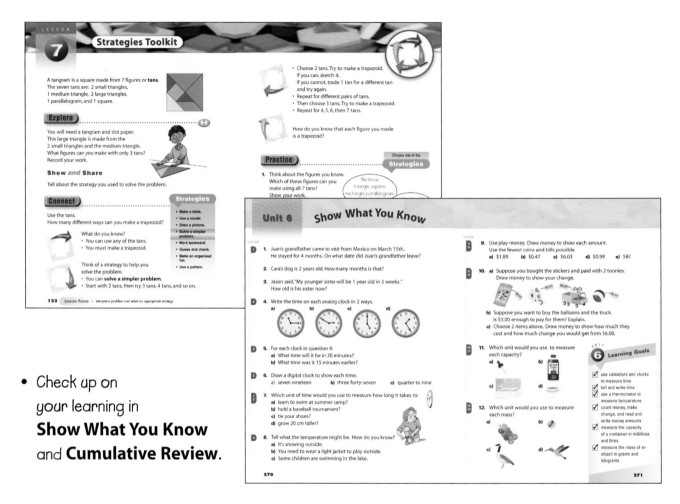

- Check up on your learning in **Show What You Know** and **Cumulative Review**.

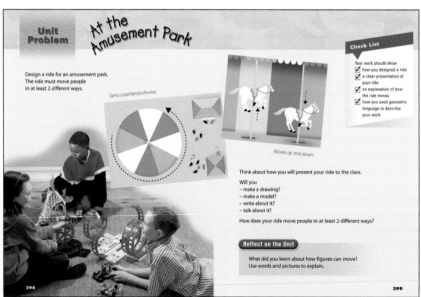

- The **Unit Problem** returns to the opening scene. It presents a problem to solve or a project to do using the math of the unit.

Explore some interesting math when you do the **Investigations**.

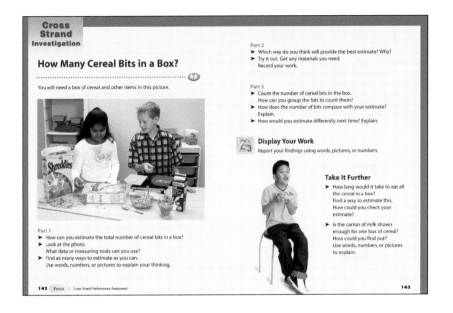

Use **Technology**.
Follow the step-by-step instructions for using a calculator or computer to do math.

Look for and  .

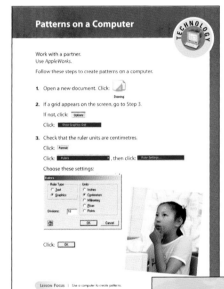

The **Glossary** is an illustrated dictionary of important math words.

Figure It Out!

You will need 12 Colour Tiles and 1-cm grid paper.

This rectangle is made of 12 tiles.

It has 4 rows of 3 tiles.

Part 1

➤ Make a rectangle using all 12 tiles.
Copy the rectangle on grid paper.
Use numbers and words to tell about your rectangle.

➤ Use the tiles to make as many different rectangles as you can.
Did you find all of them? How do you know?

➤ Copy each rectangle. Tell about it in numbers and words.
How are the rectangles the same? Different?
How can you describe a rectangle by the number of rows
and the number of tiles in each row?

Part 2

➤ Find the area of each rectangle.
What ways can you count the units?

➤ Estimate the perimeter of each rectangle.
Then find the perimeter.
How does your estimate compare with the actual perimeter?

➤ Record your results in a table.

Rectangle	Area	Perimeter Estimate	Perimeter
1	12 units	12 units	14 units
2			

➤ What do you notice about the areas of the rectangles?
Their perimeters? What patterns do you see in the table?

Display Your Work

Report your findings using words, pictures, or numbers.

Take It Further

➤ Arrange the rectangles in order from greatest perimeter to least.
➤ Look at the rectangle in the photo. It has a hole. How many different rectangles with holes can you make with 12 tiles?
Copy each rectangle on grid paper.
➤ Use the tiles to make other figures. Copy each figure on grid paper.

UNIT

1 Patterning and

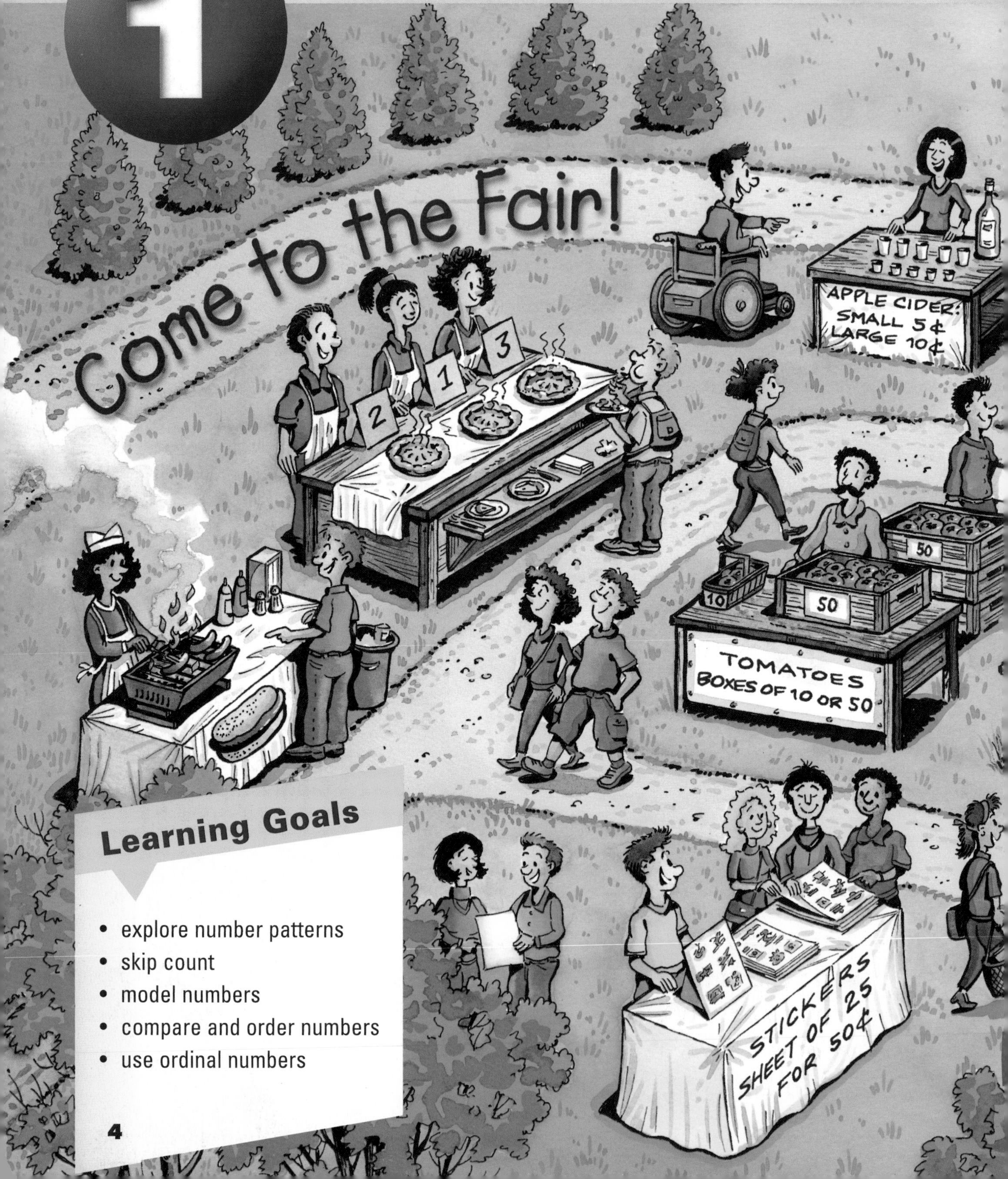
Come to the Fair!
2
1
3
APPLE CIDER:
SMALL 5¢
LARGE 10¢
50
10
50
TOMATOES
BOXES OF 10 OR 50
STICKERS
SHEET OF 25
FOR 50¢

Learning Goals

- explore number patterns
- skip count
- model numbers
- compare and order numbers
- use ordinal numbers

Place Value

Inside the picture:

GUESS HOW MANY APPLES WIN A PRIZE!

LUCY	50
KENT	59
JOSE	35
CHERYL	42
MARIKA	45

IT TAKES 40 JUGS OF SAP TO MAKE 1 JUG OF MAPLE SYRUP

Key Words

diagonal

tens digit

ones digit

Base Ten Blocks

place value

base-ten name

ordinal number

hundred

compare

order

standard form

thousand

round

You'll find colourful sights, interesting smells, and tasty foods at the fair.

Look at the picture.

- How many tomatoes are in one box?
- How do you know which pie won first prize?
- How many cups of cider could you buy for 10¢?
- What other questions could you ask about the picture?

Patterns in a Hundred Chart

At the fair, Kent guessed there were 59 apples in the basket.

59 means 5 tens and 9 ones.

the **tens digit**   the **ones digit**

You will need a copy of this hundred chart.
Find as many different patterns as you can in this hundred chart.
Record the patterns you find.

1	2	3	4	5	6	7	8	9	10
11	12	13	14	15	16	17	18	19	20
21	22	23	24	25	26	27	28	29	30
31	32	33	34	35	36	37	38	39	40
41	42	43	44	45	46	47	48	49	50
51	52	53	54	55	56	57	58	59	60
61	62	63	64	65	66	67	68	69	70
71	72	73	74	75	76	77	78	79	80
81	82	83	84	85	86	87	88	89	90
91	92	93	94	95	96	97	98	99	100

Show and Share

Share a strategy to find a pattern.
Did you look along
- rows?
- columns?
- diagonals?

Find a **diagonal** where the digits in each number add to 5. To 6. What do you notice?

row →

1	2	3	4	5	6	7	8	9	10
11	12	13	14	15	16	17	18	19	20
21	22	23	24	25	26	27	28	29	30
31	32	33	34	35	36	37	38	39	40
41	42	43	44	45	46	47	48	49	50
51	52	53	54	55	56	57	58	59	60
61	62	63	64	65	66	67	68	69	70
71	72	73	74	75	76	77	78	79	80
81	82	83	84	85	86	87	88	89	90
91	92	93	94	95	96	97	98	99	100

← diagonal

↑
column

Connect

Here are some of the patterns in a hundred chart.

- In any row, the numbers increase by 1.
  They are the counting numbers.

71	72	73	74	75	76	77	78	79	80

2
12
22
32
42
52
62
72
82
92

- In any column, the numbers increase by 10.
  The ones digits are the same and the
  tens digits increase by 1.

Look at the first 9 columns.

- In any diagonal that goes down to the left,
  the digits add to the same number.
  The tens digit increases by 1 and the
  ones digit decreases by 1.

- In any diagonal that goes down to the right,
  the tens digit increases by 1 and the
  ones digit increases by 1.

1	2	3	4	5	6	7	8	9	10
11	12	13	14	15	16	17	18	19	20
21	22	23	24	25	26	27	28	29	30
31	32	33	34	35	36	37	38	39	40
41	42	43	44	45	46	47	48	49	50
51	52	53	54	55	56	57	58	59	60
61	62	63	64	65	66	67	68	69	70
71	72	73	74	75	76	77	78	79	80
81	82	83	84	85	86	87	88	89	90
91	92	93	94	95	96	97	98	99	100

Practice

Use hundred charts.

1. a) Colour all the even numbers.
       Where are they?
    b) Use a different colour.
       Colour all the odd numbers.
       Where are they?

2. Colour the diagonal where the
    ones digit and the tens digit
    are the same in each number.

Numbers Every Day

Number Strategies

Use the doubles fact $4 + 4 = 8$
to find each sum.

$4 + 5 = \square$

$4 + 6 = \square$

$4 + 3 = \square$

$4 + 2 = \square$

3. How can you find the diagonal where the digits in each number add to 8? Colour it.

4. Choose any diagonal that goes down to the right.
Add the digits in each number.
What pattern do you see?
Check another diagonal.
Is the pattern the same? Different? Explain.

5. Colour all the numbers where the digits add to 7.
Where are these numbers?

6. Count on by 2s.
Press ②, press ⊕, then press ⊜ several times.
Record the results.
Do you see a pattern?
How is it the same as a pattern on the hundred chart?
Explain.

7. Choose a square of 4 numbers on the hundred chart.
Add the numbers in each diagonal.
What do you notice?
Repeat for other squares of 4 numbers.
Explain what you find out.

36	37
46	47

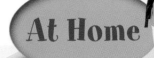

At Home

Reflect

Which pattern on the hundred chart is the most interesting?
Use pictures, words, or numbers to explain.

What number patterns can you find around your home?

Counting on a Hundred Chart

You can use patterns on a hundred chart to count.

1	2	3	4	5	6	7	8	9	10
11	12	13	14	15	16	17	18	19	20

2, 4, 6, 8, ...

How do you count on by 2s starting at 2?
How do you count on by 2s starting at 1?
How do you count back by 2s? Where could you start?

Explore

You will need a copy of this hundred chart.
How can you use this chart to count
by 10s? By 5s?
Try different starting numbers.
Try counting on, then counting back.

What patterns do you see?
Record your work.

1	2	3	4	5	6	7	8	9	10
11	12	13	14	15	16	17	18	19	20
21	22	23	24	25	26	27	28	29	30
31	32	33	34	35	36	37	38	39	40
41	42	43	44	45	46	47	48	49	50
51	52	53	54	55	56	57	58	59	60
61	62	63	64	65	66	67	68	69	70
71	72	73	74	75	76	77	78	79	80
81	82	83	84	85	86	87	88	89	90
91	92	93	94	95	96	97	98	99	100

Show and Share

Show a classmate one pattern you found.

1	2	3	4	5	6	7	8	9	10
11	12	13	14	15	16	17	18	19	20
21	22	23	24	25	26	27	28	29	30

Describe the pattern.

Counting on by 5s:
5, 10, 15, 20, 25, 30, 35

➤ To count on by 5s, start anywhere.

21	22	23	24	25	26	27	28	29	30
31	32	33	34	35	36	37	38	39	40
41	42	43	44	45	46	47	48	49	50

Start at 22.
Count on: 22, 27, 32, 37, 42, 47, …
Note the pattern in the ones digits: 2, 7, 2, 7, 2, 7, …

➤ To count back by 5s, start with a number ending in 5 or 0.

71	72	73	74	75	76	77	78	79	80
81	82	83	84	85	86	87	88	89	90
91	92	93	94	95	96	97	98	99	100

Start at 100.
Count back: 100, 95, 90, 85, 80, 75, …
Note the pattern in the ones digits: 0, 5, 0, 5, 0, 5, …

➤ To count on by 10s, start anywhere.

➤ To count back by 10s, start anywhere.

1	2	3	4	5	6	7	8	9	10
11	12	13	14	15	16	17	18	19	20
21	22	23	24	25	26	27	28	29	30
31	32	33	34	35	36	37	38	39	40
41	42	43	44	45	46	47	48	49	50
51	52	53	54	55	56	57	58	59	60
61	62	63	64	65	66	67	68	69	70
71	72	73	74	75	76	77	78	79	80
81	82	83	84	85	86	87	88	89	90
91	92	93	94	95	96	97	98	99	100

Start

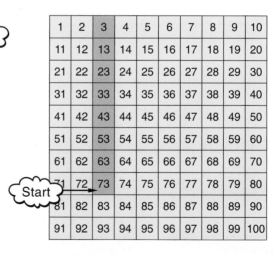

Start

Start at 8.
Count on: 8, 18, 28, 38, 48, …
Note the ones digit repeats.
The tens digit increases by 1.

Start at 73.
Count back: 73, 63, 53, 43, 33, …
Note the ones digit repeats.
The tens digit decreases by 1.

Use a hundred chart.

1. Start at 12. Count on by 2s to 26. Describe the pattern.

2. Start at 23. Count on by 5s to 53. Describe the pattern.

3. Start at 36. Count on by 10s to 96. Describe the pattern.

4. Start at 31. Count back by 2s to 17. Describe the pattern.

5. Start at 95. Count back by 5s to 55. Describe the pattern.

6. Start at 82. Count back by 10s to 22. Describe the pattern.

7. Colour a pattern on the chart.
Write the numbers you have coloured.
What pattern do you see in these numbers?

8. Start anywhere. Count on by 5s.
Put a red counter on each number you count.
Start at the same number. Count on by 10s.
Put a blue counter on each number you count.
What do you notice? Why does this happen?

9. When you count by 2s,
will you say even numbers?
Odd numbers? Both even and
odd numbers in the same count?
Explain.

Numbers Every Day

Number Strategies
Find each sum by counting
on 1, 2, or 3.

$5 + 3 = \square$

$8 + 2 = \square$

$3 + 6 = \square$

$1 + 8 = \square$

Reflect

When you start at 25 and count on by 5s,
will you say 44? 65? 71? How do you know?

LESSON

Counting on a Number Line

You can use a number line to count.

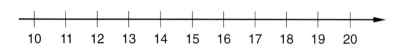
| | | | | | | | | | | |
10 11 12 13 14 15 16 17 18 19 20

10, 12, 14, 16, ...

Start at 10. Count on by 2s.
How can you show this count on the number line?

Count back by 2s. Where can you start?
How can you show this count on the number line?

Explore

You will need copies of this number line.

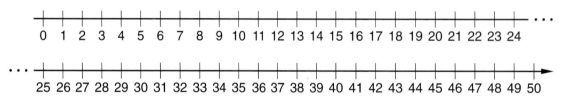
0 1 2 3 4 5 6 7 8 9 10 11 12 13 14 15 16 17 18 19 20 21 22 23 24 ...

... 25 26 27 28 29 30 31 32 33 34 35 36 37 38 39 40 41 42 43 44 45 46 47 48 49 50

Try different starting numbers.

Count on: by 2s   Count back: by 2s
         by 5s   by 5s
         by 10s   by 10s

Record how you count.

Show *and* Share

Trade number lines with a classmate.
Check each other's work.
Share the patterns you see.

Numbers Every Day

Number Strategies
Find each difference by
counting on or counting back.

5 − 2 = ☐

9 − 6 = ☐

7 − 3 = ☐

10 − 7 = ☐

12   LESSON FOCUS | Explore patterns in counting.

➤ To count on by 5s, start anywhere.

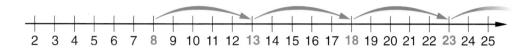

Start at 8.

Count on: 8, 13, 18, 23, ...

Note the pattern in the ones digits: 8, 3, 8, 3, ...

So, the number before 8 in the pattern is 3.

The numbers after 23 in the pattern are 28, 33, 38, 43, ...

➤ To count back by 10s, start anywhere.

Start at 66.

Count back: 66, 56, 46, 36, 26, ...

Note the pattern in the ones digits: 6, 6, 6, 6, 6, ...

Practice

1. Use a copy of this number line.
   a) Start at 31. Count on by 2s.
   What is the pattern?

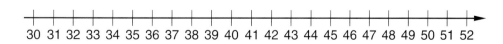

   b) Start at 50. Count back by 2s.
   What is the pattern?

2. Use a number line from 50 to 100.

    a) Start at 64. Count on by 5s. What is the pattern?

    b) Start at 99. Count back by 5s. What is the pattern?

3. Use a number line from 1 to 100.

    a) Start at 13. Count on by 10s. What is the pattern?

    b) Start at 86. Count back by 10s. What is the pattern?
       Find this pattern on the hundred chart.

For exercises 4 and 5, use a number line or a hundred chart when it helps.

4. Copy each pattern.
    Fill in the missing numbers.
    What are you counting by each time?

    a) 65, 60, 55, □, □, □   **b)** 51, 46, 41, □, □, □

    c) 60, 50, 40, □, □, □   **d)** 48, 46, 44, □, □, □

5. Copy each pattern.
    Write what comes before and after.
    How do you know?

    a) □, 24, 34, 44, □   **b)** □, 17, 19, 21, □

    c) □, 88, 86, 84, □   **d)** □, 37, 32, 27, □

6. Raisa started at 10 on a number line and counted on.
    She stopped at 50.
    What might her number pattern be?
    Is there more than one pattern?
    Show your work.

29?

Reflect

How can you use a number line to count on and count back?
Use words, pictures, or numbers to explain.

Comparing Numbers on a Number Line

You will need a copy of these number lines.
List 3 more numbers you can show on each number line.

1.

0   10   20   30   40   50   60   70   80   90   100

2.

40   45   50   55   60   65

3.

61   70   80   88

4.

50   100

Show and Share

Trade number lines with a classmate.
Draw dots on each number line to show
where your classmate's numbers go.
Write the numbers under the dots.
Check each other's work.
Explain how you placed each number.

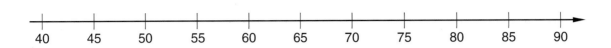
$$\begin{array}{cccccccccccc} | & | & | & | & | & | & | & | & | & | & | \rightarrow \\ 40 & 45 & 50 & 55 & 60 & 65 & 70 & 75 & 80 & 85 & 90 \end{array}$$

To place 53 on this number line:

Think: 53 is between 50 and 55.

53 is closer to 55 than to 50.

Estimate.

Mark a dot between 50 and 55, closer to 55.

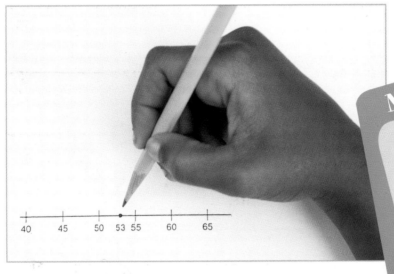

Numbers Every Day

Mental Math

Find each sum or difference.
Explain your thinking.

$3 + 5 = \square$

$1 + 9 = \square$

$8 - 2 = \square$

$6 - 3 = \square$

Practice

Use a copy of each number line.

1. Draw a dot on the number line for each number.
   Label the dot with the number.
   a) 44, 48, 56, 61

   b) 73, 78, 87, 91

2. a) Draw a dot on the number line for each number: 77, 64, 68, 73
Label the dot with the number.

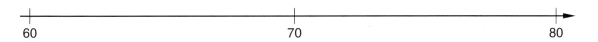

b) Which number is closest to 70?
c) Choose a number between 64 and 77.
Show it on the number line.
d) Name a number less than all the numbers in part a.

3. Estimate the number for each letter.

a)

b)

c)

4. Estimate what number the dot represents.
Explain how you know.

5. Where should 49 go on this number line?
Use numbers, words, or pictures to show your thinking.

Reflect

When you write a number on a number line,
how do you decide where it goes?
Use words, pictures, or numbers to explain.

Grouping and Counting to 100

At a school fair, there is a game to estimate
how many beads are in a jar.
At the end of fair, the beads are counted.

To count objects, you can group them into sets.

Explore

Choose a set of items.
Estimate how many items are in the set.
Group the items, then count them.
Record your work.

Show **and** Share

Show another pair of classmates
how many items are in your set.
Tell how you estimated
the number of items.
Explain how grouping helped
you count the items.

|||| |||| |||| I counted by 5s.
|||| |||| |||| 12 groups of 5
|||| |||| |||| and 4 left over.
|||| |||| |||| I counted 64.
||||

Connect

Here is one way to count a collection of beans.
Toma has 10 beans in her hand.

She estimates:
8 groups of 10 beans could be on the table.
8 tens make 80.
Toma groups the beans to check her estimate.

She counts:

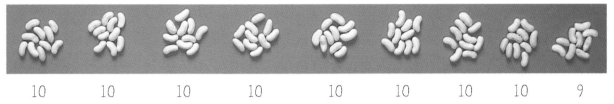

| 10 | 10 | 10 | 10 | 10 | 10 | 10 | 10 | 9 |

There are 8 groups of 10 beans and 9 leftover beans.
8 tens and 9 more make 89.
So, there are 89 beans.
Grouping in tens makes it easier to count.

Practice

1. Estimate how many buttons there are.

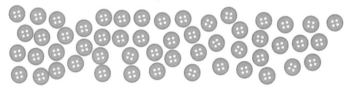

2. How many 5s are there? How many ones?
   How many pencils are there altogether?

   a)

   b)

Numbers Every Day

Calculator Skills

To start at 1 and skip count by 2s, press ⟨1⟩ ⟨+⟩ ⟨2⟩.
Then keep pressing ⟨=⟩.

Start at 2 and count by 5s.

Start at 5 and count by 2s.

What patterns do you see?

3. How many 10s are there? How many ones?
How many seeds are there altogether?

a)

b)

c)

d)

4. Suppose the seeds in question 3c and d were put in a box.
How many seeds would there be?

5. How many ones make up 10? How many tens make up 100?
Use numbers, pictures, or words to show
your thinking.

6. Selma had 67 hockey cards.
On her birthday, she got 14 more.
Use counters or cubes to show
how many hockey cards Selma has now.
Draw pictures to show your work.

7. Peter had 18 stickers.
He got 6 more packs of 10 stickers.
How many stickers does Peter have now?
How do you know?

Math Link

History

Around 1900 BCE, the
Babylonians counted by
60s because there are
60 minutes in 1 hour.

Around 700 CE, the
Hindus in India were
counting by 10s and
using the numerals we
use today.

Reflect

How can you use grouping to count objects?
Use words, pictures, or numbers to explain.

Modelling 2-Digit Numbers

Grace chose 47 on a hundred chart.

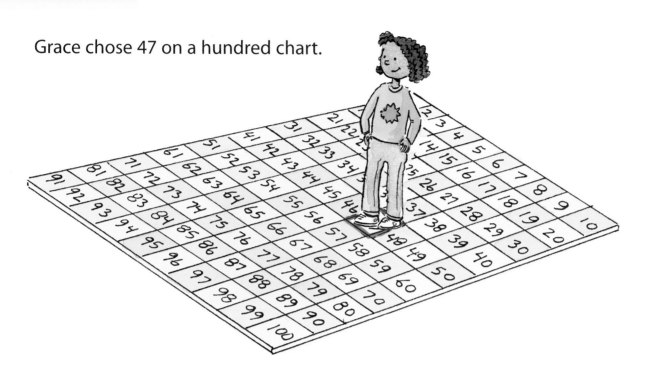

You can use **Base Ten Blocks** to model 47.

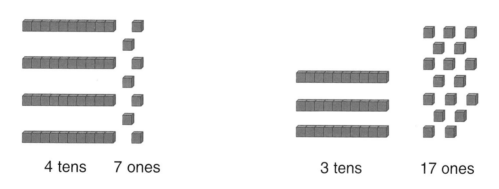

4 tens   7 ones   3 tens   17 ones

4 tens and 7 ones = 47
3 tens and 17 ones = 47

Base Ten Blocks

10   1

What other ways can you model 47?

You will need Base Ten Blocks
and a hundred chart.

➤ Choose a secret number
on the chart.
Model it with Base Ten Blocks.
Record your work.

➤ Have your partner tell
what the number is, then find it
on the hundred chart.
Have your partner model the
same number a different way.

➤ Switch roles.
Repeat this activity 5 times.

Show *and* Share

Share some models with another pair of classmates.

Connect ·

Here are some different ways to model 34.

➤ 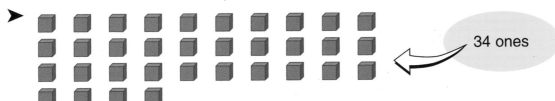 34 ones

➤ 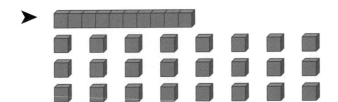 1 ten 24 ones

➤ 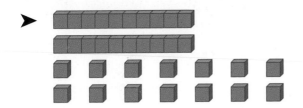 2 tens 14 ones

➤ 3 tens 4 ones

When the model has no more than 9 ones,
you can write the number on a place-value chart.

Place value helps us to understand numbers.
The *value* of each digit in a number
depends on its *place* in the number.

Tens	Ones
3	4

The value of this digit is 3 tens or 30.

The value of this digit is 4 ones or 4.

This is a place-value chart.

The **base-ten name** is 3 tens 4 ones.
In words: thirty-four

Practice

Use Base Ten Blocks when they help.

1. Write each number.

a)

b)

c)

d)

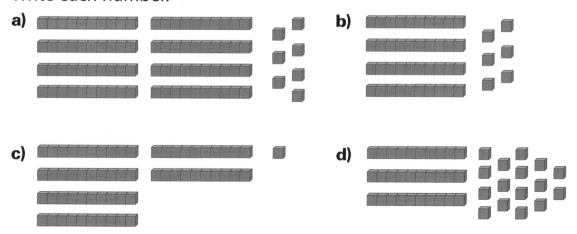

2. Draw a picture of Base Ten Blocks
to show each number.
   a) 14   **b)** 53
   c) 78   **d)** 95

3. Write each number in question 2
in words.

4. Write the base-ten name
for each number.
   a) 59   **b)** 41
   c) 23   **d)** 38
   e) 70   **f)** 96

Numbers Every Day

Mental Math

In each pair, which sum
is greater?

How can you tell
without adding?

5 + 5	or	5 + 4
3 + 3	or	4 + 4
6 + 1	or	5 + 2
3 + 0	or	4 + 0

5. Use a hundred chart.
   Choose a diagonal that goes up to the right.
   Model each number in it using the fewest blocks.
   How do the blocks change from one number to the next?
   What pattern do you see?
   Show your work.

6. Write each number as digits.
   a) sixty-four   **b)** seventy-five   **c)** fifty-three
   d) eighty   **e)** eighteen   **f)** two

7. Give the value of each underlined digit.
   a) 4<u>8</u>   **b)** <u>7</u>1   **c)** 1<u>0</u>
   d) <u>8</u>2   **e)** <u>3</u>9   **f)** 2<u>6</u>

Reflect

How can you tell the value of each digit in 99?
Use words, pictures, or numbers to explain.

Ordinal Numbers

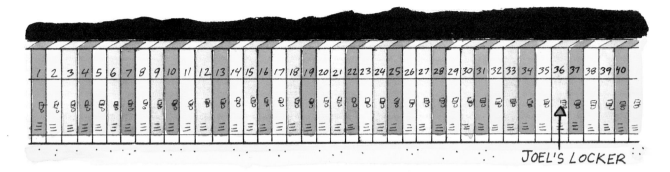

JOEL'S LOCKER

Joel's locker is the 36th locker in this hallway.
What colour is the 32nd locker?
The 21st locker? The 33rd locker?

Numbers like 36th, 32nd, 21st, and 33rd
are **ordinal numbers**.

Some Ordinal Numbers	
first:	1st
second:	2nd
third:	3rd
fourth:	4th
fifth:	5th
twelfth:	12th
twentieth:	20th
fifty-third:	53rd
eighty-first:	81st
one-hundredth:	100th

Use a hundred chart.

1. Which is:
   a) the 42nd odd number?
   b) the 19th number with a 2 in it?
   c) the 50th even number?

2. Which comes first:
   the 17th number with a 2 in it or
   the 9th number when you count by 10s?

3. Make up your own question using
   ordinal numbers on the hundred chart.

1	2	3	4	5	6	7	8	9	10
11	12	13	14	15	16	17	18	19	20
21	22	23	24	25	26	27	28	29	30
31	32	33	34	35	36	37	38	39	40
41	42	43	44	45	46	47	48	49	50
51	52	53	54	55	56	57	58	59	60
61	62	63	64	65	66	67	68	69	70
71	72	73	74	75	76	77	78	79	80
81	82	83	84	85	86	87	88	89	90
91	92	93	94	95	96	97	98	99	100

Show *and* Share

Trade problems with a classmate.
Solve your classmate's problem.
Compare your answers to all the questions on page 25.

To find the ordinal number of an item:
- Start at 1.
- Count until you reach the item.
- Name the ordinal that goes with the last number of your count.

To find the ordinal number of the person in the blue shirt:
Start at the left. Count: 1, 2, 3, 4, 5, 6, 7, 8, 9

The runner in the blue shirt is 9th.

Practice

1. Name each letter of the alphabet.
   a) the 14th letter b) the 23rd letter
   c) the 26th letter d) the 7th letter

Numbers Every Day

Calculator Skills

Count by 10s from 3 to 83.

Count by 9s from 3 to 75.

What patterns do you see?

26

2. Name each month of the year.
- **a)** the third month
- **b)** the ninth month
- **c)** the twelfth month
- **d)** the sixth month

For questions 3 and 4, use a hundred chart.

3. a) What is the 19th odd number?
- **b)** What is the 19th number with a 2 in it?
- **c)** What is the 37th even number?

4. a) Which comes first: the 10th number with a 1 in it or the 15th number when you count by 5s?
- **b)** Which comes second: the 32nd even number or the 8th number ending in a 4?

5. Suppose the first day of the year is a Friday. What day of the week will the 8th day be? The 23rd? The 44th? The 65th? Show your work.

Reflect

How do you find the ordinal number of an item?
Use words, pictures, or numbers to explain.

At Home

After you get up in the morning, what are the first 10 things you do? Make a list and write each ordinal number.

8

Modelling 3-Digit Numbers

Rajit has 178 stickers on two pages of his sticker book.

You can use Base Ten Blocks
to model this number:

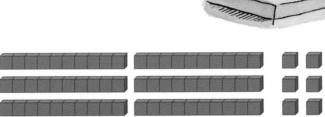

You can extend the
place-value chart to
show this number.

Hundreds	Tens	Ones
1	7	8

You will need Base Ten Blocks and a place-value chart.
➤ Choose a secret number between 100 and 1000.
Model it with Base Ten Blocks.

➤ Have your partner tell what the number is,
and write it in a place-value chart.

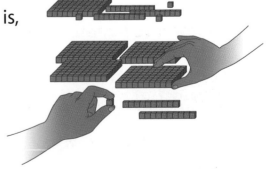

➤ Switch roles.
Repeat this activity 5 times.

Show and Share

Tell your partner how you knew
what to write in the place-value chart.

Connect

Our number system is based on groups of 10.

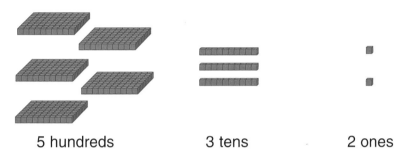		
100 **one hundred** 1 hundred = 10 tens	10 ten 1 ten = 10 ones	1 one

Here is one way to model 532.

5 hundreds	3 tens	2 ones

Hundreds	Tens	Ones
5	3	2

The value of this digit is 5 hundreds, or 500.

The value of this digit is 3 tens, or 30.

The value of this digit is 2 ones, or 2.

The base-ten name is 5 hundreds 3 tens 2 ones.
In words: five hundred thirty-two

Practice

1. Write each base-ten name, then the number.

   a)

   b)

2. Draw a picture to show each number.
   a) 417   **b)** 540   **c)** 966   **d)** 795   **e)** 128   **f)** 702

3. Write the base-ten name for each number.
   a) 582   **b)** 414   **c)** 690   **d)** 308   **e)** 500   **f)** 987

4. Write the number for each base-ten name.
   a) 9 hundreds 6 tens 2 ones
   b) 7 hundreds 8 tens
   c) 5 hundreds 7 ones
   d) 8 hundreds 8 tens 8 ones

5. Give the value of each underlined digit.
   a) 8<u>5</u>4   **b)** <u>7</u>15   **c)** 10<u>9</u>   **d)** <u>5</u>26
   e) 7<u>0</u>8   **f)** 33<u>9</u>   **g)** 35<u>0</u>   **h)** 6<u>8</u>8

6. a) How many ones make 1 ten?
   b) How many tens make 1 hundred?
   c) How many hundreds make 1000?
   d) What pattern do you see?
   e) How many thousands make 10 000?
   Show your work.

7. Draw Base Ten Blocks to show each answer.
   a) Which number is 10 more than 356?
   b) Which number is 3 less than 148?
   c) Which number is 200 more than 203?

Reflect

How does the value of each digit in 747
depend on its place in the number?
Use words, pictures, or numbers to explain.

Numbers Every Day

Number Strategies

Complete each statement.
8 is:
- 1 more than ☐
- 1 less than ☐
- 5 and ☐ more
- ☐ less than 10
- double ☐

Extending Hundred Chart Patterns

. . . .

You will need copies of these charts.

101	102	103	104	105	106	107	108	109	110
111	112	113	114	115	116	117	118	119	120
121	122	123	124	125	126	127	128	129	130
131	132	133	134	135	136	137	138	139	140
141	142	143	144	145	146	147	148	149	150
151	152	153	154	155	156	157	158	159	160
161	162	163	164	165	166	167	168	169	170
171	172	173	174	175	176	177	178	179	180
181	182	183	184	185	186	187	188	189	190
191	192	193	194	195	196	197	198	199	200

201	202	203	204	205	206	207	208	209	210
211	212	213	214	215	216	217	218	219	220
221	222	223	224	225	226	227	228	229	230
231	232	233	234	235	236	237	238	239	240
241	242	243	244	245	246	247	248	249	250
251	252	253	254	255	256	257	258	259	260
261	262	263	264	265	266	267	268	269	270
271	272	273	274	275	276	277	278	279	280
281	282	283	284	285	286	287	288	289	290
291	292	293	294	295	296	297	298	299	300

Count on by 2s, 5s, 10s, and 25s.
What patterns can you find in these charts?
Record the patterns by colouring the charts.
Write the number patterns.

Show *and* Share

Show the patterns you found to a classmate.
How are the patterns on each chart the same? Different?
How are these patterns the same as those on a 1 to 100 chart?
How are they different?

➤ To count on by 10s, start anywhere.

801	802	803	804	805	806	807	808	809	810
811	812	813	814	815	816	817	818	819	820
821	822	823	824	825	826	827	828	829	830
831	832	833	834	835	836	837	838	839	840
841	842	843	844	845	846	847	848	849	850

Start at 807.
Count on:
807, 817, 827, 837, 847, …

Note the ones digit repeats and the tens digit increases by 1.

➤ To count on by 5s, start anywhere.

901	902	903	904	905	906	907	908	909	910
911	912	913	914	915	916	917	918	919	920
921	922	923	924	925	926	927	928	929	930
931	932	933	934	935	936	937	938	939	940
941	942	943	944	945	946	947	948	949	950
951	952	953	954	955	956	957	958	959	960
961	962	963	964	965	966	967	968	969	970
971	972	973	974	975	976	977	978	979	980
981	982	983	984	985	986	987	988	989	990
991	992	993	994	995	996	997	998	999	1000

Start

Start at 943.
Count on:
943, 948, 953, 958, 963, 968, …

Note the pattern in the ones digits:
3, 8, 3, 8, 3, 8, …

Note the pattern in the tens digits:
4, 4, 5, 5, 6, 6, …

Numbers Every Day

Mental Math

Complete each skip counting pattern.

10, 20, 30, 40, □, □, □

24, 34, 44, 54, □, □, □

75, 65, 55, 45, □, □, □

97, 87, 77, 67, □, □, □

➤ To count on by 25s, start at a number that ends with 25.

801	802	803	804	805	806	807	808	809	810
811	812	813	814	815	816	817	818	819	820
821	822	823	824	825	826	827	828	829	830
831	832	833	834	835	836	837	838	839	840
841	842	843	844	845	846	847	848	849	850
851	852	853	854	855	856	857	858	859	860
861	862	863	864	865	866	867	868	869	870
871	872	873	874	875	876	877	878	879	880
881	882	883	884	885	886	887	888	889	890
891	892	893	894	895	896	897	898	899	900

901	902	903	904	905	906	907	908	909	910
911	912	913	914	915	916	917	918	919	920
921	922	923	924	925	926	927	928	929	930
931	932	933	934	935	936	937	938	939	940
941	942	943	944	945	946	947	948	949	950
951	952	953	954	955	956	957	958	959	960
961	962	963	964	965	966	967	968	969	970
971	972	973	974	975	976	977	978	979	980
981	982	983	984	985	986	987	988	989	990
991	992	993	994	995	996	997	998	999	1000

Start at 825.
Count on: 825, 850, 875, 900, 925, 950, 975, 1000

Note the pattern in the ones digits: 5, 0, 5, 0, 5, 0, 5, 0
Note the pattern in the tens digits: 2, 5, 7, 0, 2, 5, 7, 0

Practice

Use hundred charts.

1. **a)** Start at 116. Count on by 2s to 134. Write the pattern.
   b) Start at 216. Count on by 2s to 244. Write the pattern.
   c) Start at 423. Count on by 2s to 451. Write the pattern.
   d) Start at 723. Count on by 2s to 757. Write the pattern.

2. Suppose you start at 167 and count on by 2s.
   Will you say 173? 200? How do you know?
   Predict first, then check.

   OKAY...
   167,...

3. **a)** Start at 333. Count on by 5s to 383. Write the pattern.
   b) Start at 633. Count on by 5s to 698. Write the pattern.
   c) Start at 554. Count on by 5s to 604. Write the pattern.
   d) Start at 854. Count on by 5s to 914. Write the pattern.

4. Start at 137.
 a) Count on 10 times by 2s. Record your work.
 b) Count on 10 times by 5s. Record your work.
 c) Count on 10 times by 10s. Record your work.

5. a) Start at 150. Count on by 25s to 650.
  Record your work.
 b) Start at 325. Count on by 25s to 800.
  Record your work.

6. Count on by 100s to close to 1000. Write the pattern.
 a) Start at 183. b) Start at 219. c) Start at 658.
 How are these 3 patterns the same? Different?

7. Count back by 100s. Write the pattern.
 a) Start at 407. b) Start at 752. c) Start at 997.
 How are these 3 patterns the same? Different?

8. You can count from 1 to 10.
 How can you use this pattern to count on by 100s
 from 100 to 1000?

9. Start at 275. Count on by 25s to 1000.
 What pattern do you see in the ones digits?
 The tens digits? The hundreds digits?
 Show your work.

Math Link

Measurement

There are 10¢ in 1 dime.
There are 10 dimes in 1 dollar.
There are 100¢ in 1 dollar.

Reflect

How is counting from 1 to 100 the
same as counting from 100 to 1000?
How is it different?
Use words, numbers, or pictures
to explain.

Comparing and Ordering Numbers

10

Explore ....  **Game**

Who Has the Greatest Number?

You will need 2 sets of cards numbered
from 0 to 9 and game boards.

Goal: To make the greatest number

How to Play:

➤ Shuffle the cards and turn them
   face down.

➤ Players take turns to turn over
   the top card.

➤ All players write the number on each card in
   one of the spaces in the top row on the game board.

➤ Once each player has had a turn, players read aloud
   the numbers they have made.

➤ Players record each number.

➤ The player with the greatest number gets a point.
   Then the player explains why the number is the greatest.

Play 2 more rounds of the game.
Play the game again. This time, try to make the least number.

Show *and* Share

Show how you chose where to place each number
on the game board. Share your strategy.
How can you tell who has the greatest number?
The least number?

➤ You can use place value to **compare** numbers.

To compare 472 and 476:

1. Compare the hundreds digits.	2. Compare the tens digits.	3. Compare the ones digits.
4 72	4 **7** 2	47 **2**
4 76	4 **7** 6	47 **6**
Both have 4 hundreds or 400.	Both have 7 tens or 70.	2 ones are less than 6 ones.

Since 2 is less than 6,
then 472 is *less than* 476   and   476 is *greater than* 472.

You can write this as:

472 < 476   and   476 > 472

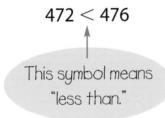
This symbol means "less than."

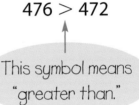
This symbol means "greater than."

➤ You can also use place value to **order** numbers.
To order 574, 384, and 578, compare each digit.

Hundreds	Tens	Ones
5	7	4
3	8	4
5	7	8

384 has the fewest hundreds, so it is the least number.
578 and 574 have the same numbers of hundreds and tens.
574 has fewer ones than 578.
So, 574 < 578

The order from least to greatest is 384, 574, 578.
The order from greatest to least is 578, 574, 384.

1. Which book has the greater number of stickers? How do you know?

a)

STICKERS 260

STICKERS 275

b)

STICKERS 943

STICKERS 940

Numbers Every Day

Number Strategies

Dustin has trouble remembering the sum of 3 + 5.

Give 3 strategies Dustin can use.

2. Copy each pair of numbers.
   Use > or < to make a true statement.
   a) 335 ☐ 281   b) 435 ☐ 462
   c) 705 ☐ 709   d) 162 ☐ 94

3. Copy each statement.
   Write a number to make each statement true.
   a) 710 > ☐   b) 984 < ☐
   c) 630 > ☐   d) ☐ < 720
   e) ☐ < 391   f) ☐ > 99

4. The number of dinosaurs in each box has 3 digits: 2, 5, and 6.
   The grey box has fewer dinosaurs than the green box.
   How many dinosaurs could there be in each box?
   How do you know?
   How many ways can you find?
   Show your work.

DINOSAURS   Dinosaurs

5. Which is the greatest number? How do you know?

a) 463	**b)** 841	**c)** 408	**d)** 724
85	926	417	720
567	721	406	729
472	627	400	726

6. Which is the least number? How do you know?

a) 968	**b)** 215	**c)** 158	**d)** 528
79	296	96	514
841	207	91	404
324	233	382	671

7. Order the numbers from least to greatest.
   a) 625, 431, 662, 523   **b)** 121, 99, 496, 407

8. Order the numbers from greatest to least.
   a) 510, 961, 847, 941   **b)** 865, 502, 969, 45

9. Write a number between 576 and 841.
   How do you know your number fits?

10. How many different 3-digit numbers can you write
   with the digits 3, 4, 7?
   Order the numbers from greatest to least.

11. Look at the numbers 263 and 460.
   How many digits do you need to compare
   to find which number is greater? Explain.

Reflect

Choose 3 different numbers between 100 and 500.
Explain how to order the numbers.

Showing Numbers in Many Ways

You will need Base Ten Blocks, a pencil, and paper.
Use models, pictures, words, and numbers.
How many different ways can you show the number 236?
Record your results.
Can you show 236 in different ways with Base Ten Blocks?

Show *and* Share

Talk about the different ways you modelled the number.

Connect

Here are different ways to show 208.
When you use digits, the number is written in **standard form**: 208

Picture:

Base-ten name: 2 hundreds 8 ones

Base Ten Blocks:

You can also use Base Ten Blocks to show 208 as

or as

Place-value chart:

Hundreds	Tens	Ones
2	0	8

Use Base Ten Blocks when they help.

1. Write each number in standard form.

   a) 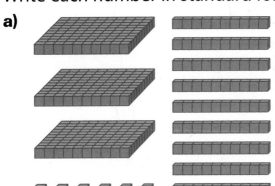   **b)**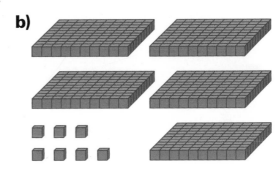

   c) sixty-seven
   d) 6 hundreds 8 tens
   e) ninety-four

2. Write the base-ten name for each number.

   a)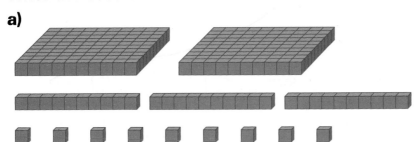

   b) 862
   c) 501
   d) sixty-seven

Numbers Every Day

Number Strategies

27 is:
   - ☐ ones
   - ☐ tens and ☐ ones
   - 3 groups of 10 less ☐
   - 1 ten and ☐ ones
   - ☐ groups of 5 and ☐ more

3. Write each number in standard form.
Then draw Base Ten Blocks to show each number
using the fewest blocks.

a)

b)

4. Show each number in 3 different ways.
a) 286   **b)** 309   **c)** 529
Compare your ways with those of your classmates.
What do you notice?

5. Draw Base Ten Blocks to show each number in 3 different ways.
a) 61   **b)** 315   **c)** 406

6. What does the zero in 308 mean?

7. Draw Base Ten Blocks.
Show 267 using exactly 24 blocks.
Explain how you did it.

Reflect

How do you know that
both pictures show 241?
Use words, numbers, or
pictures to explain.

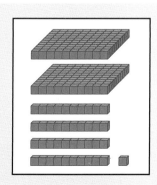
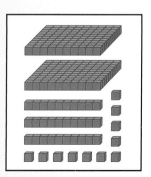

Strategies Toolkit

Explore

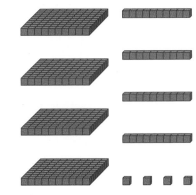

How many 3-digit numbers
can you build using
only 4 of these blocks for each number?

Show your work.

Show *and* Share

Show your classmates how you made the numbers.

Connect

Here is a similar problem, and one way to solve it.
How many 3-digit numbers can you build using
only 3 of these blocks for each number?

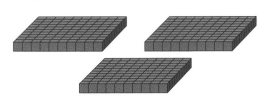 

Strategies

- **Make a table.**
- **Use a model.**
- **Draw a picture.**
- **Solve a simpler problem.**
- **Work backward.**
- **Guess and check.**
- **Make an organized list.**
- **Use a pattern.**

Understand

What do you know?
- You have to build as many
  3-digit numbers as you can.
- You may use only 3 blocks to build each number.

Plan

Think of a strategy to help you solve the problem.
- You can **make an organized list**.
- List all the numbers with 3 hundreds,
  then 2 hundreds, then 1 hundred, and so on.

Make a chart to record your list.

Hundreds	Tens	Ones	Number

- Start with 3 hundreds.
  How many numbers can you build?
  Record this in the chart.
- Repeat for all the numbers with 2 hundreds,
  then 1 hundred.

How do you know you have found all the numbers?
Think of another way you could have
solved the problem.

Practice

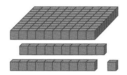

Choose one of the

Strategies

1. Use any number of
   these blocks to make as
   many numbers as you can.

2. Roll a number cube 3 times.
   Use the numbers rolled to make as many
   3-digit numbers as you can.

3. Balloons come in packages of 10, 25, and 50.
   You need 150 balloons.
   Find 5 ways you could buy the balloons.

Reflect

How did you make an organized list to solve a problem?
Use words, pictures, or numbers to explain.

How Much Is 1000?

Janny's stamp album has 10 pages.
Each page has 100 stamps.

To find how many stamps are in Janny's book,
you can count by 100s:

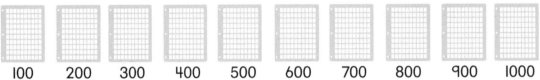

| 100 | 200 | 300 | 400 | 500 | 600 | 700 | 800 | 900 | 1000 |

10 hundreds make 1 **thousand**.

Explore

You will need a tub of pennies.
- How many desks will 1000 pennies cover?
- How many pages of this book
  will 1000 pennies cover?
- How many paper cups will 1000 pennies fill?
- How long is a line of 1000 pennies?
- How many groups of 10 are in 1000?

Choose one question to explore.
Estimate an answer, then find the answer.

Record your results.
Show your work.

Show *and* Share

Share your results with another group.
Tell about your strategies for estimating.
Show what you found out about 1000 pennies.

Connect

Here is another problem, and one way to solve it.
How many dictionaries will 1000 pennies cover?

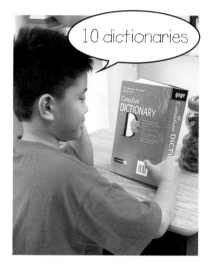

10 dictionaries

130

Make an estimate.

Cover a dictionary with pennies.

Count the pennies.

One hundred thirty pennies cover one dictionary.
This is more than 100.
Count by 100s until you reach 1000.

About:

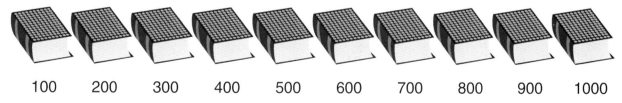

| 100 | 200 | 300 | 400 | 500 | 600 | 700 | 800 | 900 | 1000 |

When 100 pennies cover 1 dictionary,
1000 pennies cover 10 dictionaries.
Since 130 pennies covered 1 dictionary,
1000 pennies will cover fewer than 10 dictionaries.

1. Are there more than 1000 or fewer than 1000:
    a) stars in the sky on a clear night?
    b) students in your school?
    c) names in a telephone book?
    d) names on a page in a telephone book?
    e) footsteps to the principal's office?

2. Are there more than 1000 or fewer than 1000 blades of grass on a lawn? How could you find out?

3. When is 1000 a big number? Explain.

4. When is 1000 a small number? Explain.

5. How could you use hundred charts to show 1000? Explain.

Numbers Every Day

Number Strategies

Find each sum.
What patterns do you see?

2 + 2 = ☐   1 + 3 = ☐

3 + 3 = ☐   2 + 4 = ☐

4 + 4 = ☐   3 + 5 = ☐

5 + 5 = ☐   4 + 6 = ☐

Reflect

When would you like to have 1000 of something? Not like to have 1000 of something? Write about your ideas.

 14 Rounding Numbers

On a road, there are bus stops outside house number 100 and house number 200.
Suppose you live at 162. Where would you get off?
Suppose you live at 124. Where would you get off?

Explore

You will need number lines.

1. Write each number on a number line:
   21, 22, 23, 24, 25, 26, 27, 28, 29
   Is each number closer to 20 or 30?

2. Write each number on a number line:
   71, 72, 73, 74, 75, 76, 77, 78, 79
   Is each number closer to 70 or 80?

3. Write each number on a number line:
   210, 220, 230, 240, 250, 260, 270, 280, 290
   Is each number closer to 200 or 300?

Show your work.

Show and Share

Show how you found what each number was closest to.
Share any patterns in your results with a classmate.

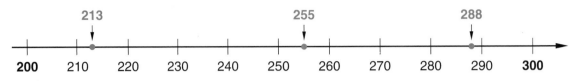

Connect

➤ You can use a number line to **round** numbers to the *nearest ten.*

213   255   288

200   210   220   230   240   250   260   270   280   290   300

213 is between 210 and 220, but closer to 210. So, to the nearest 10, 213 rounds to 210.

255 is halfway between 250 and 260. When a number is halfway between 2 tens, you round to the greater 10. So, 255 rounds to 260.

288 is between 280 and 290, but closer to 290. So, to the nearest 10, 288 rounds to 290.

➤ You can also round numbers to the *nearest hundred.*

213 is between 200 and 300, but closer to 200. So, 213 rounds to 200.

255 is between 200 and 300, but closer to 300. So, 255 rounds to 300.

288 is between 200 and 300, but closer to 300. So, 288 rounds to 300.

➤ You can round numbers without using a number line.
To round 526 to the nearest ten,

 Think:

5 26 is between 5 20 and 5 30, but closer to 530.
So, 526 rounded to the nearest ten is 530.

To round 526 to the nearest hundred,

 Think:

526 is between 500 and 600, but closer to 500.
So, 526 rounded to the nearest hundred is 500.

Numbers Every Day

Number Strategies

Complete each skip counting pattern. Tell how you did it.

155, 156, ☐, 158, ☐, ☐

40, 35, 30, ☐, ☐, 15, ☐

125, 150, 175, 200, ☐, ☐, ☐

90, ☐, 70, ☐, 50, ☐

1. Round each number to the nearest ten.
   a) 478   b) 87   c) 541   d) 751
   e) 365   f) 19   g) 55   h) 189

2. Suppose you round to the nearest ten.
   Write 5 numbers that would round to 80.

3. Round each number to the nearest hundred.
   a) 940   b) 352   c) 566   d) 137
   e) 750   f) 217   g) 788   h) 950

4. Suppose you round to the nearest hundred.
   Write 5 numbers that would round to 500.

5. Suppose you round to the nearest hundred.
   a) Write the greatest number that would round to 600.
   b) Write the least number that would round to 600.

6. Write a number that would be the same when
   you round it to the nearest ten or the nearest hundred.
   Show your work.

7. There are 378 children going to a picnic.
   Each child will have one Popsicle.
   How can you round to estimate
   how many boxes of 100 Popsicles will be needed?
   Show your work.

Reflect

Choose a 3-digit number.
Use words, pictures, or numbers to explain how to round
the number to the nearest 10 and the nearest 100.

• LESSON

1. Use a hundred chart.
   a) Start at 15. Count on by 2s to 41. Describe the pattern.
   b) Start at 27. Count on by 5s to 62. Describe the pattern.
   c) Start at 19. Count on by 10s to 99. Describe the pattern.

2. Use a number line.
   a) Start at 57. Count back by 2s to 43. What is the pattern?
   b) Start at 93. Count back by 5s to 28. What is the pattern?
   c) Start at 71. Count back by 10s to 1. What is the pattern?

3. Copy each pattern.
   Write what comes before and after.
   How do you know?
   a) ☐, 37, 39, 41, ☐   **b)** ☐, 88, 78, 68, ☐
   c) ☐, 14, 19, 24, ☐   **d)** ☐, 53, 48, 43, ☐

4. Use a number line for 1 to 100.
   a) Start at 97. Count back by 10s.
   Draw a dot on the number line for
   each number you count.
   b) What is the pattern?

5. Use a copy of the number line below.
   Draw a dot on the number line for each number: 58, 47, 66, 61
   Label the dot with the number.

43   50   60   68

6. Write each number in words.
   a) 27   **b)** 88   **c)** 51   **d)** 72   **e)** 60

7. a) January is the first month of the year.
What month of the year is April?
July? September? December?

b) Suppose Monday is the
first day of January.
What is the 9th day of January?
The 16th day? The 24th day?

c) Suppose Friday is the
first day of the year.
What will the 65th day be?
The 78th day? The 99th day?

JANUARY ✱ ✱ ✱ ✱ ✱ ✱

S	M	T	W	T	F	S
	1	2	3	4	5	6
7	8	9	10	11	12	13
14	15	16	17	18	19	20
21	22	23	24	25	26	27
28	29	30	31			

8. Model the number 758 in as many ways as you can.
Use pictures, numbers, and words.

9. Use a hundred chart that starts at 901.
Start at 902. Count on by 5s.
Colour squares to show the pattern.
Explain how you know which squares to colour.

10. Use the digits 6, 3, 9.

a) Make as many 3-digit numbers as you can.

b) Show how you can order the numbers you made.

c) Which of these numbers
is the greatest? The least?

11. Use the digits 9, 8, 2.

a) Write a number that is
a little less than 900.

b) Write a number that is
a little greater than 900.

c) Round your answers to parts a and b
to the nearest ten.

UNIT

1 Learning Goals

☑ explore number patterns
☑ skip count
☑ model numbers
☑ compare and order
numbers
☑ use ordinal numbers

Come to the Fair!

Your class is at the Fall Fair.
It's your job to solve these problems. Look at pages 4 and 5.
Use pictures, numbers, or words to show your work.

Part 1

- The basket of apples has exactly 37 apples.
  Who wins the prize for the closest guess?
  How do you know?
- Lan buys 9 sheets of stickers.
  How many stickers has she bought?
- Ms. Jessop buys 350 tomatoes to make spaghetti sauce.
  How many different ways could Ms. Jessop buy the tomatoes?
  Show your work.
- How many jugs of sap are needed to make 5 jugs
  of maple syrup?
- How many small cups of apple cider could you buy with 95¢?
  How many large cups?

Part 2

Write your own story problem about the Fall Fair.
Solve your problem. Show your work.

Part 3

Suppose you had a booth at a Fall Fair.
What would the booth be?
How would you use numbers in your booth?
Use words, pictures, or numbers to write about your booth.

Reflect on the Unit

Write one important thing you learned about place value.
Use words, pictures, or numbers to explain.

Patterns in Addition

2

National Read-A-Thon

Children across Canada have read as many books as they could in 4 weeks. The money they raised will go to charity.

Learning Goals

- describe patterns in addition and subtraction
- recall basic number facts
- develop strategies for addition and subtraction
- write, solve, and explain addition and subtraction problems

and Subtraction

Here are some results for one school.

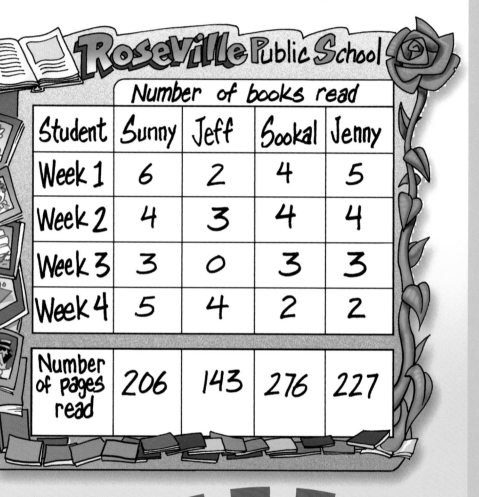

Roseville Public School

Number of books read

Student	Sunny	Jeff	Sookal	Jenny
Week 1	6	2	4	5
Week 2	4	3	4	4
Week 3	3	0	3	3
Week 4	5	4	2	2
Number of pages read	206	143	276	227

Key Words

- addition fact
- sum
- doubles
- near doubles
- subtraction fact
- related facts
- mental math
- estimate
- difference

- Who read the most pages?
- Who read the most books?
- What else can you find out from this chart?

Patterns in an Addition Chart

Isaac brought in 2 paper rolls for junk art.
Bianca brought in 5 paper rolls.
Together, they brought in 7 paper rolls.

$2 + 5 = 7$

This is an **addition fact.**
7 is the **sum**.

The addition chart below shows
addition facts up to $9 + 9$.
Use this chart to find $2 + 5 = 7$.

Explore

Look for all the patterns you can
find in the addition chart.

What do the patterns tell you
about addition?

Show and Share

Decide with your partner
how to record what you notice.
You could
• Colour number patterns
  on the chart.
• Organize lists of facts that fit
  a pattern.
• Write down your ideas.

+	0	1	2	3	4	5	6	7	8	9
0	0	1	2	3	4	5	6	7	8	9
1	1	2	3	4	5	6	7	8	9	10
2	2	3	4	5	6	7	8	9	10	11
3	3	4	5	6	7	8	9	10	11	12
4	4	5	6	7	8	9	10	11	12	13
5	5	6	7	8	9	10	11	12	13	14
6	6	7	8	9	10	11	12	13	14	15
7	7	8	9	10	11	12	13	14	15	16
8	8	9	10	11	12	13	14	15	16	17
9	9	10	11	12	13	14	15	16	17	18

There are patterns in the addition chart.
They show the ways that numbers combine in addition.

➤ When you add, the order does not matter.

$9 + 4 = 13$ $4 + 9 = 13$

➤ Adding 0 does not change the starting number.

$5 + 0 = 5$ $8 + 0 = 8$

➤ When you add two numbers that are the same,
you add **doubles**. Doubles have a sum that is even.

$2 + 2 = 4$ $5 + 5 = 10$

 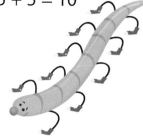

There is a pattern when you look at all the ways
to find a sum.
Here are the ways to get a sum of 14.

These numbers
increase by 1.
↓

$5 + 9 = 14$
$6 + 8 = 14$
$7 + 7 = 14$
$8 + 6 = 14$
$9 + 5 = 14$
↑

These numbers
decrease by 1.

The sum is 14 each time.

Numbers Every Day

Number Strategies

You say 2. I say 8.
You say 6. I say 4.
You say 9. I say 1.
Guess my rule.

You say 5. What will I say?
I say 7. What did you say?

1. Use the addition chart.
   List all the pairs of numbers that add to 10.
   What patterns do you see in your list of pairs?

2. List the different pairs of numbers for each sum.
   How do you know you found all the possible pairs?
   a) □ + □ = 13   b) □ + □ = 11
   c) □ + □ = 12   d) □ + □ = 15

3. Add to find each sum in the box.
   What is the pattern in the two starting numbers?
   What is the pattern in the sums?
   Predict the next two sums in the pattern.
   Check to see if you are correct.

   1 + 2 = □
   2 + 3 = □
   3 + 4 = □

4. At a playground, 9 children are on the swings
   and 7 children are on the climber.
   How many children are there altogether?

5. Write a story problem that uses an addition fact.
   Use words or pictures, then solve your problem.

6. Choose 2 even numbers less than 10. Add them.
   Repeat with another 2 even numbers.
   How many different sums can you find?
   Which numbers never appear? Why?
   Show your work.

Reflect

How do the patterns in the addition chart help you remember
some of the addition facts?

2 Addition Strategies

59

What doubles fact does the ant show?

You can use the doubles to find other facts.

 **Explore**

This addition chart
is partly filled in.
What patterns do you see?

Find ways that these patterns
can help you figure out some
addition facts.

+	0	1	2	3	4	5	6	7	8	9
0	0	1								
1	1	2	3							10
2		3	4	5					10	
3			5	6	7			10		
4				7	8	9	10			
5					9	10	11			
6					10	11	12	13		
7				10			13	14	15	
8			10					15	16	17
9		10							17	18

Show and Share

Talk to your partner
about the addition facts
in the chart.
Record any addition strategies
you talk about.

In the addition chart, the doubles are in the blue diagonal.

Adding a number to its next counting number gives a **near double**.
The green and pink diagonals show near doubles.

5 + 6 = 11

To add 5 + 6,
think of 5 + 5,
plus another 1.

The yellow diagonal in the addition chart shows **sums of 10**.
Knowing the basic facts for 10 can help you figure out other facts.

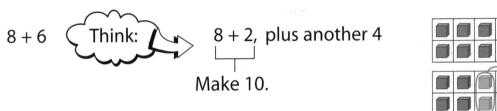

8 + 6   Think: 8 + 2, plus another 4

                        Make 10.

8 + 6 = 14

Here are some strategies for adding:
• Doubles
• Near doubles
• Make 10.

Think of other strategies you know.

1. Add.

   a) 5 + 5 = ☐   6 + 5 = ☐

   b) 7 + 7 = ☐   7 + 8 = ☐

   c) 6 + 6 = ☐   7 + 6 = ☐

   d) 8 + 8 = ☐   8 + 9 = ☐

Numbers Every Day

Number Strategies

Start at 325.

Count on by 2s to 349.

Count on by 5s to 375.

Count on by 10s to 455.

Count on by 25s to 550.

2. Add. Using doubles facts might help you.

a) $7 + 8 = \square$ **b)** $3 + 4 = \square$

c) $6 + 5 = \square$ **d)** $4 + 5 = \square$

3. Add. "Make 10" might help you.

a) $8 + 5 = \square$ **b)** $4 + 9 = \square$

c) $5 + 7 = \square$ **d)** $9 + 6 = \square$

4. Add. How can doubles help you?

a) $2 + 4 = \square$ **b)** $3 + 5 = \square$

c) $4 + 6 = \square$ **d)** $5 + 7 = \square$

e) $6 + 8 = \square$ **f)** $7 + 9 = \square$

What patterns do you see in the addition facts?

5. There were 9 children in a swimming pool.
Eight more children jumped in.
How many children are in the pool?
What strategy did you use to find out?

6. Use two or more of these numbers each time:

1, 2, 3, 4, 5, 6, 7, 8

How many different ways can you choose numbers to make 10?
How do you know you have found all the ways?
Show your work.

Reflect

What are some addition strategies you use? Use
words, pictures, or numbers to show some examples.

Subtraction Strategies

Jan has 2 single-tail goldfish and 3 double-tail goldfish.

You can write an addition fact about Jan's goldfish.

There are also two other facts you know.

$$2 + 3 = 5 \begin{cases} 5 - 3 = 2 \\ 5 - 2 = 3 \end{cases}$$ These are **subtraction facts.**

Think about subtraction as the opposite of addition.

Explore

Use the addition chart to look for subtraction facts.
Start by looking for $5 - 2 = 3$.

➤ Look for subtraction facts you already know. How do you remember these facts?

➤ Look for subtraction facts that use 10. List all of them. Describe any patterns you see.

Show and Share

Talk to your partner about strategies you use to subtract.
Think of at least two ways.
Record your ideas.

+	0	1	2	3	4	5	6	7	8	9
0	0	1	2	3	4	5	6	7	8	9
1	1	2	3	4	5	6	7	8	9	10
2	2	3	4	5	6	7	8	9	10	11
3	3	4	5	6	7	8	9	10	11	12
4	4	5	6	7	8	9	10	11	12	13
5	5	6	7	8	9	10	11	12	13	14
6	6	7	8	9	10	11	12	13	14	15
7	7	8	9	10	11	12	13	14	15	16
8	8	9	10	11	12	13	14	15	16	17
9	9	10	11	12	13	14	15	16	17	18

LESSON FOCUS | Use different strategies to recall basic subtraction facts.

You may already use counting back to help you subtract.
Here are some other strategies to subtract.

➤ Count up through 10.
$13 - 9 = \boxed{?}$
Start with 9.
You need 1 more to get 10. $\qquad$ $9 + \mathbf{1} = 10$
You need 3 more to get 13. $\qquad$ $10 + \mathbf{3} = 13$
Since $\mathbf{1 + 3 = 4}$, then $13 - 9 = 4$

*4 is the **difference** of 13 and 9.*

➤ Count back through 10.
$11 - 3 = \boxed{?}$
Start with 11.
Take away 1 to get 10: $\qquad$ $11 - 1 = 10$
Since $3 = 1 + 2$, take away 2 more: $10 - 2 = 8$
So, $11 - 3 = 8$

Practice

1. Think of doubles to subtract.
   a) $14 - 7 = \square$ $\qquad$ b) $18 - 9 = \square$
   c) $16 - 8 = \square$ $\qquad$ d) $12 - 6 = \square$

2. Subtract.
   Record each list of subtraction facts.
   a) $11 - 4 = \square$ $\qquad$ b) $18 - 9 = \square$
    $12 - 5 = \square$ $\qquad$ $17 - 8 = \square$
    $13 - 6 = \square$ $\qquad$ $16 - 7 = \square$
    $14 - 7 = \square$ $\qquad$ $15 - 6 = \square$
    $15 - 8 = \square$ $\qquad$ $14 - 5 = \square$
    $16 - 9 = \square$ $\qquad$ $13 - 4 = \square$

   Look at your answers.
   What patterns do you see?

Numbers Every Day

Number Strategies

Start at 950.
Count back by 2s to 900.
Count back by 5s to 840.
Count back by 10s to 700.
Count back by 100s to 50.

3. Subtract. Using patterns may help.

    a) 11 − 9 = ☐   **b)** 11 − 8 = ☐   **c)** 11 − 7 = ☐

    d) 11 − 6 = ☐   **e)** 11 − 5 = ☐   **f)** 11 − 4 = ☐

4. Subtract.

    a) 15 − 7 = ☐   **b)** 12 − 4 = ☐   **c)** 14 − 9 = ☐

    d) 17 − 9 = ☐   **e)** 17 − 8 = ☐   **f)** 13 − 9 = ☐

5. Subtract.

    a) 14 − 8 = ☐   **b)** 12 − 7 = ☐   **c)** 12 − 8 = ☐

    d) 14 − 6 = ☐   **e)** 15 − 9 = ☐   **f)** 13 − 7 = ☐ .

6. Subtract.

    a) 11 − 2 = ☐   **b)** 12 − 3 = ☐   **c)** 13 − 5 = ☐

    d) 12 − 9 = ☐   **e)** 13 − 8 = ☐   **f)** 17 − 6 = ☐

7. Use the addition chart.

Find all the subtraction facts that have an answer of 5.

How do you know you found all of them?

Show your work.

8. There were 17 children in line for the school bus.

Eight children got on the bus.

How many children were in line then?

9. Write a story problem that uses the subtraction fact 17 − 9.

Solve your problem.

Reflect

How can you use addition
to subtract?
Use words and numbers
to explain.

At Home

Write about when
you might need to
subtract at home.

Related Facts

Some number facts are **related**.

$$7 + 6 = 13$$
$$6 + 7 = 13$$
$$13 - 6 = 7$$
$$13 - 7 = 6$$

Why do these four facts belong together?

Explore

 Game

Make some related facts cards.
You will need about 20 triangular cards.

➤ Choose 2 numbers between 1 and 9. Add them.
➤ On a card, write each number in a corner.
  Turn the card over.
  Write all the related facts on the other side.

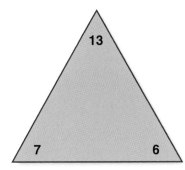

13

7   6

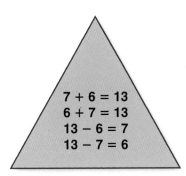

7 + 6 = 13
6 + 7 = 13
13 − 6 = 7
13 − 7 = 6

➤ Choose another pair of numbers to make another card.
➤ Continue to build your card collection.
  Include some doubles in your collection.

LESSON FOCUS | Identify and apply relationships between addition and subtraction.

65

Show *and* Share

Play these related facts games with a partner.

Show the Numbers, Tell the Facts

Take turns.
Show your partner the 3 numbers
on one side of the card.
Ask what related facts are on the back
of the card.

Show the Facts, Tell the Numbers

Take turns.
Show your partner the facts
in a set of related facts.
Ask what numbers belong in the set.

What other
games can you play
with these cards?

Connect

If you know one fact, you can use it to write other facts.

If you know $\quad 5 + 9 = 14$

then you know $\quad 9 + 5 = 14 \quad$ and you know $\quad 14 - 9 = 5$

$14 - 5 = 9$

If you know $\quad 8 + 8 = 16$

then you know $\quad 16 - 8 = 8$

Why does this doubles fact
give us only one other fact?

Practice

1. Write a set of related facts that use each set of numbers.
   a) 11, 4, 7   b) 6, 5, 11   c) 9, 9, 18   d) 3, 9, 12

2. Write the related facts for each fact.
   a) $12 - 4 = 8$ b) $5 + 9 = 14$ c) $14 - 7 = 7$ d) $5 + 7 = 12$

3. Use + or − to make each fact correct.
   a) 6 □ 8 = 14   b) 8 □ 6 = 2   c) 8 □ 7 = 1
   d) 8 □ 9 = 17   e) 9 □ 6 = 15   f) 14 □ 8 = 6

4. 8, 3, and □? are the numbers in a set of related facts.
   a) What could the missing number be?
      Write the related facts.
   b) What is another possible missing number?
      Write the related facts for this number.
   c) Explain why both numbers could work as the
      missing number.

5. Chintan read 16 books in the Read-A-Thon.
   He read 7 books in the first 2 weeks.
   How many books did Chintan read
   in the last 2 weeks?

6. Write a story problem that can be solved
   with a number fact that uses 15, 9, and 6.

7. Five is one number in a set of related facts.
   What might the other numbers be?
   Show how you found them.

8. There are 18 children in the lunch room.
   Five are from Grade 1.
   Six are from Grade 2.
   The rest are from Grade 3.
   How many children are from Grade 3?

Numbers Every Day

Number Strategies

Use the doubles fact
9 + 9 = 18 to find each sum.

9 + 8 = □

9 + 10 = □

9 + 7 = □

9 + 11 = □

Reflect

Write a set of related facts.
Use pictures, words, or numbers
to show how they are related.

Find the Missing Number

 **Explore** .... 👥 **Game**

Game: How Many Are Missing?

Goal: To find how many counters are hidden

You will need 18 counters. Take turns.
➤ Take between 10 and 18 counters.
➤ Put some counters in one hand
   and some in the other.
➤ Tell your partner how many counters you have altogether.
➤ Show how many you have in one hand.
   Ask your partner how many you have in the other hand.

Show *and* Share

What strategies did you use to find the missing number?
Share your ideas to start a class list.

 **Connect** ....

To find the missing number, think about related facts.

$8 + \square = 15$ Think: ⟶ △(15, 8, 7)   Solve: $8 + 7 = 15$

You could think subtraction.

$\square + 3 = 12$ Think: $12 - 3 = 9$ Solve: $9 + 3 = 12$

Think of other strategies you used.

1. Find each missing number. Draw a picture for each.
   a) $5 + \square = 14$ **b)** $4 + \square = 12$ **c)** $\square + 9 = 18$
   d) $17 - \square = 8$ **e)** $14 - \square = 7$ **f)** $\square - 6 = 7$

2. Find each missing number. Explain your strategy.
   a) $13 - \square = 4$ **b)** $\square - 9 = 7$ **c)** $\square - 6 = 5$

3. What number do you add to 8 to make 16?
   How do you know?

4. What number do you add to 5 to make 11? Explain.

5. Eva has 6 more animal stickers than Kris.
   Eva has 13 animal stickers.
   How many stickers does Kris have?

6. Make up a story problem that can be solved with $13 - \square = 6$.
   Solve the problem.

7. Find the missing numbers: $\square - \square = 4$.
   How many different ways can you do this?
   Show your work.

8. There are 17 soccer balls in the gym.
   Shawna takes 5 balls outside.
   Owen takes 2 balls back to the gym.
   How many soccer balls are in
   the gym now?

Reflect

Explain how you found an answer
when you played *How Many Are Missing?*

Numbers Every Day

Number Strategies

How many different ways
can you fill in the boxes?

$\square + \square = 15$

Adding and Subtracting 2-Digit Numbers

Explore

Jordan's school had a Walk-A-Thon to raise money
for an animal shelter.
The teachers had juice and water for the walkers.
They gave out 46 bottles of juice and 18 bottles of water.

How many drinks did the teachers give out?
How many more bottles of juice than water did they give out?

Show and Share

Show how you answered each question.
You might use:
• Base Ten Blocks
• a place-value mat

Tens	Ones

Record your answers
with pictures and numbers.

Numbers Every Day

Number Strategies

Here are 2 ways to break
32 into parts.

32 = 30 + 2

32 = 10 + 6 + 6 + 10

Write 5 more number
sentences that show
32 broken into parts.

There are 45 dogs in the animal shelter.
There are 37 cats at the same shelter.

➤ How many cats and dogs are there?

Find: 45 + 37
Here is one way.

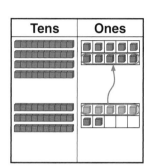

Make 10.

70 + 10 + 2 = 82
45 + 37 = 82

There are 82 cats and dogs at the animal shelter.

➤ Of the 45 dogs, 16 are puppies. How many are adult dogs?

Find: 45 − 16
Here is one way.

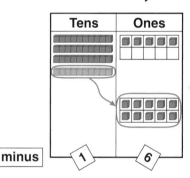

To subtract 16, take away 1 ten and 6 ones.
There are not enough ones to take away 6.
Trade 1 ten for 10 ones.

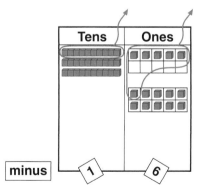

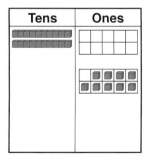

Think of other ways you can solve each problem.

Take away 6 ones.
Take away 1 ten.

45 − 16 = 29
There are 29 adult dogs.

Use Base Ten Blocks and place-value mats when they help.

1. Add.
   a) 25 + 13   **b)** 11 + 67   **c)** 30 + 28   **d)** 44 + 34

2. Add.
   a) 43 + 9   **b)** 56 + 6   **c)** 24 + 8   **d)** 67 + 5

3. Subtract.
   a) 39 − 25   **b)** 48 − 24   **c)** 57 − 23   **d)** 66 − 22

4. Subtract.
   a) 35 − 9   **b)** 74 − 8   **c)** 43 − 7   **d)** 82 − 6

5. Add or subtract.

   a) 57   **b)** 56   **c)** 50   **d)** 28
       + 27   − 29   − 23   + 46

   e) 35   **f)** 47   **g)** 16   **h)** 89
       + 19   − 20   + 78   − 62

6. Write down each list of facts as you solve them.
   a) 50 + 35   **b)** 91 − 56
       49 + 34   91 − 66
       48 + 33   91 − 76
       47 + 32   91 − 86

   What patterns do you see in your answers?
   Why do the patterns occur?

7. Find two 2-digit numbers with a sum of 30.
   How many ways can you do this?
   How do you know you have found all the ways?

8. Find two 2-digit numbers that subtract to leave 85.
   How many ways can you do this?
   Use patterns to show that you have found all the ways.

9. Children collected bottles to recycle.
   On Monday they brought in 47 bottles.
   On Tuesday they brought in 39.
   How many bottles were brought in
   on those two days?

10. There were 16 girls in the gym.
    After the boys arrived,
    there were 25 children in the gym.
    How many boys came into the gym?

11. Write a story problem that uses
    two 2-digit numbers.
    Solve the problem.

12. Make a card for each digit: 5, 3, 4, 7.
    Arrange the cards to make addition
    and subtraction problems.
    Record your problems.

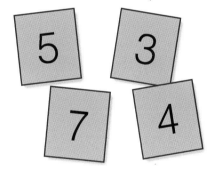

    $$\begin{array}{r} \square\square \\ +\ \square\square \\ \hline \end{array} \qquad \begin{array}{r} \square\square \\ -\ \square\square \\ \hline \end{array}$$

    How many sums and differences can you find?
    What is the greatest sum? The least difference?
    Show your work.

Reflect

Suppose a friend missed school today.
Use words, pictures, or numbers to explain to your friend
how to add and subtract two 2-digit numbers.

Using Mental Math to Add

7

When you add in your head, you do **mental math**.

Explore

The Science Centre has a special show on the science of toys.
The show has been on for 36 days.
It will be on for another 48 days.
How many days is that altogether?

Use mental math to find out.

Show and Share

Record how you added without using materials.
Share your ideas with a classmate.

Connect

Forty-nine Grade 2 children and 33 Grade 3 children went to the Science Centre.
How many children went to the Science Centre?

Think of other mental math strategies you have for adding.

Here are some mental math strategies to find 49 + 33.

➤ Add on tens,
   then add on ones.

   Think: 49 + 30 + 3

   49 + 30 = 79
   79 + 3 = 82

➤ Take from one
   to give to the other.

   Think: 49 + 1 + 32

   49 + 1 = 50
   50 + 32 = 82

   49 + 33
    ↓   ↓
   50   32

82 children went to the Science Centre.

Use mental math.

1. Add. What patterns do you see?
 a) 32 + 10   32 + 20   32 + 30   32 + 40
 b) 40 + 26   40 + 36   40 + 46   40 + 56

2. Add.
 a) 21 + 57   **b)** 31 + 57   **c)** 11 + 57   **d)** 11 + 67

3. Add.
 a) 55 + 16   **b)** 45 + 26   **c)** 35 + 36   **d)** 25 + 46

4. Add.
 a) 35 + 29   **b)** 48 + 18   **c)** 23 + 67   **d)** 16 + 55

5. How many different ways can you find 29 + 55?
 Use words, pictures, or numbers to show each way.

6. Josh and Kara were counting licence plates.
 Josh counted 49 plates from Alberta.
 Kara counted 33 plates from Ontario.
 How many licence plates did they count?

7. A passenger train has 26 cars.
 A freight train has 57 cars.
 How many cars are there altogether?

8. Write a story problem that
 you can solve using mental math.
 Solve the problem. Show your work.

Numbers Every Day

Mental Math

What number goes in each box?
Tell how you know.
 5 + 7 = 5 + 5 + □
 8 + 9 = 8 + 2 + □

Add by first making 10.
 7 + 6 = □
 4 + 8 = □
 9 + 3 = □

Reflect

Draw a picture to show how you would
add 48 + 24 in your head.

Using Mental Math to Subtract

Explore

There were 43 people skating.
Twenty-seven people left to get hot chocolate.
How many people were still skating?

Use mental math to find out.

Show *and* Share

Show how you used mental math to solve the problem.

Connect

There were 52 frogs in a pond.
Twenty-four frogs hopped away.
How many frogs were still in the pond?

Here are some mental math strategies to find $52 - 24$.

➤ Take away tens, then take away ones.

Think: $52 - 20 = 32$

Count back: $32 - 4 = 28$

➤ Add to match the ones, then subtract.

Think: Add 2 to 52 to make 54.

$54 - 24 = 30$
Take away the 2 you added.
$30 - 2 = 28$

There were 28 frogs still in the pond.

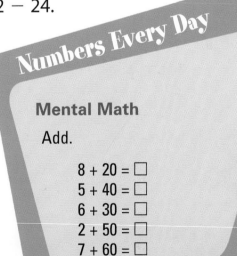

Numbers Every Day

Mental Math

Add.

$8 + 20 = \square$
$5 + 40 = \square$
$6 + 30 = \square$
$2 + 50 = \square$
$7 + 60 = \square$

Use mental math.

1. Subtract. Record each list of facts.

    a) 59 − 10   **b)** 67 − 10   **c)** 88 − 10

       59 − 20   77 − 10   78 − 20

       59 − 30   87 − 10   68 − 30

       59 − 40   97 − 10   58 − 40

    Look at each list of facts. What patterns do you see?

2. Subtract. What patterns do you see?

    a) 63 − 41   **b)** 73 − 31   **c)** 83 − 21   **d)** 93 − 11

3. Subtract.

    a)   60   **b)**   50   **c)**   40   **d)**   30

       − 28   − 28   − 28   − 28

4. Subtract.

    a)   74   **b)**   92   **c)**   67   **d)**   85

       − 56   − 18   − 38   − 47

5. How many different ways can you find 81 − 58?
Use words, pictures, or numbers to show each way.

6. There were 32 geese on a beach.
More geese flew in, and then there were 61 geese.
How many geese flew in?

7. The answer is 43.
What could the subtraction problem be?
Show your work.

Reflect

Explain how you can use mental math to subtract.

Strategies Toolkit

Explore

Gina has 25 stamps.
She has 11 more Canadian stamps than foreign stamps.
How many foreign stamps does Gina have?

Solve the problem. Use any materials you need.

Show *and* Share

Show how you solved the problem.

Connect

Jim has 23 model trucks and cars.
He has 5 more trucks than cars.
How many cars does Jim have?

Here is one way to solve this problem.

Understand

What do you know?
- Jim has 23 trucks and cars.
- He has 5 more trucks than cars.
- You want to find out how many cars Jim has.

Plan

Think of a strategy to help you solve the problem.
- You can use **guess and check**.
- *Guess* how many cars, then add 5 to find the number of trucks.
  Check to see if the total is 23.

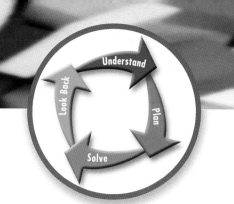

- What if you guess 10 cars?
  How many trucks would there be?
  Is the total 23?
- If it is not 23, guess again.
  Think about your next guess.
  Should it be more than your first guess or less? Why?

How many cars does Jim have?

How could you solve this problem another way?
What if you started by guessing the number of trucks?
Would you find the same answer for the number
of cars?

Practice

Choose one of the

Strategies

1. Kumail and Sasha are playing a game.
   Sasha has won 6 more cards than Kumail.
   They have won 24 cards altogether.
   How many cards has each person won?

2. Margaret uses nickels and dimes to buy a bookmark.
   It costs 65¢. Margaret paid with 8 coins.
   How many of each coin did she use?

3. At a garage sale, there are bicycles and tricycles.
   Altogether, there are 18 wheels.
   How many bicycles and tricycles are there?

Reflect

Think about one of these problems you solved.
Use words, pictures, or numbers to explain how you solved it.

Estimating Sums and Differences

When you do not need an exact answer, you **estimate**.

Glenn has $20.

As he shops, he estimates how much the items in his cart will cost.

He does not put any more in his cart when he estimates he will spend close to $20.

Explore

Jeff and May want to buy a present for their grandfather.
They count their penny collections.

Name	Jeff	May
Number of Pennies	213	488

About how many pennies do they have?
About how many more than Jeff does May have?

Numbers Every Day

Mental Math

Explain how to add 34 + 28 in your head.

Give 2 different ways.

Show *and* Share

Share your estimates with a classmate.
Did you use different strategies?
Are your estimates close enough for Jeff and May to plan
what they can buy? How do you know?

Connect

Lia has 213 red Lego blocks and 477 blue Lego blocks.
About how many blocks does Lia have?
About how many more blue blocks than red blocks are there?

Estimate: 213 + 477 and 477 − 213
Here are two ways to estimate.

Rounding First

Round to the nearest 100.

$$213 \rightarrow 200$$
$$477 \rightarrow 500$$

200 + 500 = 700
and
500 − 200 = 300

Lia has about 700 blocks.
There are about 300 more
blue blocks than red blocks.

Front-End Estimation

Use the digits in the hundreds
place. Ignore the other digits.

$$213 \rightarrow 200$$
$$477 \rightarrow 400$$

200 + 400 = 600
and
400 − 200 = 200

Lia has about 600 blocks.
There are about 200 more
blue blocks than red blocks.

These estimates are closer.
One number was rounded up, the
other was rounded down.

1. Which number is the better estimate for each sum?
   Why do you think so?

   a)   61
          $+\ 22$
          80 or 90?

   b)   54
          $+\ 13$
          60 or 70?

   c)   327
          $+\ 254$
          500 or 600?

2. Which number is the better estimate for each difference?
   Why do you think so?

   a)   72
          $-\ 41$
          30 or 50?

   b)   46
          $-\ 15$
          20 or 30?

   c)   669
          $-\ 226$
          400 or 500?

3. Look at these numbers:
         26, 53, 95, 148, 153, 256
   Which two numbers will give the sum that is closest to 200?
   How do you know? Show your work.

4. Suppose you start at 0.
   Estimate how many times you add 145 to get 900.
   Explain how you found your answer.
   Check with a calculator.

5. Faizal had 136 books. He gave away 25.
   Faizal thinks he now has about 80 books. Is he close?
   How do you know?

6. Write a problem you would *not* solve by estimating.
   Explain why not. Solve the problem. Show your work.

Reflect

Explain the difference between guessing and estimating.
Use examples to show your thinking.

Adding 3-Digit Numbers

St. Mark's School sells T-shirts for gym classes.
236 children ordered blue T-shirts.
175 children ordered red T-shirts.

How many T-shirts were ordered?

Use any materials you need to solve this problem.

Show *and* Share

Show how you found the total number of T-shirts.
Share your strategy with another pair of classmates.

Connect

The school also sells hats.
It needs 257 blue hats and 165 white hats.
How many hats is that?

Find: 257 + 165

Here is one way to add
257 and 165.

Hundreds	Tens	Ones

Step 1.
Combine the groups.
Make 10.

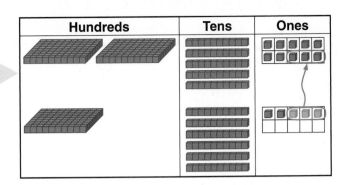

Step 2.
Trade 10 ones for 1 ten.

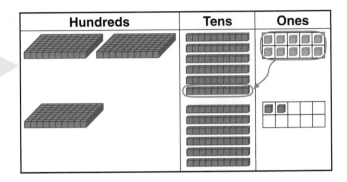

Step 3.
Trade 10 tens for 1 hundred.

$257 + 165 = 400 + 20 + 2 = 422$

There are 422 hats.

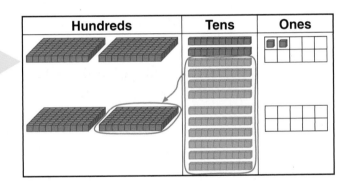

Think of other ways to solve the problem.

Practice

Use Base Ten Blocks and place-value mats when they help.

1. Add.

a)
$$\begin{array}{r} 269 \\ + 217 \\ \hline \end{array}$$

b)
$$\begin{array}{r} 258 \\ + 158 \\ \hline \end{array}$$

Numbers Every Day

Mental Math

Add. Explain your strategy.

$57 + 42 = \square$

$49 + 51 = \square$

$25 + 34 = \square$

$85 + 49 = \square$

2. Add. See how many you can do mentally.

a) 350 + 22   **b)** 832 + 65   **c)** 407 + 13

d) 403 + 29   **e)** 768 + 24   **f)** 643 + 71

3. Add.

a)   340
    + 270

b)   271
    + 459

c)   382
    + 148

d)   293
    + 237

4. Add.

a) 290 + 561   **b)** 372 + 479   **c)** 502 + 349   **d)** 177 + 674

5. A family reunion was held in a park.
There were 137 children and 218 adults.
How many lunches were needed
for the people at the reunion?
Show how you solved the problem.

6. Write a story problem that can be solved
by adding two 3-digit numbers.
Solve the problem.

7. Find two 3-digit numbers with a sum of 217.
How many ways can you do this?
How do you know you have found all the ways?
Show your work.

8. Hannah's family went on a vacation.
The first day they drove 256 km.
The next day they drove 45 km farther than the first day.
How far did they drive over the 2 days?

Reflect

How is adding 3-digit numbers like adding 2-digit numbers?
How is it different?

Subtracting 3-Digit Numbers

Canada has 39 national parks.
The oldest is Banff National Park in Alberta.
In 1883, railroad workers discovered hot springs in Banff.
Today, visitors go to see the mountain peaks, rivers, lakes, and waterfalls.

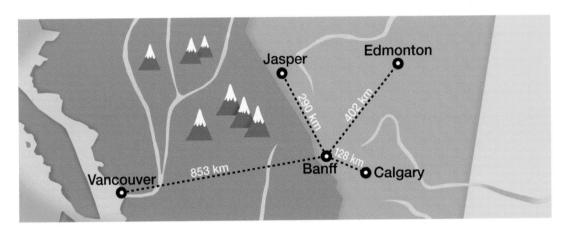

Explore

Use the sketch map above.
The Lee family went to Banff from Jasper.
The Gurza family went to Banff from Calgary.
Which family travelled farther? How much farther?

Solve the problem.
Here are some ways to record your work.
• Draw a picture of the materials you used.
• Write numbers to show your steps.

Show **and** Share

Share with another pair of classmates one important step
that helped you solve the problem.

Georgia lives in Jasper. Her cousin Kelly lives in Vancouver.
They met in Banff for a hiking vacation.
How much farther than Georgia did Kelly travel?

From the map, Georgia travelled 290 km.
Kelly travelled 853 km.

Find: 853 − 290

Here is one way to subtract.

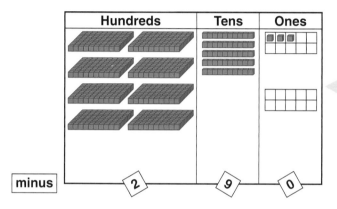

To subtract 290, take away
2 hundreds 9 tens 0 ones.

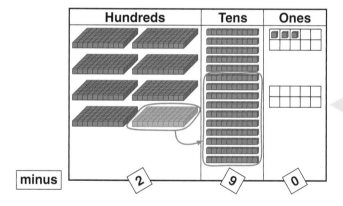

There are not enough tens
to take away 9 tens.
Trade 1 hundred for 10 tens.

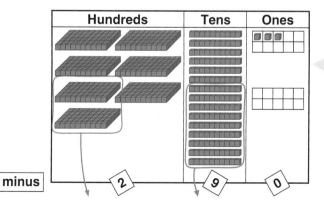

Take away 2 hundreds.
Take away 9 tens.

853 − 290 = 563
Kelly travelled 563 km farther
than Georgia.

Here is one more problem.
Jay travelled 402 km from Edmonton to Banff.
Then he travelled 128 km from Banff to Calgary.
How much farther was the trip from Edmonton?

Find: 402 − 128

Here is one way to subtract.

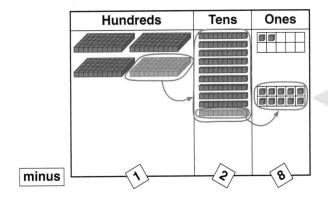

To subtract 128, take away
1 hundred 2 tens 8 ones.
There are not enough tens
to take away 2 tens.
Trade 1 hundred for 10 tens.
There are not enough ones
to take away 8 ones.
Trade 1 ten for 10 ones.

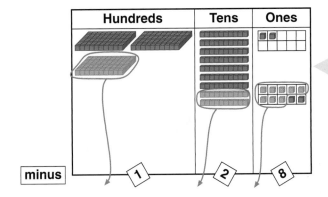

Take away 1 hundred.
Take away 2 tens.
Take away 8 ones.

402 − 128 = 274
The trip from Edmonton
was 274 km farther.

Practice

Use Base Ten Blocks when you need to.

1. Subtract.

a)

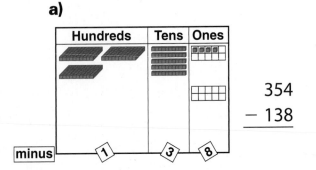

354
− 138

b)

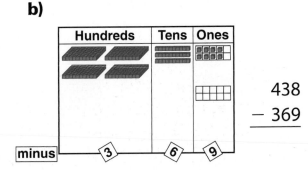

438
− 369

2. Subtract.
   a) 876 − 23   **b)** 923 − 10   **c)** 635 − 22   **d)** 599 − 86

3. Subtract.
   a) 756 − 49   **b)** 830 − 21   **c)** 687 − 39   **d)** 940 − 35

4. Subtract.
   a) 483 − 156   **b)** 557 − 230   **c)** 654 − 327   **d)** 701 − 374

5. Subtract.

a) 200	**b)** 300	**c)** 400	**d)** 500
− 82	− 183	− 284	− 285

6. Find two 3-digit numbers that subtract to leave 123. How many ways can you do this? Show your work.

7. A campground is 475 km from the Kapurs' home. Before lunch the Kapurs drove 238 km. How far do they still have to drive? Show how you solved the problem.

8. At a flea market, a stall had 456 comic books. The stall keeper sold 285 comic books. How many were left? How do you know?

9. Write a story problem that can be solved using 652 − 328. Solve the problem. Explain your strategy.

Reflect

Use words, pictures, or numbers to explain how to find 300 − 157.

Numbers Every Day

Number Strategies

Use 50 + 45 = 95 to find these sums.

49 + 45 = ☐
51 + 45 = ☐

Find.

40 + 35 = ☐
38 + 35 = ☐
42 + 35 = ☐

13

A Standard Method for Addition

Every day, people solve problems by adding numbers.
They don't always have Base Ten Blocks to use.
They don't always have a calculator.

There are many ways to add numbers by recording
your work on paper.

Explore

Tio helped at the school book fair on Monday and Tuesday.
He sold books and
counted bookmarks.
Tio added to find his totals.

Do each addition your own way.
Is Tio correct?
How did Tio do each addition?

At the Book Fair   Tio T.

Book Sales   Bookmarks Counted

Monday 25   With tassels 257

Tuesday +39   Magnetic + 138
        64   395

Show *and* Share

Share with a classmate how you added.

Connect

➤ Tio spent 44 minutes at the book fair
   on Monday.
   He spent 38 minutes at the book fair
   on Tuesday.
   How long did Tio spend at the book fair?

Find: 44 + 38
Estimate first: 40 + 40 = 80

- Use mental math.
  Take from one number to give to the other.
  38 + 2 + 42
  38 + 2 = 40
  40 + 42 = 82

- Here is another way to add.

Add the ones.	Trade 10 ones for 1 ten.	Add the tens.
44 + 38	1 44 + 38 2	1 44 + 38 82
12 ones	12 ones = 1 ten + 2 ones	

44 + 38 = 82
Tio spent 82 minutes at the book fair.

➤ Tio chose 2 books at the fair.
  One book had 163 pages. The other had 175 pages.
  How many pages altogether?

Find: 163 + 175
Estimate first: 200 + 200 = 400
Here is one way to add.

Add the ones.	Add the tens.	Add the hundreds.
163 + 175 8	1 163 + 175 38	1 163 + 175 338
	13 tens; trade 10 tens for 1 hundred	

163 + 175 = 338
Tio's books had a total of 338 pages.

Here is this addition on a place-value mat.

Hundreds	Tens	Ones

Numbers Every Day

Mental Math

Leah subtracts 52 – 37 like this:
$52 - 32 = 20$
$20 - 5 = 15$
Explain her method.

Use Leah's method to subtract.
$43 - 17 = \square$
$87 - 48 = \square$
$45 - 26 = \square$

Practice

1. Show three different ways to add 27 + 39.

2. Add. What patterns do you see?

   a) $\begin{array}{r} 40 \\ + 21 \\ \hline \end{array}$ b) $\begin{array}{r} 50 \\ + 22 \\ \hline \end{array}$ c) $\begin{array}{r} 60 \\ + 23 \\ \hline \end{array}$ d) $\begin{array}{r} 70 \\ + 24 \\ \hline \end{array}$

3. Add. Try to do these mentally.

   a) $\begin{array}{r} 82 \\ + 6 \\ \hline \end{array}$ b) $\begin{array}{r} 83 \\ + 7 \\ \hline \end{array}$ c) $\begin{array}{r} 84 \\ + 8 \\ \hline \end{array}$ d) $\begin{array}{r} 85 \\ + 9 \\ \hline \end{array}$

4. Add. Try to do these mentally.

   a) $\begin{array}{r} 400 \\ + 7 \\ \hline \end{array}$ b) $\begin{array}{r} 501 \\ + 6 \\ \hline \end{array}$ c) $\begin{array}{r} 602 \\ + 5 \\ \hline \end{array}$ d) $\begin{array}{r} 703 \\ + 4 \\ \hline \end{array}$

5. Add. Use mental math if you can.

   a) $\begin{array}{r} 51 \\ + 33 \\ \hline \end{array}$ b) $\begin{array}{r} 26 \\ + 39 \\ \hline \end{array}$ c) $\begin{array}{r} 47 \\ + 59 \\ \hline \end{array}$ d) $\begin{array}{r} 65 \\ + 48 \\ \hline \end{array}$

6. Add.

   a) $\begin{array}{r} 510 \\ + 90 \\ \hline \end{array}$ b) $\begin{array}{r} 485 \\ + 15 \\ \hline \end{array}$ c) $\begin{array}{r} 326 \\ + 74 \\ \hline \end{array}$ d) $\begin{array}{r} 607 \\ + 93 \\ \hline \end{array}$

7. Add.

   a) $\begin{array}{r} 285 \\ + 264 \\ \hline \end{array}$ b) $\begin{array}{r} 202 \\ + 429 \\ \hline \end{array}$ c) $\begin{array}{r} 358 \\ + 474 \\ \hline \end{array}$ d) $\begin{array}{r} 699 \\ + 133 \\ \hline \end{array}$

8. The Grade 3 class planted tulips at the front of the school.
   They planted 256 red tulips and 371 yellow tulips.
   How many tulips were planted?
   Explain how you solved this problem.

9. **a)** Grade 2 and Grade 3 children rode on a bus to visit a museum.
   There were 19 Grade 2 children.
   There were 25 Grade 3 children.
   How many children were on the bus?
   b) Twenty-seven Grade 4 children joined the
   Grades 2 and 3 children for lunch at the museum.
   How many children were there for lunch?
   How do you know?

10. Use the digits 2, 3, and 4.
    How many 3-digit numbers can you make?
    Add pairs of these numbers.
    How many different sums do you get?
    Show your work.

11. Parkside School was collecting things to recycle.
    Children brought in 277 cans and 125 bottles.
    How many things were brought in?

12. Write a story problem that can be solved
    using 356 + 248. Solve the problem.

Reflect

You know several ways to add.
Which way do you like best? Why?

At Home

Ask 3 adults how they add.
Write down what you
found out about adding.

A Standard Method for Subtraction

There are many ways to subtract numbers by recording your work on paper. In this lesson, you will learn one way.

Explore

Both Joe and his older sister Angie
are in the Read-A-Thon.
Joe is reading a book with 42 pages.
He is on page 18.

Angie is reading a book with 245 pages.
She is on page 164.

Joe works out how much more
they still have to read.

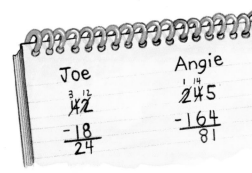

Is Joe correct?
How do you know?

Show and Share

Share your ideas with a classmate.
Explain how Joe's method works.

Connect

Joe's method works for 2-digit and 3-digit subtraction.

Find: 342 − 186

➤ Here is how the subtraction would start on a place-value mat.

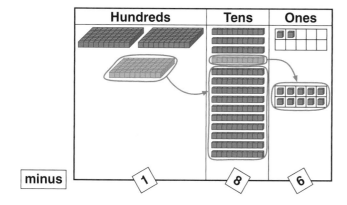

Numbers Every Day

Calculator Skills

The ⑦ key is broken on Julia's calculator.

How could Julia display 77 on her calculator?

How could she calculate 75 − 17?

➤ Here is another way to subtract 186 from 342.

| You cannot subtract the ones. You need more ones. | 34**2** − 18**6** |

Trade 1 ten for 10 ones.
Subtract the ones.
You cannot subtract the tens.
You need more tens

```
    3 12
  3 4̸ 2̸
−  1 8 6
  ───────
        6
```

Trade 1 hundred for 10 tens.
Subtract the tens.

```
   2 13 12
  3̸ 4̸ 2̸
− 1 8 5
  ───────
    5 6
```

Subtract the hundreds.

```
   2 13 12
  3̸ 4̸ 2̸
− 1 8 6
  ───────
  1 5 6
```

Find: 500 − 254

You cannot subtract the ones.
There are no tens to trade.
Go to the hundreds.

$$\begin{array}{r} 50\mathbf{0} \\ -\ 25\mathbf{4} \\ \hline \end{array}$$

Trade 1 hundred for 10 tens.	Trade 1 ten for 10 ones. Subtract the ones.	Subtract the tens. Subtract the hundreds.
$$\begin{array}{r} {}^{4}\ {}^{10} \\ \cancel{5}\ \cancel{0}\ 0 \\ -\ 2\ 5\ 4 \\ \hline \end{array}$$	$$\begin{array}{r} {}^{4}\ {}^{9}_{\cancel{10}}\ {}^{10} \\ \cancel{5}\ \cancel{0}\ \cancel{0} \\ -\ 2\ 5\ 4 \\ \hline 6 \end{array}$$	$$\begin{array}{r} {}^{4}\ {}^{9}_{\cancel{10}}\ {}^{10} \\ \cancel{5}\ \cancel{0}\ \cancel{0} \\ -\ 2\ 5\ 4 \\ \hline 2\ 4\ 6 \end{array}$$

 Use a calculator to check the answers to both problems.

Practice

1. Subtract. What patterns do you see?

   a) $\begin{array}{r} 85 \\ -\ 23 \\ \hline \end{array}$ b) $\begin{array}{r} 75 \\ -\ 24 \\ \hline \end{array}$ c) $\begin{array}{r} 65 \\ -\ 25 \\ \hline \end{array}$ d) $\begin{array}{r} 55 \\ -\ 26 \\ \hline \end{array}$

2. Subtract.

   a) $\begin{array}{r} 90 \\ -\ 21 \\ \hline \end{array}$ b) $\begin{array}{r} 80 \\ -\ 32 \\ \hline \end{array}$ c) $\begin{array}{r} 70 \\ -\ 43 \\ \hline \end{array}$ d) $\begin{array}{r} 60 \\ -\ 54 \\ \hline \end{array}$

3. Show 3 different ways to find 75 − 37.

4. Subtract.

   a) $\begin{array}{r} 456 \\ -\ 234 \\ \hline \end{array}$ b) $\begin{array}{r} 528 \\ -\ 413 \\ \hline \end{array}$ c) $\begin{array}{r} 382 \\ -\ 140 \\ \hline \end{array}$ d) $\begin{array}{r} 843 \\ -\ 211 \\ \hline \end{array}$

5. Subtract.

   a) $\begin{array}{r} 400 \\ -\ 125 \\ \hline \end{array}$ b) $\begin{array}{r} 600 \\ -\ 244 \\ \hline \end{array}$ c) $\begin{array}{r} 500 \\ -\ 317 \\ \hline \end{array}$ d) $\begin{array}{r} 700 \\ -\ 488 \\ \hline \end{array}$

6. Subtract.
a) 450 − 271   b) 603 − 455   c) 700 − 482   d) 356 − 238

7. Prya and Jody are collecting donations for the Terry Fox Run.
Prya has collected $82.
Jody has collected $49.
a) Who collected more money? Explain.
b) How much more did she collect?

8. Ali was at a yard sale. He had 90¢.
Ali bought a book for 25¢ and a car for 50¢.
His mother gave him another 19¢.
How much money did Ali have then? How do you know?

9. Jamie is collecting Popsicle sticks for a project.
He bundles them to count them easily.
He has 2 bundles of 100, 2 bundles of 10, and 5 ones.
Jamie needs 455 sticks.
How many more sticks does Jamie need to collect?

10. Zane, Sunny, and Michelle were playing video games.
Zane's score was 456. Sunny's score was 285.
Michelle's score was 369.
a) How many points does Sunny need to tie Michelle?
b) How many points do Michelle and Sunny need to tie Zane?
c) Make up your own problem about these scores.
Solve your problem.
Show your work.

11. Write your own story problem where you subtract two
3-digit numbers to solve it. Solve the problem.

Reflect

When you subtract 2 numbers, how do you know
when to trade? Use an example to explain.

Show What You Know

1 2

1. Add.

   a) $5 + 9 = \square$ **b)** $8 + 7 = \square$ **c)** $6 + 8 = \square$ **d)** $9 + 9 = \square$

2. Mia has two number cubes.
Each number cube has the numbers 3, 4, 5, 6, 7, and 8.
She rolls both number cubes and adds the numbers.
What possible sums might Mia get?

3

3. Subtract.

   a) $15 - 6 = \square$ **b)** $17 - 9 = \square$ **c)** $16 - 8 = \square$ **d)** $18 - 9 = \square$

4

4. Find all possible subtraction facts for each difference.

   a) 1   **b)** 2   **c)** 3   **d)** 4

How do you know you have found all of them?

5

5. Find each missing number.

   a) $6 + \square = 15$ **b)** $\square + 7 = 14$ **c)** $17 - \square = 9$ **d)** $\square - 8 = 7$

6

6. Ari started an addition chart.
Use a copy of this chart.
Use patterns to complete
the chart.
Write about the patterns
you see.

+	3	6	9	12	15	18	21	24
5			14			23		
10		16			25			
15	18			27				
20			29					

11 13

7. Add.

   a)   25   **b)**   47   **c)**   156   **d)**   349
        + 36   + 19   + 232   + 267

7 8

8. Use mental math to add or subtract.

   a)   61   **b)**   72   **c)**   48   **d)**   89
        + 8   - 3   + 22   - 20

9. Explain how you use mental math to find the sum and the difference.

a) 38 + 45 = ☐ **b)** 50 − 18 = ☐

10. Look at these numbers: 37, 89, 51, 62, 98, 23

a) Estimate which two numbers have the sum that is closest to 100.

b) Estimate which two numbers have the difference that is closest to 50.

11. The classroom floor was retiled. Four hundred seventy-six red tiles and 385 yellow tiles were needed. How many tiles were needed?

12. Subtract.

a)	b)	c)	d)
78	90	385	500
− 23	− 52	− 256	− 187

13. There were 750 children at summer camp. After one week, 252 children went home. How many children were left at the camp?

14. The answer is 376. What might the problem be? Show several problems.

15. Use these numbers: 2, 3, 4, 5, 8, 9
Arrange the numbers
to make the greatest possible sum.
The least possible sum.

```
   ☐ ☐ ☐
 + ☐ ☐ ☐
 ―――――――
```

UNIT

2 Learning Goals

☑ describe patterns in addition and subtraction
☑ recall basic number facts
☑ develop strategies for addition and subtraction
☑ write, solve, and explain addition and subtraction problems

National Read-A-Thon

It's almost time to report on the Read-A-Thon.

This table shows the results from another school.

Woodlawn Public School

Number of books read

Student	Stanley	Jadan	LaToya	Susan
Week 1	2	4	5	3
Week 2	3	2	6	3
Week 3	4	0	3	2
Week 4	1	3	2	1
Number of pages read	214	237	298	228

Use the tables on pages 55 and 100.

Part 1

- Estimate to find which group of children read the most pages.
  Explain how you know.
- How many pages did Jeff and Sookal read altogether?
- Who read more pages, LaToya or Jadan? How many more pages?
- Who read more books, LaToya or Jadan? Explain how you know.

Part 2

There are two kinds of prizes for the Read-A-Thon.
- One for any child who reads from 10 to 15 books
- One for any child who reads from 16 to 20 books

Decide which children should get each prize.
Use words, pictures, or numbers to explain your answers.

Part 3

Think of another way to award a prize at the Read-A-Thon.
What could it be and who would get it?

Reflect on the Unit

What are some important things you know about adding and subtracting? Give at least two examples to show your thinking.

UNIT 3

Geometry

At the Beach

Learning Goals

- describe, name, and sort figures and solids
- describe angles
- build solids
- explore congruent figures and congruent solids
- solve geometry problems

Key Words

attributes

parallel

vertex (vertices)

angle

right angle

regular figure

trapezoid

parallelogram

rhombus

Venn diagram

congruent

pyramid

prism

face

base

edge

net

Look at the picture.

- How are some of the figures the same? Different?
- How are some of the solids the same? Different?
- What else can you say about the picture?

Describing Figures

Look around the classroom. Point out figures with straight sides and curved sides. How else can you describe the figures you see?

 **Explore**

Choose one of these figures. Keep your choice secret.

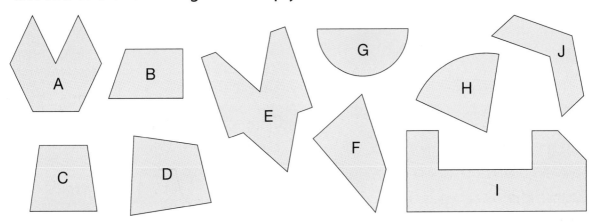

➤ Describe the figure to your partner in as many ways as you can. Have your partner guess the figure.

➤ Trade roles.

Repeat this activity 4 times.

Show and Share

Talk with another pair of classmates.
Share some of the ways you described the figures.
How many sides do they have?
Are the sides curved or straight?

....

An **attribute** is a way to describe a figure.
Here are some attributes of figures.

➤ The lengths of the sides

These figures have some sides
the same length.

These figures have all sides
the same length.

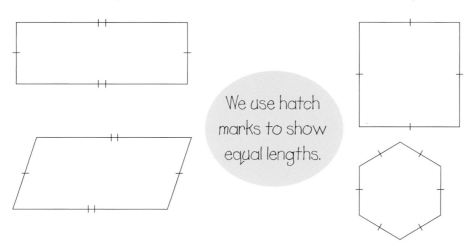

We use hatch
marks to show
equal lengths.

➤ The direction of the sides

These figures have at least
one pair of **parallel** sides.
These sides are always the
same distance apart and
never meet.

These figures have
no parallel sides.

We use arrows to show
parallel lines.

Use large cutouts of these figures for questions 1 and 2.

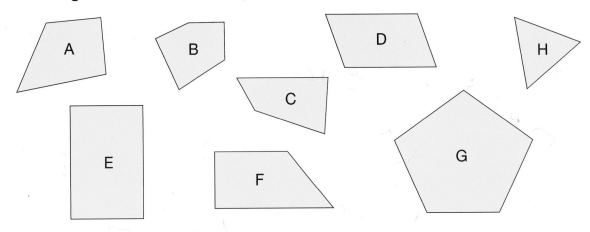

1. Which figures have:
   a) all sides the same length?
   b) some sides the same length?
   c) parallel sides?

2. Choose 2 figures above.
   Sketch figures like them on dot paper.
   How are the figures the same? Different?
   Write about what you see.

 3. Use a geoboard.
   How many different figures can you make
   with only 2 parallel sides?
   Draw your figures on dot paper.
   Write about each figure.

Reflect

How can you tell if a figure has
parallel sides?
Use words or pictures to explain.

Numbers Every Day

Mental Math

Copy this number sentence.
Fill in all the numbers that
make the sentence true.

$$\square + \square = 10$$

How do you know you
have found all the
ways?

Describing Angles

Explore •

You will need a geoboard, geobands, and dot paper.

Make each figure on a geoboard. Then draw it on dot paper.
- a figure that has a corner smaller than the corners in a square
- a figure that has a corner larger than the corners in a square
- a figure that has a corner that matches the corners in a square

Show *and* Share

Share your figures with a classmate.
Which figures have all the same corners?
Which figures have more than one type of corner?
Did any figure have three types of corners?

Connect •

➤ Two sides of a figure meet at a **vertex**.
The two sides make an **angle**.
This figure has four angles.

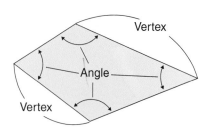

We show an angle with an arc.

➤ When the sides make a square corner at the vertex, the angle is a **right angle**.
These figures have right angles.

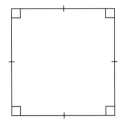 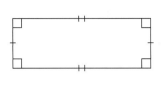 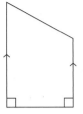

 This is how we show a right angle.

These figures have angles that are greater than a right angle.

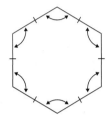 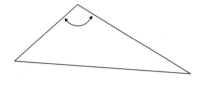 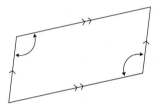

These figures have angles that are less than a right angle.

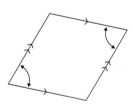 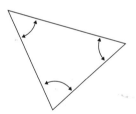 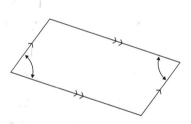

Practice

Use a piece of paper with a square corner when it helps.

1. Which angle is less than a right angle? A right angle? Greater than a right angle?

a)

b)

c)

2. Look at the figures below. Find a figure with:
   a) four right angles
   b) two right angles
   c) no right angles
   d) only one angle larger than a right angle

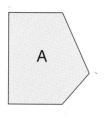 A

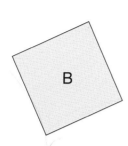 B

 C

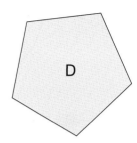 D

3. Sketch objects in your classroom that do not have any right angles. Name each object you sketch.

4. Use a geoboard.
   Try to make a figure with:
   a) only 1 right angle
   b) only 2 right angles
   c) only 3 right angles
   Draw each figure on dot paper.
   Tell how you made each figure.

5. How can you draw a right angle without using dot paper?

Reflect

When you see an angle, how can you tell if it is a right angle?
Use words and pictures to explain.

Numbers Every Day

Number Strategies

Which number am I?

I have:
- 3 tens and 2 ones
- 1 ten
- 10 ones
- 4 tens and 12 ones
- 2 fewer tens than 32

Naming Figures

Explore

You will need geoboards, geobands, and dot paper.

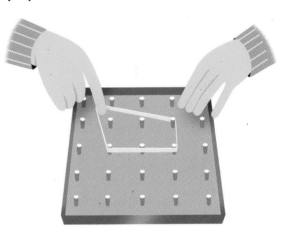

➤ Make a figure on the geoboard.
   Have your partner describe the figure.
➤ Copy the figure on dot paper.
   Write about the figure.
➤ Trade roles.
Repeat this activity until you have 6 figures.

Show *and* Share

Share the figures you made with another pair of classmates.
How are they alike? Different?
Name any figures you know.

Connect

Here are some figures you know.

This is a triangle.
It has 3 sides.
It has 3 angles.

This is a rectangle.
It has 4 sides.
It has 4 right angles.
Opposite sides have
the same length.

This is a square.
It has 4 sides.
It has 4 right angles.
All sides have the
same length.

A regular
figure has all
sides equal
and all angles
equal.

➤ Here are some other figures with 4 sides.

A **trapezoid** has 2 parallel sides.

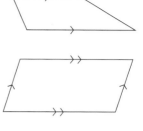

A **parallelogram** has 2 pairs of parallel sides.

A **rhombus** is a parallelogram with all sides equal.

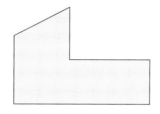

➤ Here are some figures with more than 4 sides.

A pentagon has 5 sides.   A hexagon has 6 sides.

A regular pentagon has 5 equal sides and 5 equal angles.

A regular hexagon has 6 equal sides and 6 equal angles.

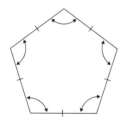

We use the same arc to show equal angles.

Practice

1. Use a geoboard. Make these figures.
   Draw the figures on dot paper.
   a) 2 different trapezoids   **b)** 2 different parallelograms
   c) 2 different rhombuses   **d)** 2 different pentagons

2. Use the figures below. Find:
   a) a rhombus   **b)** a parallelogram
   c) a trapezoid   **d)** a hexagon

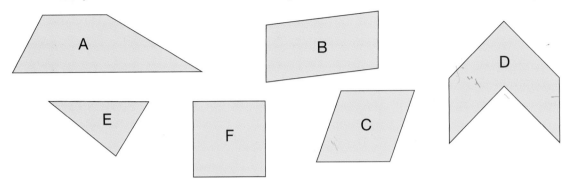

3. Use a geoboard.
   a) Make a square inside a rectangle.
   b) Make a triangle and a square that share an angle.
   c) Make a rhombus and a triangle that share a side.
   Draw your figures on dot paper.

4. Use a geoboard.
   Make 3 different figures with 4 sides.
   Draw the figures on dot paper.
   How are the figures the same? Different?
   Write all you know about each figure.

5. Use a geoboard.
   Make a figure with 7 sides.
   Draw the figure on dot paper.
   Write about the figure.
   Tell about its sides and angles.

Reflect

How is a rectangle like a parallelogram?
How is it different?
Use words and pictures to explain.

Numbers Every Day

Mental Math

Skip count to find each missing number.

5 nickels = ☐ cents
5 dimes = ☐ cents
5 quarters = ☐ cents
5 toonies = ☐ cents

4 Sorting Figures

You will need large cutouts of the figures below.

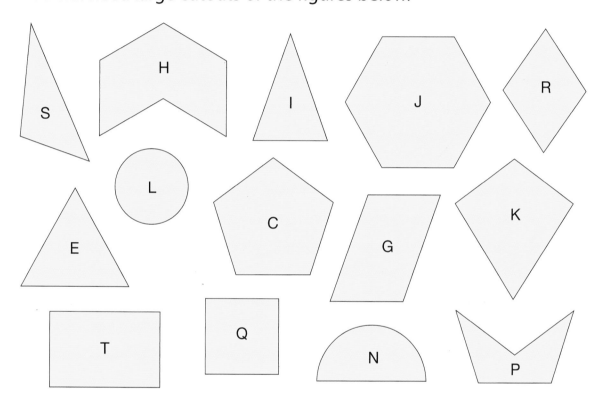

➤ Sort the figures into two or more groups.
   Record your sorting.

➤ Repeat the activity.
   Sort the figures a different way.
   Record the sorting.

Show and Share

Talk about the attributes you used to sort.
What did you do with a figure that did not belong?

LESSON FOCUS | Compare and sort figures.

Connect

You can use a **Venn diagram** to sort.

➤ This is a Venn diagram.

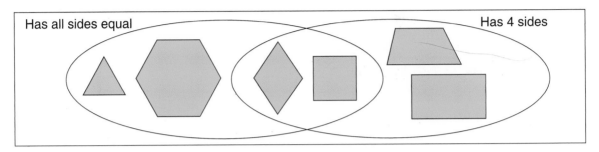

The figures in the loop on the left have all sides equal.
The figures in the loop on the right have 4 sides.
The figures in the middle have 4 equal sides.

The sorting rule is:

Figures with all sides equal and figures with 4 sides

➤ The Venn diagram below shows figures with parallel sides
and figures with right angles.
The figures in the middle have parallel sides *and* right angles.
The figures outside the loops have no parallel sides
and no right angles.

The sorting rule is:

Figures with parallel sides and
figures with right angles

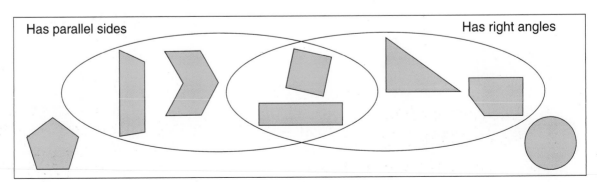

For questions 1 and 2, use the figures from *Explore*.

1. Copy this Venn diagram. Make it large.
   Choose 2 attributes.
   Sort the figures in the Venn diagram.
   Have a classmate tell your sorting rule.

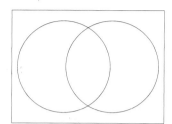

2. Work with a partner.
   Take turns to choose a secret attribute.
   Find a set of figures with that attribute.
   Ask your partner to add a figure to the set.
   Or, your partner could sketch a figure that belongs.
   If the figure does not belong, tell your partner to try again.
   Ask your partner to guess the attribute.

3. Draw a Venn diagram on dot paper.
   Label one loop: Right angle
   Label the other loop: Five angles
   Sketch 3 different figures in each loop
   and 3 figures in the middle.

4. Draw a large Venn diagram
   with two separate loops.
   Which figures could go in each loop?
   Sketch the figures.
   Label each loop.
   Explain your work.

Reflect

Choose two attributes.
Choose 5 different figures.
Use words or pictures to show
how to sort the figures.

Numbers Every Day

Number Strategies

Suppose you start at 18 and
count back by 2s.
Will you say 4? 5?
How do you know?

Suppose you start at 17
and count back by 2s.
Will you say 2? 3?
How do you know?

Congruent Figures

Use large cutouts of these figures:

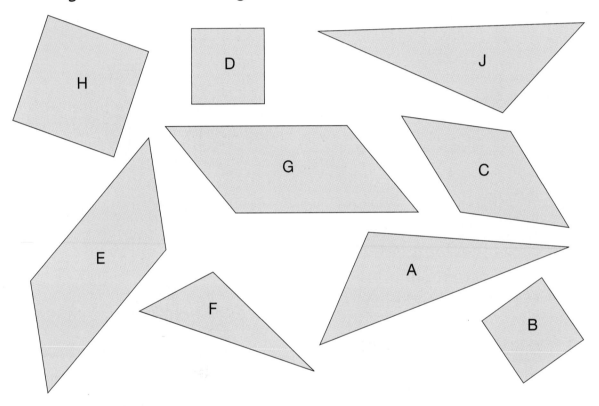

➤ Look at the squares.
  How are they the same? Different?
  Record your ideas.
➤ Repeat the activity for the triangles.
➤ Repeat the activity for the parallelograms.

Show *and* Share

Share your answers with another pair of classmates.
How do you know if two figures are exactly the same?

When two figures have the same shape and size, the figures are **congruent**.

➤ Congruent figures have equal matching sides and equal matching angles.

These pentagons are congruent.
They have the same size and shape.

These rectangles are *not* congruent.
They have the same shape but different sizes.

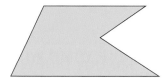

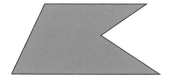

➤ To show two figures are congruent, place one figure on top of the other. If they coincide, they are congruent.

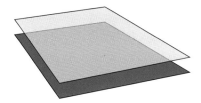

➤ You may need to flip or turn the figures to show they are congruent. If you cannot move the figures:

Trace one figure. Place it on top of the other figure.

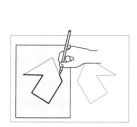

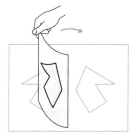

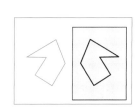

If the tracing coincides with the other figure, the figures are congruent.

1. Use a geoboard.
   a) Make 2 congruent triangles.
   b) Make 2 congruent parallelograms.
   c) Make 2 congruent trapezoids.
   Draw the figures on dot paper.

2. Use a geoboard.
   a) Make 2 different triangles that share one side.
   b) Make 2 different triangles that share one angle.
   Draw the figures on dot paper.

3. Use a geoboard. Make this parallelogram. Make as many congruent parallelograms as you can.
   Record your results on dot paper.
   Use a different colour for each parallelogram.

4. Find pairs of congruent figures.
   How do you know they are congruent?

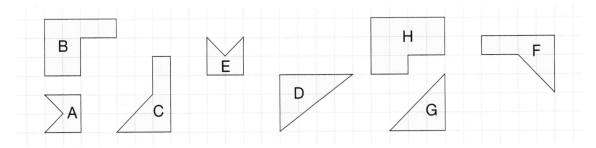

Reflect

How can you tell if 2 figures are congruent?
Use dot paper. Draw 2 figures that are congruent.
Draw 2 figures that are *not* congruent.

Numbers Every Day

Calculator Skills

When you use a calculator to count on by 2s, it is an "add 2 maker".
How do you make your calculator a:
• "subtract 2 maker"?
• "doubles maker"?

Making Pictures with Figures

Artists use figures to create interesting pictures.
This picture is called *Swinging*.
Wassily Kandinsky painted it in 1925.

Which figures have been put together to make other figures?

Explore

You will need Pattern Blocks and dot paper.
Take 3 Pattern Blocks.

➤ Put the blocks next to each other to make a figure.
Be sure the sides of the blocks touch.
Draw the figure.
Count the number of sides in the figure.
Record your work in a table.

➤ Use the same 3 blocks to make a different figure.
Draw the figure.
How many sides does it have?

➤ Use the same blocks to make as many different figures as you can.
Record each figure.

Figure	Number of Sides
	4

LESSON FOCUS | Make a picture from figures.

Show *and* Share

Share your results with a classmate.
Can your classmate make a different figure with your blocks?
With more sides? With fewer sides?

Many figures may be made from other figures.

With 2 congruent triangles,
you can make a parallelogram.

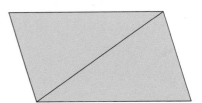

With 3 congruent triangles,
you can make a trapezoid.

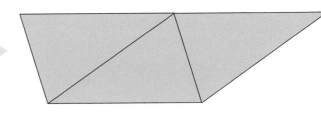

With a square and a triangle
that have one side the
same length, you can make a
pentagon.

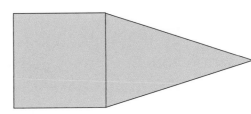

Practice

1. Use Pattern Blocks to make a picture.
    Trace or copy the picture.
    Write about your picture.
    Which figures did you use?
    Are any figures congruent?
    How do you know?

2. Use 2 different Pattern Blocks each time.
Make a figure with:
   a) 1 pair of parallel sides
   b) 2 pairs of parallel sides
   c) 3 pairs of parallel sides
   d) No parallel sides
Sketch each figure you made.

3. Use 4 green Pattern Blocks.
How many different figures can you make using 4 green triangles?
How many sides does each figure have?
Each triangle must have at least one side
fully touching another triangle.
Sketch each figure.
Record the number of sides.

4. Use a copy of this picture.
What figures do you see?
Are any of them congruent? How do you know?

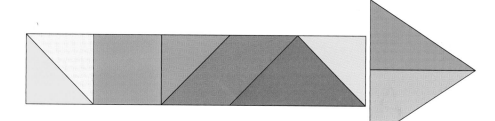

Reflect

Use dot paper. Draw a triangle with
all sides different lengths.
Draw a congruent triangle.
Cut out the triangles.
Draw the different figures you can make
by putting these triangles together.

Strategies Toolkit

A tangram is a square made from 7 figures or **tans**.
The seven tans are: 2 small triangles,
1 medium triangle, 2 large triangles,
1 parallelogram, and 1 square.

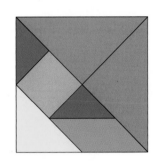

Explore

You will need a tangram and dot paper.
This large triangle is made from the
2 small triangles and the medium triangle.
What figures can *you* make with only 3 tans?
Record your work.

Show *and* Share

Tell about the strategy you used to solve the problem.

Connect

Strategies

- **Make a table.**
- **Use a model.**
- **Draw a picture.**
- **Solve a simpler problem.**
- **Work backward.**
- **Guess and check.**
- **Make an organized list.**
- **Use a pattern.**

Use the tans.
How many different ways can you make a trapezoid?

Understand

What do you know?
- You can use any of the tans.
- You must make a trapezoid.

Plan

Think of a strategy to help you
solve the problem.
- You can **solve a simpler problem**.
- Start with 2 tans, then try 3 tans, 4 tans, and so on.

Solve

- Choose 2 tans. Try to make a trapezoid.
  If you can, sketch it.
  If you cannot, trade 1 tan for a different tan
  and try again.
- Repeat for different pairs of tans.
- Then choose 3 tans. Try to make a trapezoid.
- Repeat for 4, 5, 6, then 7 tans.

Look Back

How do you know that each figure you made
is a trapezoid?

Practice

Choose one of the

Strategies

1. Think about the figures you know.
   Which of these figures can you
   make using all 7 tans?
   Show your work.

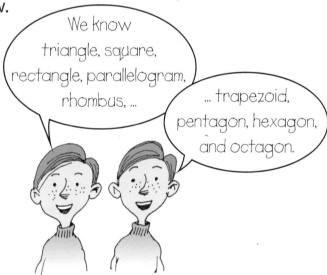

We know triangle, square, rectangle, parallelogram, rhombus, ...

... trapezoid, pentagon, hexagon, and octagon.

2. Try to make a square with
   2 tans, 3 tans, 4 tans, 5 tans,
   6 tans, and 7 tans.
   What did you find out?

Reflect

Which figures were easiest to make with tans?
Which figures were the hardest? Why?
Write about your ideas.

Identifying Prisms and Pyramids

This is a **pyramid**.

This is a **prism**.

How are they the same?
How are they different?

Explore

Choose a solid.
Keep your solid secret.
Describe the solid to your partner
in as many ways as you can.
Have your partner guess the solid.
Trade roles.
Repeat this activity 4 times.

Show *and* Share

Share with your partner how you identified each solid.
Which attributes did you use?

➤ A pyramid has 1 **base**.
The base is a **face**.
The shape of the base tells the name of the pyramid.
A pyramid also has triangular faces.

This is a square pyramid.
It has 5 faces:
1 square
4 triangles

This is a hexagonal pyramid.
It has 7 faces:
1 hexagon
6 triangles

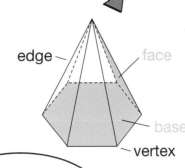

For pyramids and prisms, the **edges** meet at a **vertex**.

➤ A prism has 2 congruent bases.
The shape of the bases tells the name of the prism.
A prism also has rectangular faces.

This is a triangular prism.
It has 5 faces:
2 triangles
3 rectangles

This is a pentagonal prism.
It has 7 faces:
2 pentagons
5 rectangles

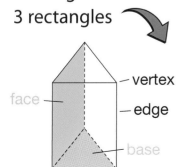

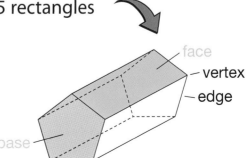

➤ When two solids have the same size and shape, they are congruent.
Here are two congruent rectangular pyramids.

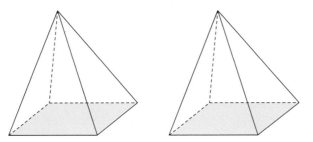

Use models when they help.
Use these pictures for questions 1 to 3.

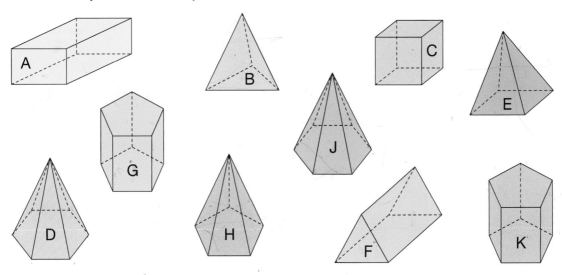

1. Use the solids above.
   Name each prism. Tell how you know.
   Write how many faces, edges, and vertices it has.

2. Use the solids above.
   Name each pyramid. Tell how you know.
   Write how many faces, edges, and vertices it has.

3. Use the solids above.
   a) Which pyramids are congruent? How do you know?
   b) Which prisms are congruent? How do you know?

4. Which solid has each set of faces? How do you know?

a)

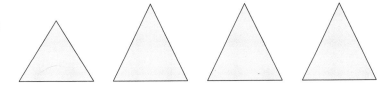

b)

c)

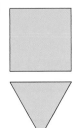 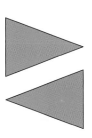

5. Two faces of a solid are shown.
What could the solid be? How do you know?

a)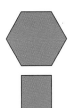

b)

c)

6. A prism and a pyramid have the same number of vertices.
What type of prism and pyramid could they be?
Is there more than one answer?
How do you know?
Show your work.

Numbers Every Day

Mental Math

Find each missing number.
Explain your strategy.

$$10 - \square = 8$$
$$5 + \square = 9$$
$$2 + 3 + 5 = \square$$
$$7 + 3 - 2 = \square$$

Reflect

How are prisms and pyramids alike?
Different?
Use words or pictures to explain.

Sorting Solids

Explore ·

Use models of these solids.

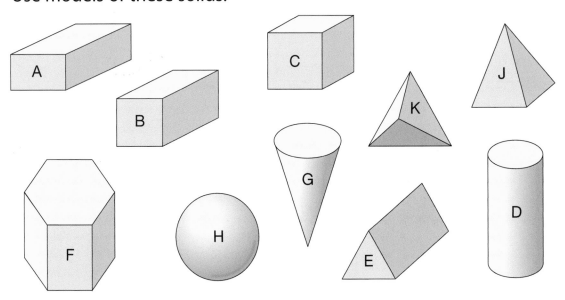

➤ Choose 2 attributes. Keep them secret.
➤ Sort some of the solids.
  Use a Venn diagram if you wish.
➤ Ask your partner to tell what the attributes are. Record the attributes.
➤ Trade roles.
  Repeat the activity for 2 different attributes.

Show *and* Share

Show another pair of classmates one way you sorted.
Ask your classmates to tell the attributes you used.

➤ Here are some attributes of solids you know.

A cube has all faces congruent.
It has:
8 vertices
12 edges
6 faces

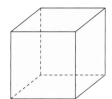

This triangular pyramid has
all faces congruent. It has:
4 vertices
6 edges
4 faces

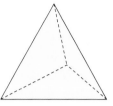

A rectangular prism has:
8 vertices
12 edges
6 faces

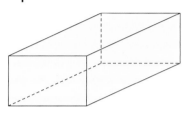

A square pyramid has:
5 vertices
8 edges
5 faces

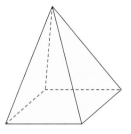

➤ One way to sort these solids is in a Venn diagram,
with these attributes:

• Has 8 vertices

• Has all faces congruent

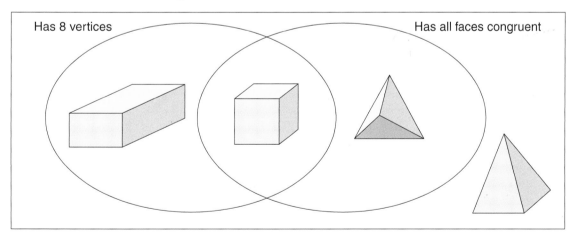

The square pyramid has neither of these attributes.
It is placed outside the loops.

The sorting rule is:

Solids with 8 vertices and solids with all faces congruent

Use solids when they help.

1. Navjit sorted these solids.
What sorting rule did he use?
How would you label the loops?

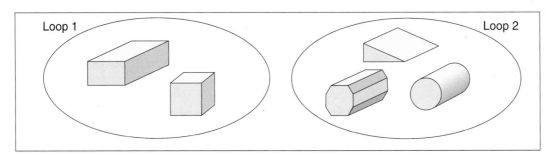

2. a) Sort the solids below, in a
copy of this Venn diagram.
How did you know where
to put each solid?

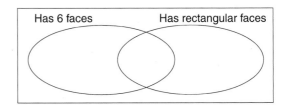

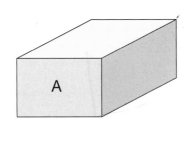  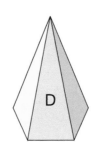 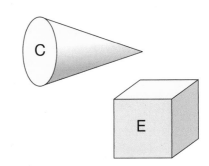

b) Choose a different solid.
Where does it belong in the Venn diagram? Explain.

Math Link

Patterning

There is a pattern in the numbers of edges, faces,
and vertices of a solid.
When you add the numbers of vertices and faces,
the sum is 2 more than the number of edges.

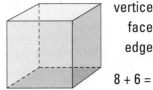

vertices = 8
faces = 6
edges = 12

8 + 6 = 12 + 2

3. Look at the solids below. Find 2 attributes.
Sort the solids. Use the letters to help record your sorting.
Write your sorting rule.

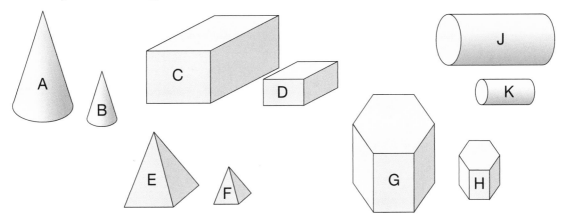

4. Use the solids above.
Choose 2 different attributes.
Sort the solids. Use the letters to help record your sorting.
Write your sorting rule.

5. Choose 2 solids from question 3.
How are these solids the same? Different?

6. Tell which solid is described. Explain how you know.
Is there more than 1 solid each time?
   a) I have 5 vertices and 5 faces.
   b) I have 6 faces.
   c) I have 5 faces.
   Three of my faces are rectangles.
   d) I have 12 edges.
   All my faces are congruent.

Reflect

Choose 5 different solids.
Choose 2 attributes.
Sort the solids. Use words and pictures
to explain how you sorted these solids.

Numbers Every Day

Number Strategies

Skip count to find how many cents.
   • 4 dimes and 3 nickels
   • 3 quarters and 2 dimes
   • 2 quarters and 4 nickels
   • 4 quarters, 3 dimes,
     and 2 nickels

Making Models from Figures

You can use different figures
to build models of solids.
These students built
a gingerbread house.
Which figures can you see
in the house?

Explore

You will need several cardboard cutouts of the figures below,
and sticky tape. Your teacher will give you more cutouts.
Make your own model.

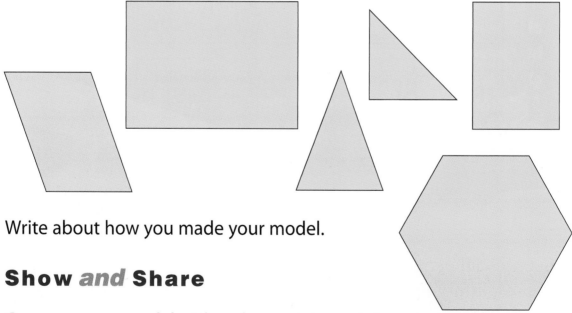

Write about how you made your model.

Show and Share

Compare your model with a classmate's model.
How are the models the same? Different?

Taping each edge of a cutout can be hard to do.
We can make a model from one cutout.
This cutout is called a **net**.

➤ This box is a rectangular prism.
It can be cut so it is in one piece.

This is a net for the box.

➤ Here is another net for a
rectangular prism.
It also shows all the faces of the
rectangular prism joined in 1 piece.
Some faces are congruent.

A net can be folded to make a model
of a solid.

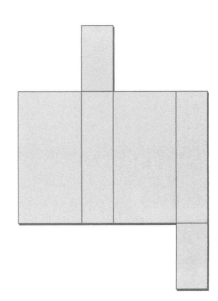

1. Use a large copy of this net.
   Colour the congruent faces the same colour.
   Fold the net.
   Where are the congruent faces
   on your model?

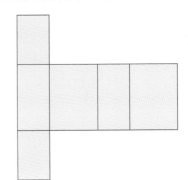

2. Use a cereal box.
   Cut along some edges until you can
   lay the cardboard flat.
   Which figures do you see in your net?
   Which attributes do the figures have?

3. Use a large copy of this net.
   Predict which sides will meet
   when you fold the net.
   Fold the net to check.
   What do you notice about
   the lengths of the sides that join?

4. Which picture shows a net for a cube? How do you know?
   Use any materials you think will help. Show your work.

   a)   b)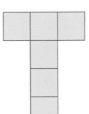

Reflect

The net of a rectangular prism has
6 rectangles.
When you see 6 rectangles in a picture,
how can you tell if it is a net?
Use words and pictures to explain.

Number Strategies

Estimate each sum.
Explain your strategy.

156 + 233
407 + 108
38 + 150
198 + 49

11 Making a Structure from Solids

This is an inuksuk:
An inuksuk is a stone structure made by the Inuit.
The head looks like a triangular prism.
The arms look like rectangular prisms.

Look at structures in your neighbourhood or school. What solids can you find?

Explore

You will need many different solids, and glue or sticky tape.
Use the solids to make a structure.
Sketch a picture of your structure.
Write about how you made your structure.

Show and Share

Show your structure to another pair of classmates. Ask them to find congruent solids and congruent figures. Match the objects in your classmates' sketch with the objects in their structure.

Connect

Here is a sandcastle Jasmine made.

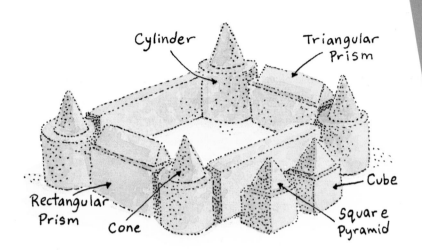

Numbers Every Day

Number Strategies

Estimate each difference.
Explain your strategy.

$$233 - 156$$
$$407 - 108$$
$$150 - 38$$
$$198 - 49$$

Jasmine wrote about how she built it:

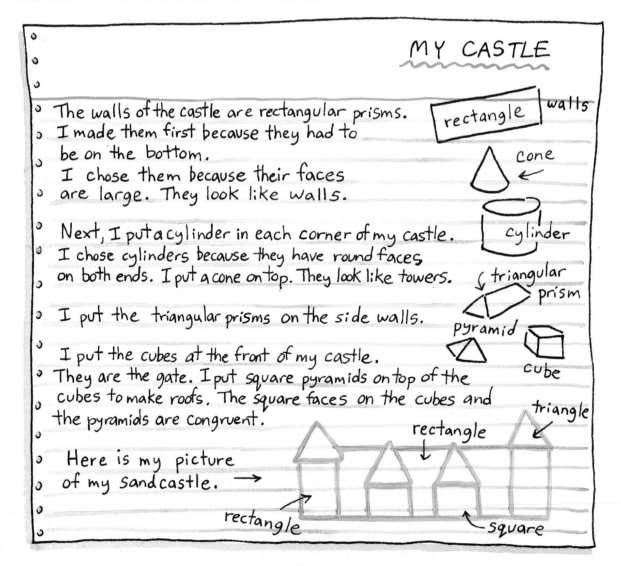

MY CASTLE

The walls of the castle are rectangular prisms. I made them first because they had to be on the bottom. I chose them because their faces are large. They look like walls.

Next, I put a cylinder in each corner of my castle. I chose cylinders because they have round faces on both ends. I put a cone on top. They look like towers.

I put the triangular prisms on the side walls.

I put the cubes at the front of my castle. They are the gate. I put square pyramids on top of the cubes to make roofs. The square faces on the cubes and the pyramids are congruent.

Here is my picture of my sandcastle. →

rectangle walls

cone

cylinder

triangular prism

pyramid

cube

triangle

rectangle

rectangle

square

1. Make a structure using no more than 10 solids.
   a) Sketch your structure.
   b) Explain how you built it.

2. These buildings are made of many solids.
   a) How many solids can you find?
   b) Name each solid.
   c) How many are pyramids? Prisms?

3. Build a bridge from solids. Sketch your bridge. Write about the solids you used and why you used them.

4. Use Pattern Blocks. Build a tower 15 cm high. Use the fewest Pattern Blocks. Which blocks did you use? What attributes do they have? Show your work.

At Home

Reflect

When you look at a structure, how do you find out which solids it is made of? Use words and pictures to explain.

Choose a building near your home. Sketch a picture of it. Write about the solids that make up the building.

LESSON

1. How are these figures alike? How are they different?

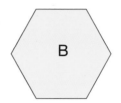  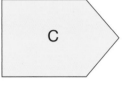

2. Use figures A and C above. Tell about the angles in each figure.

3. Name each figure. Write all that you know about it.

a) 　　b) 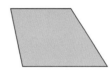 　　c)

d) 　　e) 　　f)

4. Use large cutouts of the figures below.
Choose 2 attributes.
Sort the figures in a Venn diagram.

   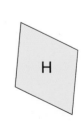

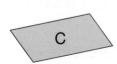  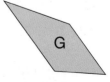

5. Look at the figures in question 4.
Which figures are congruent? How do you know?

138

6   **6.** Use 4 blue Pattern Blocks.
Make as many different figures as you can.
Make sure that sides of the blocks touch each other.
Trace each figure you make.

8   **7.** Name the solids below.
How are they alike? Different?

10   **8.** Sketch the faces of each solid in question 7.

8
9   **9.** Identify each solid below.
Choose 2 attributes.
Sort the solids. Write the sorting rule.

   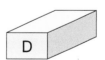 

9
11   **10.** Find solids like those in question 9.
Build a structure.
Sketch your structure,
then write about it.
Did you use congruent solids?
How do you know?

UNIT

3 **Learning Goals**

☑ describe, name, and sort
figures and solids
☑ describe angles
☑ build solids
☑ explore congruent figures
and congruent solids
☑ solve geometry problems

At the Beach

Design a sand castle.

Use any solids to make a model of your sand castle.
Sketch a picture of your model.
Write about your model.

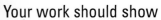

Your work should show
- ☑ how you used solids to make a model of a sand castle
- ☑ a picture that matches your model
- ☑ a clear explanation of how you made your model
- ☑ the names of the solids you used, and why you chose them

Reflect on the Unit

How are figures and solids the same? Different?
Use words and pictures to explain.

Cross Strand Investigation

How Many Cereal Bits in a Box?

You will need a box of cereal and other items in this picture.

Part 1

➤ How can you estimate the total number of cereal bits in a box?
➤ Look at the photo.
  What data or measuring tools can you use?
➤ Find as many ways to estimate as you can.
  Use words, numbers, or pictures to explain your thinking.

Part 2

➤ Which way do you think will provide the best estimate? Why?
➤ Try it out. Get any materials you need.
  Record your work.

Part 3

➤ Count the number of cereal bits in the box.
  How can you group the bits to count them?
➤ How does the number of bits compare with your estimate?
  Explain.
➤ How would you estimate differently next time? Explain.

Display Your Work

Report your findings using words, pictures, or numbers.

Take It Further

➤ How long would it take to eat all the cereal in a box?
  Find a way to estimate this.
  How could you check your estimate?

➤ Is the carton of milk shown enough for one box of cereal?
  How could you find out?
  Use words, numbers, or pictures to explain.

Multiplication

Here Comes the Band!

Learning Goals

- model multiplication and division
- find strategies to multiply and divide
- recall basic multiplication and division facts
- pose and solve problems using multiplication and division
- use a calculator to find patterns in numbers

and Division

In a parade, there are many bands.

Key Words

- multiplication sentence
- times
- equal groups
- array
- factor
- product
- row
- column
- division sentence
- divisible
- related facts

- How many people are in this band?

- How did you find out?

- How else can you find out how many people are in the band?

- How many different ways can you find out how many are in the band?

Relating Multiplication and Addition

Explore

Kia has 3 strips of stickers.
There are 5 stickers on each strip.
Find ways to show how many stickers Kia has.
Record your work.

Show *and* Share

Share your results with a classmate.
Make up a problem like the sticker problem.
Solve the problem with your classmate.

Connect

Aaron has 4 strips of stickers.
There are 3 stickers on each strip.
How many stickers does Aaron have?

To find how many stickers:

➤ You can model the stickers with Snap Cubes, then count.

Count: 1,   2,   3,   4,   5,   6,   7,   8,   9,   10, 11, 12

➤ You can add.
   $3 + 3 + 3 + 3 = 12$
   Think: 4 groups of 3 added = 12

This is an
addition sentence.

$3 + 3 + 3 + 3 = 12$

➤ You can multiply.

$4 \times 3 = 12$

Think: 4 groups of $3 = 12$

Another way to say this is "4 **times** 3 equals 12."

Aaron has 12 stickers.

Equal groups have the same number of things in each group.

When you have equal groups, you can add or multiply to find how many altogether.

This is a multiplication sentence.

$4 \times 3 = 12$

Practice

Use counters or Snap Cubes when they help.

1. For which pictures can you write a multiplication sentence? Explain.

a)

b)

c)

2. Write an addition sentence and a multiplication sentence for each picture. The first one is done for you.

a)

$3 + 3 = 6$

$2 \times 3 = 6$

b)

c)

3. Write a multiplication sentence for each addition sentence, then draw a picture.
   a) $7 + 7 + 7 = 21$
   b) $1 + 1 + 1 + 1 + 1 + 1 = 6$
   c) $5 + 5 = 10$
   d) $2 + 2 + 2 + 2 + 2 + 2 + 2 = 14$

4. Write an addition sentence for each multiplication sentence, then draw a picture.
   a) $2 \times 6 = 12$
   b) $3 \times 3 = 9$
   c) $4 \times 1 = 4$

5. How many legs are there altogether?
   How many different ways can you find out?
   Show your thinking.

6. a) Kayla uses straws and pipe cleaners
      to make triangles.
      She must not bend the straws.
      How many straws will Kayla need
      to make 4 triangles?
   b) Suppose Kayla makes 4 squares.
      Will she need more or fewer straws?
      How do you know?

7. Can you write a multiplication sentence for this picture?
   How do you know?

Reflect

When can you use a multiplication sentence to find how many?
Use words, pictures, or numbers to explain.

2 Using Arrays to Multiply

Explore

You need 12 counters.
How many different ways can you arrange the counters
in equal rows?

➤ Begin with 2 counters in each row.
➤ Write a multiplication sentence and
an addition sentence for each way.
Record your work.

Show and Share

Share your results with another
pair of classmates.
Did you find all the ways to arrange
the counters?
How do you know?
What patterns did you find?

Numbers Every Day

Number Strategies

40 − 20 = 20

Use this doubles fact to find
each difference.

40 − 21 = ☐

40 − 19 = ☐

42 − 20 = ☐

An **array** shows objects arranged in equal rows.

➤ Here are 2 arrays that show 15 counters.
You can use an addition sentence and
a multiplication sentence to tell how many counters.

3 rows of 5
5 + 5 + 5 = 15
3 groups of 5
3 × 5 = 15

5 rows of 3
3 + 3 + 3 + 3 + 3 = 15
5 groups of 3
5 × 3 = 15

➤ You can use an array to multiply.
To find 6 × 4, make an array of 6 rows of 4.

6	×	4	=	24
↑		↑		↑
rows		counters in each row		total number of counters

In a multiplication sentence, the numbers you multiply are **factors**.
The answer is the **product**.

6 × 4 = 24
factor factor product

Practice

1. Write a multiplication sentence for each array.

a)

b)

c)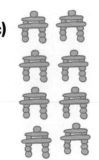

2. Use counters. Make arrays to show:
   a) 2 rows of 7 and 7 rows of 2
   b) 1 row of 6 and 6 rows of 1
   Write a multiplication sentence for each array.

3. Use counters. Make an array to find each product.
   a) 3×2　　b) 2×3　　c) 1×7　　d) 7×1
   What do you notice about the products?

4. In Alysa's garden, there are 5 rows of tomato plants.
   There are 4 plants in each row.
   How many plants are there in all?
   Show how you found out.

5. In a store, there are 4 rows of comedy videos
   and 2 rows of cartoon videos.
   There are 6 videos in each row.
   How many videos are there in all?

6. Find each missing number.
   How are the products in each pair the same? Different?
   a) $3 \times 6 = 18$　　b) $5 \times 2 = 10$　　c) $4 \times 7 = 28$
   　 $6 \times 3 = \square$　　　 $2 \times 5 = \square$　　　 $7 \times \square = 28$

7. a) How many ways can you arrange 6 counters in equal rows?
   　 How do you know you have found all the ways?
   b) Arrange 7 counters in equal rows.
   　 How many ways can you do this? Explain.
   Show your work.

Reflect

How can you use an array to multiply?
Make up an example. Use words, pictures, or numbers
to explain how you multiply.

Multiplying by 2 and by 5

 **Explore** ··  Game

You will need a spinner, a paper clip as a pointer,
a number cube labelled 1 to 6, 2-cm grid paper, and counters.

Product Cover-Up

How to play:

➤ Use 2-cm grid paper.
Each player makes the
product card below.
Write these products
anywhere on your card.

➤ Roll the number cube,
then spin the spinner.
Use the numbers to write
a multiplication sentence.

• The number cube
gives the first factor.

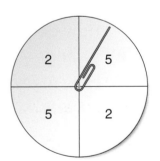

Products			
4	15	10	8
25	12	30	6
10	20	5	2

• The spinner gives the second factor.
On the product card, cover the product
with a counter.

➤ Take turns.
The first person to cover one row wins.

➤ Play the game again.
This time, the spinner gives the first factor
and the number cube gives the second factor.

Show *and* Share

Which strategies did you use to multiply by 2 and by 5?

Connect

➤ Multiply 7 × 2.
  • One way to multiply is to skip count on a number line.

   Start at 0. Count on by 2s seven times: 2, 4, 6, 8, 10, 12, 14
   7 × 2 = 14

  • Another way to multiply 7 by 2 is to use doubles.
   Double 7 is 14.

➤ Multiply 2 × 7.
Skip count on a number line.

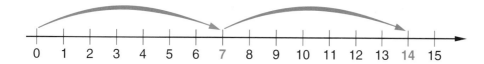

Start at 0. Count on by 7s two times: 7, 14
2 × 7 = 14

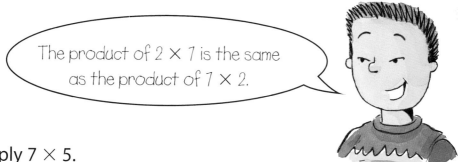

The product of 2 × 7 is the same as the product of 7 × 2.

➤ Multiply 7 × 5.
Here is one way to multiply 7 by 5.

Skip count on a
hundred chart. Start at 5.
Count on by 5s until you
have counted 7 numbers:
5, 10, 15, 20, 25, 30, 35
7 × 5 = 35

1	2	3	4	5	6	7	8	9	10
11	12	13	14	15	16	17	18	19	20
21	22	23	24	25	26	27	28	29	30
31	32	33	34	35	36	37	38	39	40

Practice

Use counters when they help.

1. Write a multiplication sentence
for each picture.
The first one is done for you.

a)

3 groups of 2
$3 \times 2 = 6$

b)

c)

2. Use a hundred chart to multiply.
What patterns do you see in the products?

a) 1×2 b) 2×2

c) 3×2 d) 4×2

e) 5×2 f) 6×2

3. When you multiply by 2, is the product
ever an odd number?
How do you know?

4. Use a number line to multiply.
What patterns do you see in the products?

a) 1×5 b) 2×5

c) 3×5 d) 4×5

e) 5×5 f) 6×5

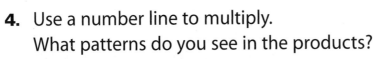

5. When you multiply by 5, is the product ever an odd number? Explain.

6. Multiply.

a) 2×4 **b)** 5×6 **c)** 7×2 **d)** 2×7

e) 5×1 **f)** 2×3 **g)** 5×7 **h)** 2×1

7. Françoise has 6 pairs of shoes.
How many shoes does she have?
Show your work with pictures and numbers.

8. Stelios buys 3 packets of stamps.
Each packet has 5 stamps.
How many stamps does Stelios buy?

9. Barbara bought tickets for 4 children and 2 adults.
Carlos bought tickets for 2 children and 3 adults.
Who spent more money?
How much more? How do you know?

Movie Matinee
Child $2.00 / Adult $5.00

Reflect

What strategies do you use to multiply by 2 and by 5? Use words, pictures, or numbers to explain.

At Home

Make groups of nickels. Each group can have at most 7 nickels. Write a multiplication sentence to find how many cents are in each group of nickels.

Multiplying by 10

Explore

There are 10 candles in a box.
Shireen bought 4 boxes.
How many candles did Shireen buy?
Show your work.

Show and Share

Share your answer with another pair of classmates.
What strategies did you use to multiply by 10?
Make up a similar problem with your partner, then solve it.

Connect

There are 6 packages of balloons.
There are 10 balloons in each package.
How many balloons are there?

Think: 6 packages of 10 balloons is 6 × 10.

Here are 3 ways to multiply by 10.
➤ Use Base Ten Blocks and skip count.

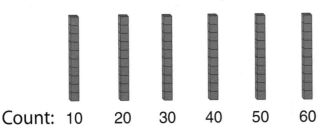

Count: 10   20   30   40   50   60
6 × 10 = 60

➤ Skip count on a number line.

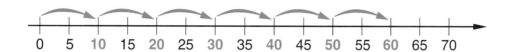

Start at 0. Count on by 10s six times: 10, 20, 30, 40, 50, 60
6 × 10 = 60

➤ Use patterns and place value.

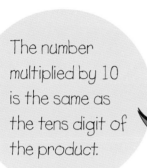

The number multiplied by 10 is the same as the tens digit of the product.

$1 \times 10 = 10$
$2 \times 10 = 20$
$3 \times 10 = 30$
$4 \times 10 = 40$
$5 \times 10 = 50$
$\mathbf{6} \times 10 = \mathbf{6}0$
$7 \times 10 = 70$

The ones digit of the product is always 0.

Practice

1. Write a multiplication sentence for each picture.

a)
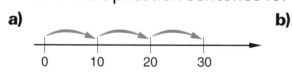

b)

1	2	3	4	5	6	7	8	9	10
11	12	13	14	15	16	17	18	19	20
21	22	23	24	25	26	27	28	29	30
31	32	33	34	35	36	37	38	39	40
41	42	43	44	45	46	47	48	49	50

2. Write a multiplication sentence for each sum.
  a) 10 + 10
  b) 10 + 10 + 10 + 10 + 10 + 10

3. Multiply.

   a) 5×10 **b)** 7×10

   c) 10×1 **d)** 1×10

   e) 10×2 **f)** 6×10

   g) 10×3 **h)** 4×10

4. You have 5 dimes and 6 nickels.
How much money do you have?
How do you know?
Show your work.

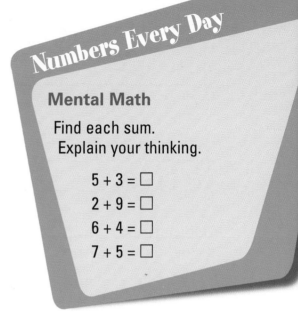

Numbers Every Day

Mental Math

Find each sum.
Explain your thinking.

$5 + 3 = \Box$

$2 + 9 = \Box$

$6 + 4 = \Box$

$7 + 5 = \Box$

5. There will be 10 people at
Philip's birthday party.

  a) Look at the price list for
party items. How much will
each set of items cost?

    • 10 party hats

    • 10 balloons

    • 10 plates

    • 10 napkins

  b) Will 35¢ be enough to buy
10 cups? Explain how you know.

Items	Price
Party hat	6¢
Balloon	2¢
Cup	4¢
Napkin	1¢
Plate	5¢

6. Write a story problem you can solve by multiplying by 10.
Solve your problem. Show your work.

7. Draw as many different arrays
as you can to show the product 20.
Write a multiplication sentence for each array.

Reflect

When you multiply by 10, how can you write the
product without counting or using an array?
Use words, pictures, or numbers to explain.

5 Multiplying by 1 and by 0

Explore ···

You will need paper plates and counters.

➤ Mark makes waffles for his family.

He puts each waffle on a different plate.
Mark uses 5 plates.
How many waffles does Mark make?
How can you use a multiplication sentence to show this?

➤ Mark has 3 empty plates.
How many waffles are on these plates?
How can you use a multiplication
sentence to show this?

Show *and* Share

Show your work to a classmate.
What is special about multiplying by 1?
What is special about multiplying by 0?

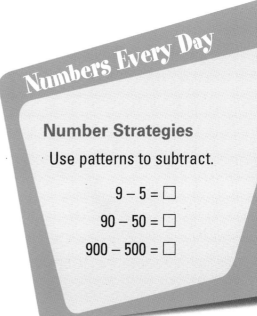

Numbers Every Day

Number Strategies
Use patterns to subtract.

$9 - 5 = \square$

$90 - 50 = \square$

$900 - 500 = \square$

➤ Marie made pancakes for her friends.

She put 1 pancake on each plate.
Marie used 6 plates.
How many pancakes did Marie make?

Think: 6 groups of 1 is 6 × 1.

$$6 \times 1 = 6$$

plates   pancake   pancakes
in all

Also, 1 × 6 = 6

When 1 is a factor, the product is always the other factor.

➤ Marie had 5 empty plates.

How many pancakes are on these plates?

Think: 5 groups of 0 is 5 × 0.

$$5 \times 0 = 0$$

plates   pancakes   pancakes
in all

Also, 0 × 5 = 0

When 0 is a factor, the product is always 0.

Practice

1. Multiply.
   a) 0 × 6   b) 1 × 5   c) 0 × 7   d) 1 × 3

2. Jessica buys 6 single-scoop ice cream cones.
How many scoops of ice cream does Jessica buy?
Show your answer using pictures and numbers.

3. Mario has 3 empty ice cream cones.
How many scoops of ice cream does Mario have?
Write a multiplication sentence.

4. Find each missing number.
   a) $6 \times \square = 6$ **b)** $\square \times 3 = 0$ **c)** $\square \times 5 = 5$ **d)** $2 \times \square = 0$

5. Write a story problem that can be solved by multiplying by 0.
Give your problem to a classmate to solve.

6. Mark puts these fruits on his waffle:
   • one strawberry
   • twice as many raspberries as strawberries
   • three times as many blueberries as raspberries
   How many raspberries are on the waffle?
   How many blueberries?
   How do you know?

7. **a)** Is it easier to solve 24×1 or 24×2? Explain.
   b) Is it easier to solve 6×0 or 66×0? Explain.

Reflect

What are quick ways to multiply by 0 and multiply by 1?
Use words, pictures, or numbers to explain.

Using a Multiplication Chart

You have looked at patterns in a hundred chart.
Some patterns helped you multiply.
Patterns in a multiplication chart can also help you multiply.

Explore

Use a copy of this multiplication chart.
Some products you already know have been filled in.

x	0	1	2	3	4	5	6	7	8	9
0	0	0	0	0	0	0	0	0	0	0
1	0	1	2	3	4	5	6	7	8	9
2	0	2	4	6	8	10	12	14	16	18
3	0	3	6			15				
4	0	4	8			20				
5	0	5	10	15	20	25	30	35	40	45
6	0	6	12			30				
7	0	7	14			35				
8	0	8	16			40				
9	0	9	18			45				

For example, $3 \times 2 = 6$

What patterns do you see?
On a copy of this chart, fill in the missing products.
What patterns do you see in the completed chart?

Show *and* Share

Show your completed chart to another pair of classmates.
What strategies did you use to find the products?
Talk about the patterns you found.

Here are some patterns in the multiplication chart.

➤ The **row** and **column** for the same factor have the same numbers.

Here are the row and column for factor 5.
They show that:

$5 \times 3 = 15$ and $3 \times 5 = 15$

$5 \times 6 = 30$ and $6 \times 5 = 30$

x	0	1	2	3	4	5	6	7
0						0		
1						5		
2						10		
3						15		
4						20		
5	0	5	10	15	20	25	30	35
6						30		
7						35		

➤ To fill in a row or column, skip count by the first number in the row or column.

To fill in the row or column for factor 2, start at 0, then count on by 2s:
0, 2, 4, 6, 8, 10, 12, 14

x	0	1	2	3	4	5	6	7
0			0					
1			2					
2	0	2	4	6	8	10	12	14
3			6					
4			8					
5			10					
6			12					
7			14					

➤ Here is another strategy to fill in the chart.
To find 4×6, find 2×6, then double it.

$2 \times 6 = 12$

$2 \times 6 = 12$

$4 \times 6 = 24$

$$\begin{array}{r} 12 \\ + 12 \\ \hline 24 \end{array}$$

1. Use a copy of a multiplication chart.
   a) Colour blue the products in the row and column for factor 2.
   b) Colour red the products in the row and column for factor 3.
   c) Colour green all the products with factor 6.
   What patterns do you see in the numbers you coloured?

2. Multiply.
   a) 3×6 b) 6×3 c) 7×5 d) 5×7
   e) 3×3 f) 6×6 g) 7×7 h) 7×6

3. Rabia bought 4 bags of oranges.
   Each bag had 6 oranges.
   How many oranges did Rabia buy?

4. How many days are there in 4 weeks?
   How do you know?

5. Here is part of a multiplication chart.
   The figures ♥, ●, ▲, and ■
   represent numbers.
   a) What number does each figure represent?
   b) What is the sum ♥ + ● ?
   c) What is the sum ▲ + ● ?
   d) Order the figures from least value to greatest value.
   Show your work.

x	2	3	4	5
2	4	6	▲	10
3	6	●	12	■
4	8	12	16	20
5	♥	15	20	25

6. Use a copy of a multiplication chart.
   Colour in a design on the chart.
   Write the multiplication sentence for each product you coloured.
   Give your sentences to a classmate.
   She uses these sentences to draw your design on another multiplication chart.

7. You will need a deck of cards with the 8s, 9s, 10s, and the face cards removed. An ace card counts as 1.

Card Products

How to play:
➤ The dealer shuffles the cards and divides them into two equal piles. Each player gets one pile.
➤ Each player turns over 2 cards and finds the product. The player with the greater product takes all the cards, and puts them at the bottom of her pile.
➤ The game ends when one player runs out of cards.

8. You will need a spinner like this one, a paper clip as a pointer, 2-cm grid paper, and counters.

Square Numbers

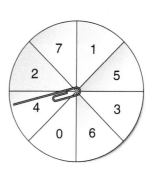

How to play:
➤ Use 2-cm grid paper. Each player makes a product card like this:
➤ Spin the pointer. Find the product of the number and itself. On the product card, cover the product with a counter.
➤ Take turns. The first person to cover his card wins.

0	1	4	9
16	25	36	49

Reflect

How can you use a chart to multiply? Use words and numbers to explain.

Numbers Every Day

Calculator Skills

Use only the numbers ③ and ⑤.

Show 68 on your calculator.

Strategies Toolkit

Explore

Karlee has 3 T-shirts and 2 pairs of pants.
How many different outfits can
Karlee make? Show your work.

Show and Share

Show how you found the outfits.
Explain your strategy.

Connect

Ben is getting a new bike. He can choose
a racing bike, a mountain bike, or a BMX bike.
He can choose: blue, black, silver, or red
How many different bikes can Ben choose?

Understand

What do you know?
- There are 3 different bikes.
- There are 4 different colours.
- You want to find how many
  different bikes are possible.

Plan

Think of a strategy to help you
solve the problem.
- You could **make a table**.
- Here are the bikes that are blue.
  Copy and complete the table
  for each of the other colours.

Strategies

- **Make a table.**
- **Use a model.**
- **Draw a picture.**
- **Solve a simpler problem.**
- **Work backward.**
- **Guess and check.**
- **Make an organized list.**
- **Use a pattern.**

Colour	Bike
blue	racing
blue	mountain
blue	BMX

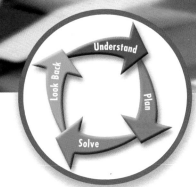

There are 3 bikes that are blue.
How many bikes are there for
each of the other colours?
How many different bikes are there in all?

How can multiplication help you to
solve the problem?

Practice

Choose one of the

Strategies

1. Each day, Zakia takes 1 fruit and 1 vegetable
   for her snack.
   - For the vegetable, she can choose either
     celery or carrot.
   - For the fruit, she can choose an apple, a
     kiwi, a pear, or an orange.
   How many different snacks can Zakia make?

2. Make a children's menu.
   Include foods and drinks on the menu.
   A meal has 1 food item and 1 drink item.
   How many different meals can you make
   from your menu?

Reflect

How does making a table help to solve a problem?
Can you solve the problem without completing the table?
Explain.

Modelling Division

Explore

You will need 18 counters.

➤ Arrange 18 counters into groups of 6.
   How many groups are there?
   Record your work with pictures and numbers.
➤ Arrange 15 counters into 3 equal groups.
   How many counters are in each group?
   Record your work.

Show and Share

Share your work with another pair of classmates.
How did you find out how many groups?
How did you find out how many counters in each group?

Connect

Janet has 12 pencils.

➤ Janet arranges the pencils into groups of 4.
   How many groups are there?

   Put 4 pencils in each group.

   Count how many groups.
   There are 3 groups of 4.

   This is division by grouping.

You write: 12   ÷   4   =   3

↑ number of pencils   ↑ number in each group   ↑ number of groups

This is a division sentence.

You say, "12 divided by 4 is 3."

➤ Now Janet arranges the pencils into 6 equal groups. How many pencils are in each group?

Share the pencils among 6 groups.

Count how many pencils are in each group. There are 6 groups of 2.

You write: 12   ÷   6   =   2

↑ number of pencils   ↑ number of groups   ↑ number in each group

This is division by sharing.

You say, "12 divided by 6 is 2."

Practice

Use counters when they help.

1. Find the number of groups. Then write a division sentence.
   The first one is done for you.
   a) Make groups of 2.   b) Make groups of 1.   c) Make groups of 4.

5 groups of 2
10 ÷ 2 = 5

2. Find the number in each group.
Then write a division sentence.

a) Make 2 equal groups.

b) Make 3 equal groups.

c) Make 1 group.

3. Kathryn has 24 stickers.
She shares them equally among 6 people.
How many stickers does each person get?

4. Omar puts 21 stamps in equal groups.
He puts more than 1 stamp in each group.
What is the greatest number of groups
Omar can make?
How many stamps would be in each group?
How do you know?

5. Write a story problem for each situation.
Solve the problem.

a) You know the number of groups.
You need to find out how many
are in each group.

b) You know how many are in
each group.
You need to find out
how many groups.

Numbers Every Day

Mental Math

In each pair, which product
is greater? How can you
tell without multiplying?

6×3 or 6×2
7×2 or 2×7
5×1 or 4×1
3×0 or 5×0

Reflect

Describe two kinds of division problems.
Give an example of each kind.

Using Arrays to Divide

You will need 16 counters.

There are 16 children in the gym.
They line up in equal rows.
How many children could be in each row?
How many different ways can you find?
Use counters to model each way.
Record each model.

Show and Share

Share your answers with another
pair of classmates.
How many different ways could the
children line up in equal rows?
Write a division sentence for each way.

Numbers Every Day

Number Strategies

30 is:

- ☐ tens and ☐ ones
- 1 ten and ☐ ones
- ☐ groups of 5
- ☐ ones

Connect

There are 8 drum dancers.
They will dance onto the stage
in equal rows.
How many dancers could be in each row?

Make an array to show each way.
Write a division sentence for each way.

2 rows of 4

4 rows of 2

1 row of 8

8 rows of 1

8 ÷ 1 = 8
1 row of 8 dancers

8 ÷ 2 = 4
2 rows of
4 dancers

8 ÷ 4 = 2
4 rows of
2 dancers

8 ÷ 8 = 1
8 rows of 1 dancer

Practice

Use counters when they help.

1. Copy each division sentence.
   Use the array to complete the sentence.
   a) 12 ÷ 2 = ☐   b) 20 ÷ 4 = ☐

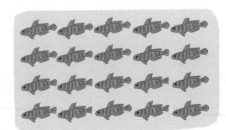

2. Write a division sentence for each array.

a)  **b)**  **c)**

3. Use counters. Make an array for each division sentence.
   a) $12 \div 3 = 4$ **b)** $7 \div 1 = 7$ **c)** $25 \div 5 = 5$ **d)** $42 \div 7 = 6$

4. Copy and complete each division sentence.
   a) $12 \div 4 = \square$ **b)** $21 \div 7 = \square$ **c)** $10 \div 5 = \square$ **d)** $36 \div 6 = \square$

5. The choir sings on stage.
   a) There are 24 chairs in 6 equal rows.
       How many chairs are in each row?
   b) Suppose there are 24 chairs in 4 equal rows.
       How many chairs are in each row?
   Draw an array to show each answer.

6. There are 12 drummers and 15 horn players.
   a) Can they form equal rows of 2? How do you know?
   b) Can they form equal rows of 3? How do you know?
   c) What other equal rows can they form?
   Show your work.

7. Write a story problem that you can solve by
   drawing an array to divide. Solve your problem.
   Show your work.

Reflect

How can you use an array to divide?
Use words and pictures to explain.

Dividing by 2, by 5, and by 10

Explore

You will need 31 counters.

➤ Thirty children are working on a project. How many children will be in each group if there are:
- 5 equal groups?
- 10 equal groups?
- 2 equal groups?

Show your work.

➤ Suppose 31 children work on the project. Can they make:
- 5 equal groups?
- 10 equal groups?
- 2 equal groups?

How do you know?
Show your work.

Show *and* Share

Share your work with another pair of classmates.
How did you find how many children were in each equal group?
How did you know you could not make equal groups
with 31 children?

➤ There are 20 children in Mr. Carlson's class.
Can Mr. Carlson make 5 equal groups?
2 equal groups?
How many children will be in each group?

You can use an array to model the groups.

Mr. Carlson can make
5 groups of 4 children.

20 can be divided into
5 groups of 4.
You say 20 is **divisible** by 5.

20 is also divisible by 4.

Mr. Carlson can make
2 groups of 10 children.

20 can be divided into
2 groups of 10.
20 is divisible by 2.

20 is also divisible by 10.

➤ There are 23 children in Miss Dawson's class.
Can Miss Dawson make groups of 5? Groups of 10?

23 is 4 groups of 5,
with 3 left over.
23 is not divisible by 5.

Miss Dawson cannot make
groups of 5.

23 is 2 groups of 10,
with 3 left over.
23 is not divisible by 10.

Miss Dawson cannot make
groups of 10.

Practice

1. Divide. Use the array to help you.
   a) $8 \div 2 = \square$
   b) $35 \div 5 = \square$
   c) $50 \div 10 = \square$

2. Find each missing number.
   a) $12 \div 2 = \square$
   b) $5 \div 5 = \square$
   c) $14 \div 2 = \square$
   d) $35 \div 5 = \square$
   e) $30 \div 10 = \square$
   f) $6 \div 2 = \square$
   g) $90 \div 10 = \square$
   h) $20 \div 5 = \square$

3. Divide.
   a) $12 \div 2$
   b) $2 \div 2$
   c) $35 \div 5$
   d) $50 \div 10$
   e) $15 \div 5$
   f) $40 \div 10$
   g) $4 \div 2$
   h) $10 \div 5$

4. Fourteen children work in groups of 2.
   How many groups are there?

5. Draw an array to show each division.
   a) $15 \div 2$
   b) $18 \div 5$
   c) $32 \div 10$
   d) $32 \div 5$

6. Zoe bought 3 baskets of strawberries.
   Each basket held 10 strawberries.
   Zoe and 4 friends share the strawberries equally.
   How many strawberries does each person get?
   Show your work.

Math Link

Measurement

To find how many dimes are in 70¢, divide by 10.
To find how many nickels are in 30¢, divide by 5.

Use a copy of a hundred chart for questions 7 to 9.

1	2	3	4	5	6	7	8	9	10
11	12	13	14	15	16	17	18	19	20
21	22	23	24	25	26	27	28	29	30
31	32	33	34	35	36	37	38	39	40
41	42	43	44	45	46	47	48	49	50
51	52	53	54	55	56	57	58	59	60
61	62	63	64	65	66	67	68	69	70
71	72	73	74	75	76	77	78	79	80
81	82	83	84	85	86	87	88	89	90
91	92	93	94	95	96	97	98	99	100

7. a) Colour blue the numbers that are divisible by 2.
    b) What patterns do you see in the ones digits?
    c) How can you tell if a number is divisible by 2?

8. a) Colour green the numbers that are divisible by 5.
    b) What patterns do you see in the ones digits?
    c) How can you tell if a number is divisible by 5?

9. a) Colour yellow the numbers that are divisible by 10.
    b) What patterns do you see?
    c) How can you tell if a number is divisible by 10?

10. Copy the Venn diagram below.
    Sort these numbers: 4, 12, 17, 24, 25, 30, 32, 45, 50
    What is true about the numbers
    where the loops overlap?

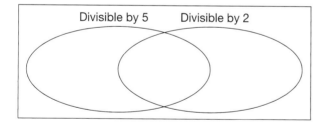

Reflect

Choose a number between 20 and 50.
How can you tell, by looking,
if the number is divisible by 2, 5, or 10?
Use words, pictures, or numbers to explain.

Numbers Every Day

Number Strategies

$3 \times 2 = 6$

How can you use this result to find 3×4?

Use pictures and words to explain.

Relating Multiplication and Division

Explore

You will need 1-cm grid paper.

➤ Choose any product from the
multiplication chart.
Keep the product secret.

➤ Use grid paper.
Draw an array for the product.

➤ Show the array to your partner.
Ask your partner to write a multiplication
sentence and a division sentence for the array.

➤ Trade roles. Continue until each of you has made 5 different arrays.

Record your work.

x	1	2	3	4	5	6	7
1	1	2	3	4	5	6	7
2	2	4	6	8	10	12	14
3	3	6	9	12	15	18	21
4	4	8	12	16	20	24	28
5	5	10	15	20	25	30	35
6	6	12	18	24	30	36	42
7	7	14	21	28	35	42	49

Show *and* Share

Show your work to another pair of classmates.
How are the multiplication and division sentences
for each array related?

Connect

Kamil used a different multiplication chart.
He chose the product 50.
He made this array.

There are 5 rows of 10.
You can write this multiplication sentence: $5 \times 10 = 50$
You can write this division sentence: $50 \div 5 = 10$

LESSON FOCUS | Find related multiplication and division facts.

You can also turn the array to show 10 rows of 5.

There are 10 rows of 5.
You can write this multiplication sentence:
$10 \times 5 = 50$
You can write this division sentence:
$50 \div 10 = 5$

These four number sentences are **related facts**.

$5 \times 10 = 50$
$10 \times 5 = 50$
$50 \div 10 = 5$
$50 \div 5 = 10$

When you know one number fact, you can write related facts.

Practice

Use counters when they help.

1. Write a multiplication sentence and a division sentence for each picture. Part of the first one is done for you.

   a)

   $4 \times 3 = 12$
   $12 \div 3 = \square$

   b)

   c)

   d)

2. Use related facts to find each missing number.

   a) $7 \times 6 = 42$ **b)** $6 \times 5 = 30$ **c)** $7 \times 7 = \square$ **d)** $6 \times \square = 24$

        $42 \div 6 = \square$ $30 \div 6 = \square$ $49 \div 7 = \square$ $24 \div 6 = \square$

3. Write the related facts for each set of numbers.

   a) 3, 5, 15   **b)** 4, 7, 28   **c)** 7, 5, 35   **d)** 3, 6, 18

4. Divide. How can you use multiplication facts to help you?

   a) $9 \div 3$ **b)** $15 \div 3$ **c)** $28 \div 4$ **d)** $4 \div 4$

   e) $30 \div 6$ **f)** $12 \div 6$ **g)** $14 \div 7$ **h)** $42 \div 7$

5. Concentration

   Your teacher will give you a set of cards.

   Arrange the cards face down on a table.

   Take turns to choose 2 cards.

   If the cards represent related facts, keep them.

   The player with the most cards at the end of the game wins.

👫 **Game**

6. Mrs. Bowski tries to arrange her class into work groups.
When she makes groups of 6 or of 4, she has 1 child left over.
Mrs. Bowski has fewer than 30 children in her class.
How many children might be in Mrs. Bowski's class?
How do you know?

Numbers Every Day

Number Strategies

Order each set of numbers from least to greatest.

- 87, 99, 42, 21, 55
- 91, 26, 30, 80, 72
- 47, 20, 53, 68, 63
- 42, 18, 85, 57, 36

Reflect

Show 3 different ways to find $21 \div 7$.
Use words, numbers, or pictures
to explain each way.

Number Patterns on a Calculator

You will need a 4-function calculator.
Use the calculator to create number patterns.
These keystrokes are for the TI-108.

➤ Press: [ON/C] [7] [+] [=] [=] [=] [=] [=] [=] [=]
Record what you see on the screen. Look for patterns.

Choose a different start number.
Repeat this activity.

➤ Press: [ON/C] [8] [1] [−] [9] [=] [=] [=] [=] [=] [=]
Record what you see on the screen. Look for patterns.

Choose a start number between 85 and 99.
Repeat this activity.

Show *and* Share

Share your patterns with another pair of classmates.
What do your patterns show?

Connect

➤ A calculator can do repeated addition.
This is counting on.
Press: [ON/C] [6] [+] [=] [=] [=] [=] [=] [=] [=] [=] [=] [=]
You will see: 6   12 18 24 30 36 42 48 54 60
This is 6 multiplied by: 1   2   3   4   5   6   7   8   9   10

There is a pattern in the ones digits: 6, 2, 8, 4, 0, 6, 2, 8, 4, 0

➤ A calculator can do repeated subtraction.
This is counting back.
Press: [ON/C] [4] [8] [−] [8] [=] [=] [=] [=] [=] [=]
You will see: 48   40 32 24 16 8   0

➤ A calculator can do repeated multiplication.
Press: [ON/C] [3] [×] [=] [=] [=] [=] [=]
You will see: 3   9   27   81   243 729

Practice

For questions 1 to 4:
• Press the keys.
• Write what you see on the screen.
• Write about the patterns you see.

1. [ON/C] [5] [+] [=] [=] [=] [=] [=] [=] [=] [=] [=] [=]

2. [ON/C] [1] [0] [0] [−] [1] [0] [=] [=] [=] [=] [=] [=] [=] [=] [=] [=]

3. [ON/C] [9] [+] [=] [=] [=] [=] [=] [=] [=] [=] [=] [=]

4. [ON/C] [2] [×] [=] [=] [=] [=] [=] [=] [=] [=]

5. Start at 42. Keep subtracting 7 until you reach 0.
How many 7s did you subtract?
What division sentence does this show?

6. Work with a partner.
The goal is to reach 40.
Press 2. Take turns.
Each person enters [+] or [×],
then either 2 or 5, then [=].
If one of you goes over 40, begin again.
The person who makes 40 wins.

For questions 7 and 8, tell if you would multiply
or divide to find the answer. Find the answer.

7. Two hundred ten children signed up for baseball.
   Each team has 15 players.
   How many teams can be made?

8. A mini-soccer league has teams of 12 players.
   There are 8 teams in the league.
   How many players are there?

9. The product of two numbers is 16.
   What are the two numbers?
   How many different answers are there?
   How do you know you have found all the answers?

10. Write a story problem for each situation.
    Solve the problem.
    Write the answer in a number sentence.
    a) Twelve dogs and 3 dog walkers
    b) Five skipping ropes and 15 children

Reflect

Randy said, "When I use division
to find an answer, I could also find the
answer by using subtraction."
Do you think Randy is correct? Use
words, pictures, or numbers to explain.

Numbers Every Day

Number Strategies

Use the doubles fact 6 + 6 = 12
to find each sum.

6 + 5 = ☐

6 + 4 = ☐

6 + 7 = ☐

6 + 8 = ☐

Show What You Know

LESSON

1 2 8 9

1. Write a multiplication sentence and a division sentence for each picture.

   a)

   b)

2

2. Draw a picture to find each product.
   a) 6×0 **b)** 1×4 **c)** 7×5 **d)** 4×2 **e)** 5×10

3 4 5

3. Multiply.
   a) 3×6 **b)** 4×7 **c)** 7×1 **d)** 6×6
   e) 10×7 **f)** 6×4 **g)** 2×6 **h)** 5×0

6

4. Natalie buys 3 CDs. Each CD costs $7.
   How much does Natalie spend on CDs?

8 9 10

5. Divide.
   a) $12 \div 2$ **b)** $21 \div 7$ **c)** $10 \div 5$ **d)** $36 \div 6$
   e) $4 \div 1$ **f)** $18 \div 3$ **g)** $28 \div 4$ **h)** $80 \div 10$

8 9

6. There are 20 beads on a necklace. Every 4th bead is gold.
   How many gold beads are on the necklace?

11

7. Write related facts for each set of numbers.
   a) $2, 4, 8$ **b)** $3, 7, 21$ **c)** $5, 6, 30$ **d)** $5, 5, 25$

6 11

8. What might each missing number be?
   How many answers can you find?
   a) $\square \times \square = 12$ **b)** $\square \div \square = 1$

10

9. Which of these numbers are
divisible by 5? By 2?
How do you know?
2, 5, 9, 10, 14, 15, 20, 21, 26
Copy this Venn diagram.
Sort the numbers.

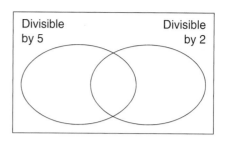

Divisible
by 5   Divisible
                   by 2

1
8

10. There are 6 flowers in one bunch.
Brittany wants 42 flowers.
How many bunches should she buy?
Write a multiplication sentence and
a division sentence.

12

11. Use a calculator.
a) Press: ON/C 8 + = = = = = = = = = =
b) Press: ON/C 7 2 − 8 = = = = = = = = =
Write what you see on the screen.
Write about the patterns.

7

12. There are 4 toys in one package.
There are 6 toys in another package.
How many different ways could
Addison buy 24 toys?
Show your work.

6

13. Connor was picking up rocks
on the beach.
He put 4 rocks into each of
6 large bags. He put 3 rocks
into each of 5 small bags.
How many rocks did Connor collect?
How do you know?

U N I T

4 Learning Goals

✓ model multiplication
and division
✓ find strategies to multiply
and divide
✓ recall basic multiplication
and division facts
✓ pose and solve problems
using multiplication
and division
✓ use a calculator to find
patterns in numbers

Here Comes the Band!

Part 1

A marching band has 48 people.
They march in equal rows.
How many different ways can the band be arranged?
Write a multiplication sentence for each way.
Show your work.

Part 2

➤ Thirty band members perform on stage.
You will set up chairs for them.
  • There must be equal rows of chairs.
  • There must be at least 2 chairs
    in each row.
  How many ways can you set up the chairs?
  Write a division sentence for each way.

➤ What problems might you have
if the band has 31 members? Explain.

Part 3

Suppose you are the bandleader
for a day.
  • You choose how many band members
    will play that day.
  • Choose a number.
  • Show all the different ways
    you could arrange your band members
    into equal rows.
    Write a multiplication sentence and
    a division sentence for each way.

Check List

Your work should show
  ☑ all the ways to arrange
    the band members in
    equal rows
  ☑ correct multiplication
    and division sentences
  ☑ a clear explanation of
    why 31 band members
    might be a problem
  ☑ how you used
    mathematical language
    and symbols correctly

Reflect on the Unit

How are multiplication and division related?
Use words, pictures, or numbers to explain.

UNIT

1 1. Count on by 5s.
Press ⬜5️⃣⬜, press ⬜➕⬜, then press ⬜🟰⬜ several times.
Record the results.
What pattern do you see?
How is it the same as a pattern on a hundred chart?
Explain.

2. Copy each pair of numbers.
Use > or < to make each statement true.
a) 73 ⬜ 730   b) 874 ⬜ 851
c) 934 ⬜ 936   d) 208 ⬜ 199

3. Draw Base Ten Blocks to show each number in 3 different ways.
a) 47   b) 385   c) 907   d) 420

2 4. Find each missing number. Explain your strategy.
a) 9 + ⬜ = 12   b) 18 − ⬜ = 9   c) ⬜ + 5 = 13   d) ⬜ − 7 = 8

5. Add or subtract.
a) 368 + 292   b) 409 + 567   c) 734 − 576   d) 801 − 699

6. A shopkeeper had 738 balloons. She sold 579.
How many were left? Explain your strategy.

3 7. Use dot paper.
Draw two different figures that have two parallel sides.
a) Describe their sides.
b) Describe their angles.
c) Write their names.

8. Name each figure. Find pairs of congruent figures.
How do you know the figures are congruent?

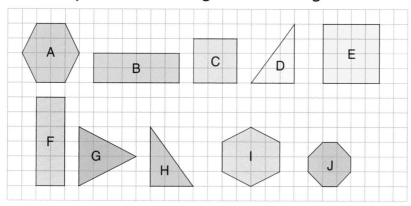

9. Identify each solid. Sort the solids in a Venn diagram.
Write the sorting rule.

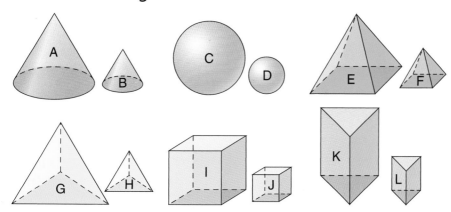

10. Multiply.
a) 6×3 **b)** 7×7 **c)** 0×9 **d)** 2×1 **e)** 5×7 **f)** 4×6

11. Divide.
a) $18 \div 6$ **b)** $24 \div 4$ **c)** $42 \div 7$ **d)** $25 \div 5$ **e)** $14 \div 2$ **f)** $10 \div 1$

12. There are 8 muffins in one package.
Laila wants 56 muffins.
How many packages should she buy?
Write a multiplication sentence and a division sentence.

Sorting and Data

Using Data to Answer Questions

Books Read in April

Angie	📖 📖 📖 📖 📖 📖 📖 📖 📖
Shane	📖 📖 📖
Paul	📖 📖 📖 📖 📖
Jason	📖 📖 📖 📖 📖 📖
Deanna	📖 📖 📖 📖 📖 📖 📖

📖 Represents 1 book

Lunch	Number of Students
Pizza	ⅣⅣ IIII
Burger and fries	ⅣⅣ III
Tuna sandwich	IIII
Taco	ⅣⅣ
Submarine	ⅣⅣ I

Learning Goals

- sort and classify objects and data
- collect and organize data
- draw graphs
- interpret graphs
- conduct surveys

Management

Key Words

data

attribute

Venn diagram

pictograph

bar graph

circle graph

tally mark

tally chart

key

scale

horizontal axis

vertical axis

survey

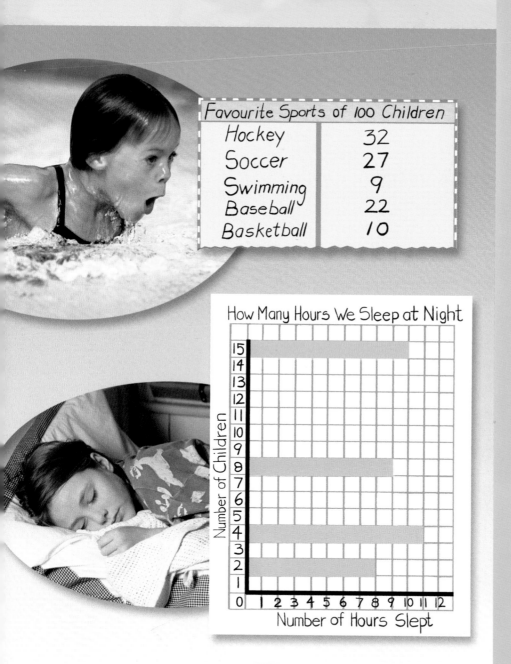

Favourite Sports of 100 Children	
Hockey	32
Soccer	27
Swimming	9
Baseball	22
Basketball	10

How Many Hours We Sleep at Night

Number of Children

Number of Hours Slept

These graphs and charts show data about Grade 3 students.

What can you find out from each graph and chart?

191

1

Sorting by Two Attributes

You can sort in many ways.
In Unit 3, you sorted by shape:

Triangle   Rectangle   Rectangle   Irregular octagon

Shape is an **attribute**.
What other attributes can you think of?

You will need Attribute Blocks.
➤ Choose 10 Attribute Blocks. Pick 2 attributes.
➤ Sort the blocks. Record the sorting.
➤ What other ways could you sort the same Attribute Blocks?
  Record each sorting.

Show and Share

Show one sorting to another pair of classmates.
Have them find your sorting rule.

Numbers Every Day

Mental Math

Which number goes in each box? Tell how you know.

$6 + 6 + 6 = 6 \times \square$

7×4 is $\square$ more than 6×4.

3×5 is $\square$ less than 4×5.

$\square \times 4 = 0$

Here are 2 ways to sort these 6 Attribute Blocks.

➤ Using a chart
The blocks are sorted by size and shape.

Shape \ Size	Big	Small
Triangle	▲	▲
Circle	●	
Square		■
Hexagon		⬡
Rectangle	▬	

193

➤ Using a Venn diagram

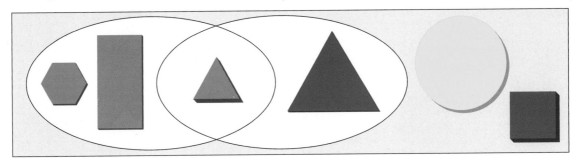

In the left loop, all blocks are red.
In the right loop, all blocks are triangles.
In the overlap, all blocks are red triangles.
Blocks that are not red and are not triangles are outside the loops.

Practice

Use these blocks for questions 1 to 4.

1. Use a large copy of this chart.
   Sort the blocks above in this chart.

Size / Thickness	Big	Small
Thin		
Thick		

2. Use 2 different attributes.
   Sort the blocks above in a chart.

3. Use a large copy of this
   Venn diagram.
   Sort the blocks above in this
   Venn diagram.

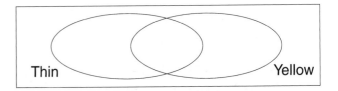

4. Use 2 different attributes.
   Sort the blocks above in a Venn diagram.

5. a) Sort these vehicles. Use 2 attributes.

b) Choose 2 different attributes.
Sort the vehicles another way.
Show your work.

6. a) How have these numbers been sorted?

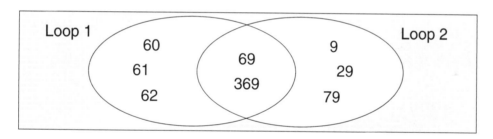

Loop 1 | Loop 2
60 | 69 | 9
61 | 369 | 29
62 | | 79

b) What other numbers could you write in each loop?
c) What numbers would you write outside the loops?

Reflect

You have used a chart and a
Venn diagram to sort.
When is it better to use a
chart? A Venn diagram?
Use examples to explain.

At Home

What things do you sort
at home?
Draw a chart or Venn diagram
to show how you sort them.

Sorting by Three Attributes

Explore ··

You will need Attribute Blocks.
Choose 10 Attribute Blocks. Pick 3 attributes.
Use a Venn diagram like this to sort the blocks.

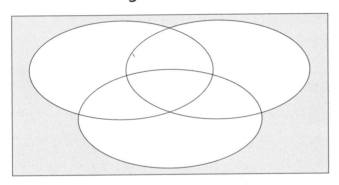

Show *and* Share

Share your sorting with another pair of classmates.
How did you label each loop?
How did you know where to put each block?

Connect ··

Look at these 8 Attribute Blocks.

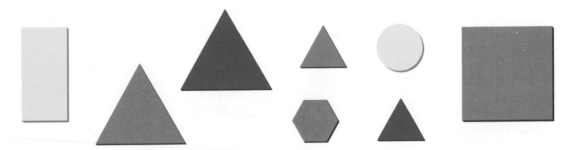

Here is one way to sort them.

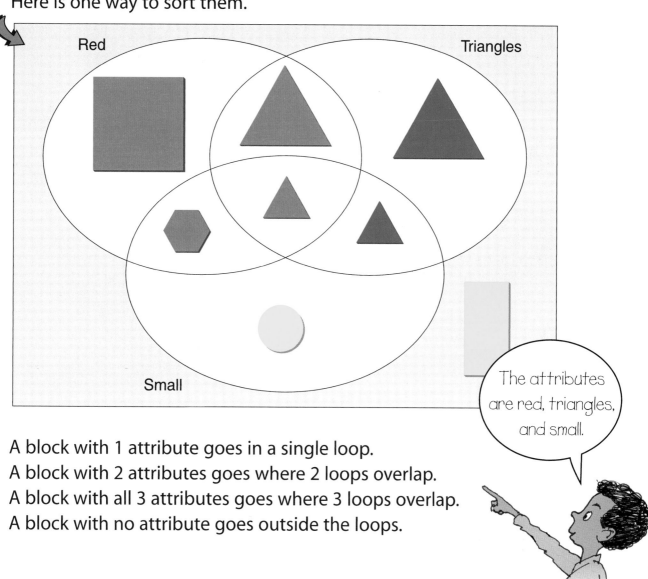

A block with 1 attribute goes in a single loop.
A block with 2 attributes goes where 2 loops overlap.
A block with all 3 attributes goes where 3 loops overlap.
A block with no attribute goes outside the loops.

Practice

Use a large copy of each Venn diagram.
1. Choose 10 Attribute Blocks.
   Sort them in this Venn diagram.

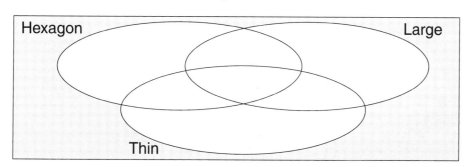

2. Sort 10 Attribute Blocks in a Venn diagram.
Use these attributes: Thin, Blue, and Square
Try to find a block for each space.

3. a) This Venn diagram was drawn to sort Attribute Blocks.
What is wrong with the Venn diagram?
Can you find a block for each space? Explain.

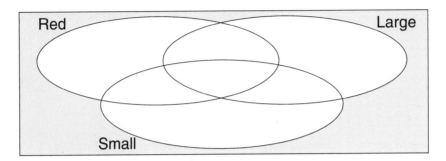

b) How can you correct the Venn diagram?

4. a) How were these blocks sorted? How do you know?

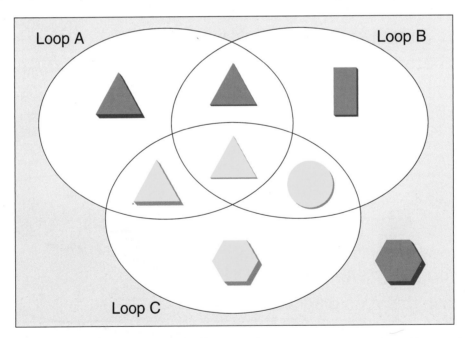

b) Write a label for each loop.

5. Choose 10 books from the classroom.
Choose 3 attributes. Sort the books.
Explain how you sorted them.

Patterning

You use attributes when you make patterns.
In this pattern, 3 attributes change: position, colour, and shape

What comes next?

6. Suppose you use this Venn diagram
   to sort 10 classmates.
   Two loops do not overlap.
   Who could go in each of these loops?
   In the third loop?
   Write about your sorting.

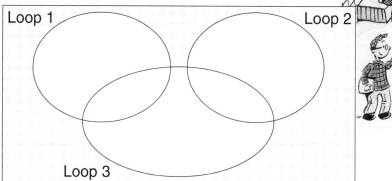

Reflect

A Venn diagram with
3 overlapping loops has 7 spaces.
When you sort with it,
sometimes 1 or more spaces are empty.
Draw a Venn diagram to show items
sorted this way.

Numbers Every Day

Number Strategies

Find each sum.

19 + 15
27 + 43
48 + 26

Which strategies did
you use?

Interpreting Graphs

These 2 graphs show the same data.

Videos Rented in One Store on One Day

Pictograph

Bar Graph

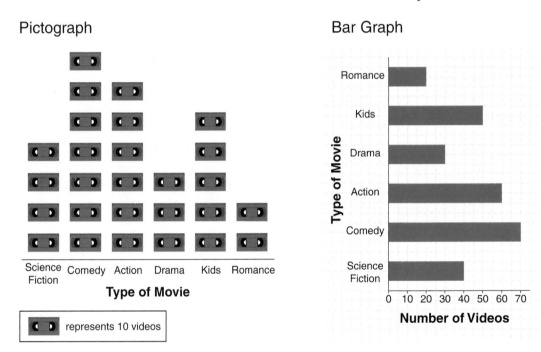

Look at each graph.
List all the things you know
from looking at each graph.

Show *and* Share

Share your list with another pair
of classmates.
Which type of movie is most popular?
Least popular?
Which graph is easier to read? Why?

Numbers Every Day

Mental Math

Find the missing numbers
in each number pattern.

226, ☐, ☐, 223, 222, ☐

☐, ☐, 172, 170, ☐

☐, 395, ☐, 385, 380, ☐

1000, ☐, 800, 700, ☐, ☐

Connect

These 2 graphs show the videos rented by 1 family over 4 months.

Videos Rented by the Cheung Family

Pictograph

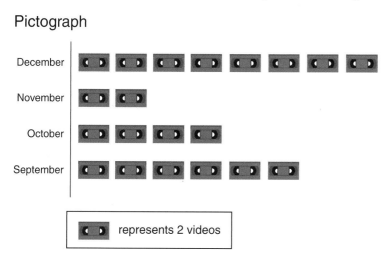

| | represents 2 videos |

Bar Graph

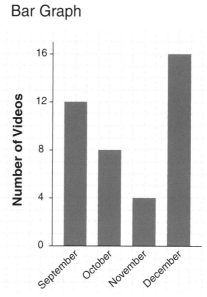

➤ You can use the **pictograph** to find how many videos were rented in December:

Since [ ] represents 2 videos, count by 2s.

December [ ] [ ] [ ] [ ] [ ] [ ] [ ] [ ]

Count: 2, 4, 6, 8, 10, 12, 14, 16

So, 16 videos were rented in December.

➤ You can use the **bar graph** to find how many videos were rented in September:

The top of the September bar lines up with 12.

So, 12 videos were rented in September.

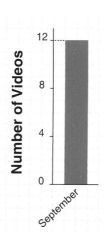

1. Write three things you know from this pictograph.

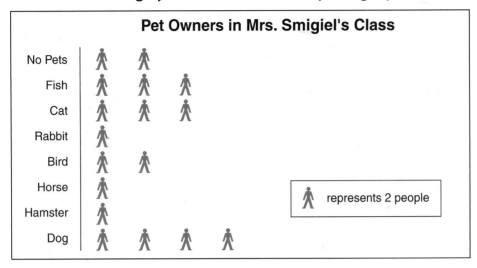

Pet Owners in Mrs. Smigiel's Class

🕴 represents 2 people

2. Some children were asked
to name their favourite animal.

a) How many children like dogs?

b) List the animals from
most popular to least popular.

c) How many children were
asked? How do you know?

d) Write what else you know
from this graph.

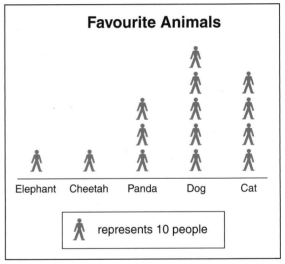

Favourite Animals

Elephant   Cheetah   Panda   Dog   Cat

🕴 represents 10 people

3. Children from three Grade 3 classes
were asked to tell their eye colour.

a) Which eye colour is
most common? Least common?

b) How many more blue eyes
are there than hazel?

c) How many more brown eyes
are there than green?

d) Make up your own question
about this graph.
Trade questions with a classmate.
Answer the question.

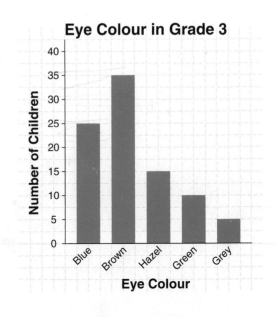

Eye Colour in Grade 3

Number of Children

Blue   Brown   Hazel   Green   Grey

Eye Colour

4. Children in a Grade 3 class
collected leaves.
   a) How is this graph different
   from the graph in question 3?
   b) Which type of leaves did
   the class collect the most of?
   c) How many leaves were
   collected in all?
   d) How many maple leaves
   were collected?
   e) How many leaves
   were not hickory or oak?
   f) Write a question about
   this graph.
   Answer your question.
   Show your work.

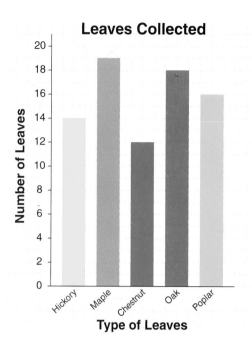

5. Which chart below
matches this pictograph?
How do you know?

Pizza Served at Lunchtime

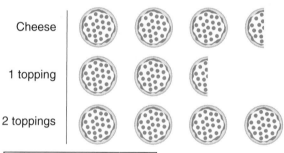

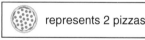

represents 2 pizzas

A	
Type	**Number**
Cheese	10
1 topping	8
2 toppings	12

B	
Type	**Number**
Cheese	7
1 topping	5
2 toppings	8

C	
Type	**Number**
Cheese	7
1 topping	6
2 toppings	8

Reflect

Which graph is easier to read: a bar graph or a pictograph?
Use words, pictures, or numbers to explain.

Interpreting Circle Graphs

These 2 graphs show the same data.

Our Favourite Things to Do after School

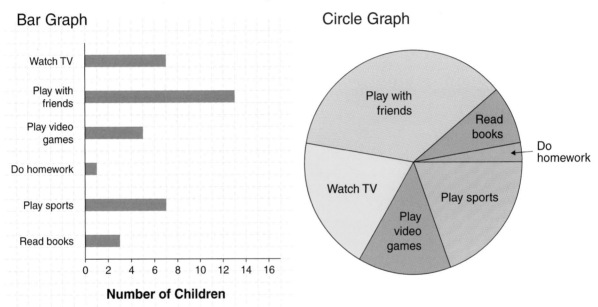

➤ Look at each graph.
List all the things you know from looking at each graph.
➤ Write a question about each graph.
Trade questions with your partner.
Answer your partner's questions.
Show your work.

Show *and* Share

Share your list with another pair of classmates.
Which graph tells you more?
What does the bar graph show
that the circle graph does not show?

Numbers Every Day

Calculator Skills

Make a pattern with
only even numbers.
Tell how you did it.
What is the
pattern rule?

These graphs show the sports played by the children
in two Grade 3 classes.

The Sports We Play

Bar Graph

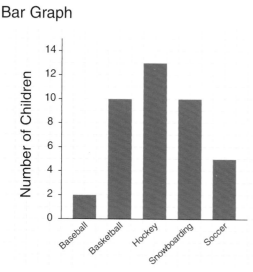

Circle Graph

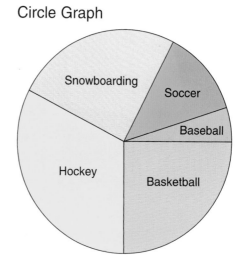

➤ You can use the bar graph to find
how many children play soccer.
The top of the soccer bar is halfway
between 4 and 6.
So, 5 children play soccer.

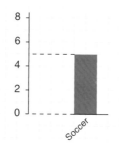

➤ You cannot use the **circle graph** to
find how many children play a sport.
The circle graph shows the fraction of
all the children who play each sport.
  • The fraction of the children
    who play basketball is about
    one-fourth.
  • The fraction of the children who
    play hockey is about one-third.

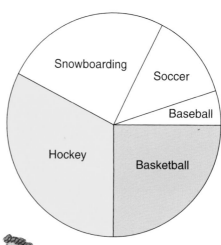

1. Write 3 things you know from this graph.

Our Favourite Colours

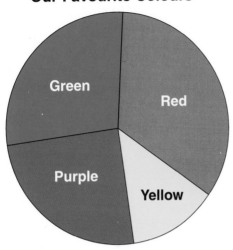

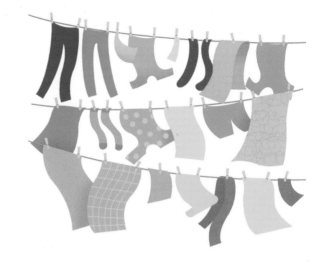

How Lynne Spent Her Day

2. a) What does this graph show?
   b) How did Lynne spend
      the most time? The least time?
   c) What did Lynne do about
      one-quarter of the time?
   d) Which 2 things together
      took about one-half of the time?
   e) What else do you know
      from this graph?

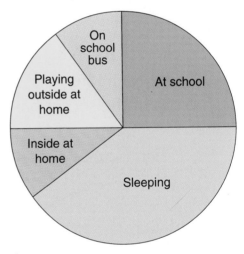

3. a) What does this graph show?

   b) How do most children
      get to school?
      How do you know?
   c) Write what else you know
      from this graph.
   d) Write a question about
      this graph.
      Answer your question.
   Show your work.

How We Get to School

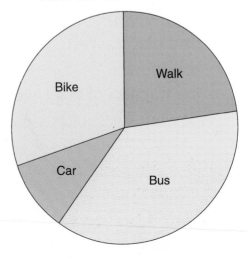

4. Sita counted the bugs she saw in her backyard. Which circle graph below shows the same data as this bar graph? How do you know?

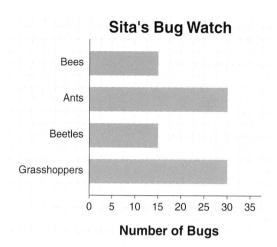

Sita's Bug Watch

Number of Bugs

a)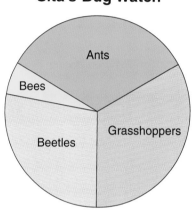

Sita's Bug Watch

b)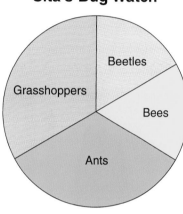

Sita's Bug Watch

c)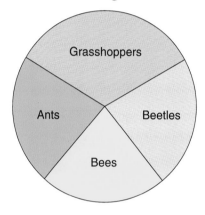

Sita's Bug Watch

5. Can you use the correct circle graph in question 4 to find out how many bees Sita saw? Explain.

6. Suppose you wanted to graph the favourite TV shows of your classmates. Would you draw a circle graph or a bar graph? Explain.

At Home

Reflect

What can you find out from a circle graph? Use words, pictures, or numbers to explain.

Find bar graphs and circle graphs in newspapers and magazines. What can you find out from these graphs?

Drawing Pictographs

What types of movies do your classmates like best?

On the chalkboard, draw a **tally mark** beside the type of movie you like best.

Our Favourite Movies

Comedy II
Action III
Kids
Science Fiction III
Drama
Mystery

Explore

➤ Use the **tally chart** on the board.
Draw a pictograph to show the movie data.
Let one picture represent more than 1 movie.
You choose how many movies 1 picture represents.

➤ Write 4 questions you can answer from the graph.
Answer your questions. Show your work.

Show *and* Share

Trade graphs and questions with another pair of classmates.
Use their graph to answer their questions.
Check each other's work.

The children in a Grade 3 class chose 1 of 3 ice cream flavours. Here are the data.

Our Favourite Ice Cream Flavours

Ice Cream Flavours	Tally	Number of Children
Cotton Candy	|||| |||| ||	12
Tiger Tiger	|||| ||||	9
Chocolate	||||	5

To draw a pictograph

➤ Choose a picture:

Choose how many items the picture will represent, so the graph is not too large.

This is called a **key**: represents 2 children.

➤ For each flavour, draw one for each 2 children.

Count by 2s to find the number of pictures to draw.

Cotton Candy:
Count: 2, 4, 6, 8, 10, 12

Tiger Tiger:
Count: 2, 4, 6, 8, 9

Draw one-half of an ice cream cone for 1 child.

Chocolate:
Count: 2, 4, 5

➤ Draw the pictograph.

Favourite Ice Cream Flavours

Cotton Candy

Tiger Tiger

Chocolate

 represents 2 children

209

1. Yoshi asked his classmates for their favourite fruit. This is his tally chart.

Our Favourite Fruit		
Fruit	Tally	Number of Children
Apple	IIII	4
Orange	HHT HHT	10
Banana	HHT II	7
Pear	II	2
Strawberry	HHT IIII	9
Other	IIII	4

   a) Draw a pictograph. Use 1 picture to represent 2 children.
   b) Why did Yoshi include "Other" in his list?
   c) Which fruit was the most popular? The least popular?
   d) What else do you know from the pictograph?

2. Here is a tally chart.

?	Tally	Number of Children
?	HHT HHT II	12
?	HHT HHT I	11
?	IIII	4
?	HHT HHT HHT III	18

   a) Make up a story about these data. Copy the chart, then complete it.
   b) Draw a pictograph. Use 1 picture to represent 2 children.
   c) What can you tell from the graph?

3. The students in two Grade 3 classes chose their favourite recess game.

   a) Draw a pictograph. Use 1 picture to represent 2 children.
   b) What do you know from the graph?
   c) Suppose you collected the same data from your classmates. How do you think the results would compare?

Game	Number of Children
Skipping	14
Tag	9
Hopscotch	4
Soccer	15
Hide and Seek	10

4. Scott found how many people in Grades 1 to 6 wear glasses.
   a) Draw a pictograph.
   b) How did you choose the key?
   c) Write all that you know from the graph.
   d) Write a question about the graph. Answer your question.
   Show your work.

Grade	Children Who Wear Glasses
1	15
2	5
3	25
4	40
5	30
6	10

5. Madhu found out how many children in her school watched the Canadian hockey team play. The team won a gold medal.
   a) Draw a pictograph. Let 1 picture represent 5 children.
   b) Draw another pictograph. Let 1 picture represent 10 children.
   c) How does changing the key change the graph?
   d) Which graph is easier to read? Explain.

Grade	Children Who Watched the Game
1	25
2	40
3	35
4	55
5	65
6	50

Reflect

When you draw a pictograph, how do you decide what key to use? Use words, pictures, or numbers to explain.

Drawing Bar Graphs

Explore

You will need grid paper and a ruler.

For a school project,
Anna timed how long she spent
on each activity on Saturday.
Draw a bar graph to show Anna's data.
Write about what you know
from the graph.

What I Did on Saturday

Activity	Time in Minutes
Listening to music	90
Playing video games	20
Reading for fun	50
Watching TV	170
Watching videos	40
Using the computer	30

Show *and* Share

Compare graphs with another pair of classmates.
How are the graphs the same? Different?

Connect

One hundred children chose their favourite home activity.

➤ To draw a bar graph,
choose a **scale**.

- All the numbers in the table
  end in 0 or 5.
- So, choose a scale of
  1 square represents 5 children.
- Count by 5s to find
  the number of squares
  in each bar on the graph.

Favourite Things to Do at Home

Activity	Number of Children
Listening to CDs	15
Listening to the radio	10
Playing video games	5
Reading for fun	20
Using a computer	10
Watching TV	40

Activity	Number of Children	Count by 5s	Number of Squares
Listening to CDs	15	5, 10, 15	3
Listening to the radio	10	5, 10	2
Playing video games	5	5	1
Reading for fun	20	5, 10, 15, 20	4
Using a computer	10	5, 10	2
Watching TV	40	5, 10, 15, 20, 25, 30, 35, 40	8

➤ Here is another way to find the number of squares in each bar on the graph.
Since all the numbers in the table are divisible by 5, divide each number by 5.

Activity	Number of Children	Number of Squares
Listening to CDs	15	$15 \div 5 = 3$
Listening to the radio	10	$10 \div 5 = 2$
Playing video games	5	$5 \div 5 = 1$
Reading for fun	20	$20 \div 5 = 4$
Using a computer	10	$10 \div 5 = 2$
Watching TV	40	$40 \div 5 = 8$

➤ Write the activities on the **horizontal axis**.
➤ Write the number of children on the **vertical axis.**

The graph shows watching TV is the favourite activity. Its bar has the most squares.

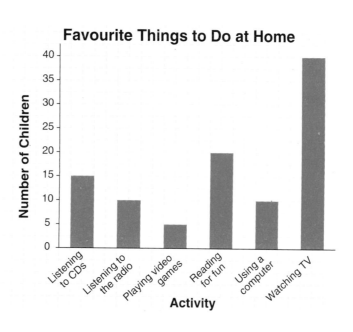

Favourite Things to Do at Home

Practice

1. Stefan had a bag of coloured candy. He counted each colour.

Stefan's Candy

Colour	Tally	Number
Brown	‖‖	5
Red	‖‖ ‖‖ ‖	12
Yellow	‖‖ ‖‖	10
Blue	‖‖ ‖	6
Orange	‖‖ ‖‖	9
Green	‖‖ ‖	7

a) Draw a bar graph.
   Use a scale of 1 square represents 2 candies.

b) Write 3 things you know from the graph.

2. The children in a Grade 3 class estimated the time they took to get to school.

a) Draw a bar graph.

b) Compare your graph with a classmate's graph. Do both graphs match? Explain.

c) How many children take the greatest time?

d) One child takes only 5 minutes. Does he or she live closest to the school? Explain.

How Long It Takes to Get to School

Time in Minutes	Number of Children
5	1
10	2
15	8
20	7
25	5
30	0
35	3
40	0
45	2

3. Write your full name and those of 5 classmates.
Make a tally chart for the letters in the names.
   a) Draw a bar graph.
   b) How many letters are there in the names?
   c) Which letter appears most often? Only once?
   d) Which letters are vowels? Consonants?
   e) Write a question about the letters in the names.
      Answer the question.
   Show your work.

4. On a calendar, mark the birthdays of you and your classmates.
   a) Draw a bar graph.
   b) Which month has the most birthdays? The fewest birthdays?
   c) How many students had birthdays during the
      summer vacation?
   d) What else do you know from the graph?

5. The chart shows the top speeds of some animals.

Animal	Speed in Kilometres per Hour
Human	45
Greyhound	63
Quarter horse	76
Lion	80
Canada goose	100
Cheetah	113

   a) Round each speed to the nearest 10.
   b) Draw a bar graph of the rounded data.
   c) Write what you know from the graph.

Reflect

How are bar graphs and pictographs alike? Different?
Use pictures and words to explain.

Strategies Toolkit

Explore

Shane had nickels, dimes, and quarters.
He bought a used comic book for 25¢.
He did not get any change.
How many different ways could
Shane pay for the comic book?

Show and Share

Show your classmates how you solved the problem.

Connect

Amy had pennies, nickels, and dimes.
She bought a pencil for 20¢.
Amy did not get any change.
How many different ways could
Amy pay for the pencil?

Strategies

- **Make a table.**
- **Use a model.**
- **Draw a picture.**
- **Solve a simpler problem.**
- **Work backward.**
- **Guess and check.**
- **Make an organized list.**
- **Use a pattern.**

What do you know?
- Amy paid 20¢.
- Amy used pennies, nickels, and dimes.

Think of a strategy to help you solve the problem.
- You can **solve a simpler problem**.
- Use play money.

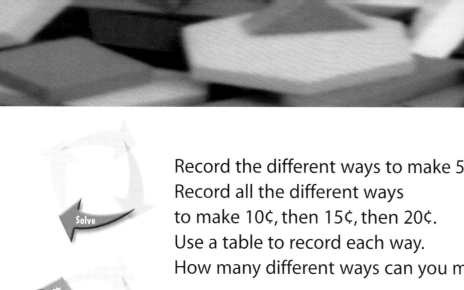

Solve

Record the different ways to make 5¢.
Record all the different ways
to make 10¢, then 15¢, then 20¢.
Use a table to record each way.
How many different ways can you make 20¢?

Look Back

How could you have solved this problem
another way?

Practice

Choose one of the

Strategies

1. Show 4 ways you could make 55¢
   with six or fewer coins.

2. The pizzas in Tony's Restaurant have these toppings:
   pepperoni, mushroom, and green pepper
   You can choose 1, 2, or 3 toppings.
   How many different pizzas can you make?

3. What number am I?
   • I have two digits.
   • I am less than 90.
   • I am more than 20.
   • The sum of my digits is not even.
   • My ones digit is one more than my tens digit.
   How many numbers did you find?

Reflect

Tell about a time when you had to buy something with coins.
How did you decide which coins to use?

Collecting Data

Explore

You will need a metre stick.
In your group, whose knee is
farthest from the ground?
Use a metre stick to find out.
Record your data in a table.

Student	Ground to Knee

*Round each length
to the nearest
centimetre.*

Show *and* Share

Share your results with
another group.
Whose knee is farthest
from the ground?
Closest to the ground?
Whose knees are farther from the ground than yours?
Whose knees are closer to the ground than yours?

Connect

Data are facts or information.
You collect data to learn about people and things.

To collect data, begin with these questions:
- WHAT do you want to know?
- WHAT question will you ask?
- WHOM will you ask?
- HOW will you show what you find out?

You can collect data from friends and family.

➤ You can record data in tally charts and tables.

OUR BIRTHDAYS	
MONTH	NUMBER OF BIRTHDAYS
JANUARY	II
FEBRUARY	III
MARCH	HHT II

BIRDS SPOTTED ON SPRING DAYS	
DAY	NUMBER OF BIRDS
1	4
2	9
3	3

➤ You can show data in graphs.

Practice

1. Work with the class.
   How long did it take you to get to school this morning?
   a) Record your time on the board.
   b) Who took the longest time?
      How do you know?
   c) Who took the shortest time?

2. Work with the class.
   Are you left-handed or right-handed?
   a) Record your answer on the board.
   b) How many children are left-handed?
   c) How many children are right-handed?
   d) Are there more right-handed or left-handed children?

Numbers Every Day

Calculator Skills

Make a pattern with only odd numbers. Tell how you did it. What is the pattern rule?

219

3. Work with a partner. Use a measuring tape to find out.
   a) Which is longer: your leg or your arm?
   b) Which is shorter: around your waist or around your head?
   c) Which is longer: elbow to wrist or elbow to shoulder?
   Record your work in a table.

4. Which season do you and your classmates like best?
   a) Record your favourite season on the board.
   b) Record all the data in a tally chart.
   c) Make a table from your tally chart.
   d) What did you find out? Write to explain.
   Show your work.

5. Kumar's teacher wrote these data on the board.
   a) What question do you think she asked the class?
   b) Draw a graph to show these data.

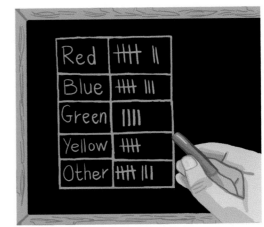

Red								
Blue									
Green					
Yellow						
Other									

6. Write a question to find out:
   a) what pets the class has
   b) the class' favourite ice cream
   c) the TV show most watched by the class

Reflect

Look at all the *Practice* questions above. Why might someone want to know the answer to one of these questions? Explain.

At Home

Choose something you would like to know about everyone at home.
Ask a suitable question.
Write what you found out.

9 Conducting a Survey

Think about your answers to these questions:

How many people live in your home?

How many hours do you sleep at night?

Do you prefer to watch sports or take part in sports?

What is your favourite sport?

Would your classmates' answers be different? Explain.

Explore

➤ Choose one of these topics:
  • Buttons on classmates' clothes
  • Classmates' favourite piece of clothing
  • Colours each classmate is wearing
➤ In your group, discuss:
  • what question you will ask
  • whom you will ask
  • what answers you might get
  • how you will record the answers
➤ Ask the question.
  Record the answers.
  Show your data in a chart and a graph.

Which is your favourite sport to play?

Hockey –

Baseball –

Basketball –

Volleyball –

Soccer –

Other –

Show *and* Share

Share your findings with another group.
Show your chart and graph. Tell what you found out.

When you ask a question to find out about something, you are **conducting a survey**.
Angie conducted a survey to find out the favourite after-school activity of children in her grade.
She gave choices with her question to help record the answers.
Angie asked:

> Which is your favourite after-school activity?
> play with brother/sister/friend ____ read ____ play with pets ____
> do homework ____ use the computer _____

Each student in Grade 3 answered the question.

➤ Angie made this tally chart:

Grade 3s Favourite After-School Activities

Activity	Tally	Number
Play with brother/sister/friend	卌 卌 卌 卌 卌 I	26
Read	卌 卌 III	13
Play with pets	卌	5
Do homework	卌 III	8
Use the computer	卌 卌	10

➤ Angie drew this bar graph:

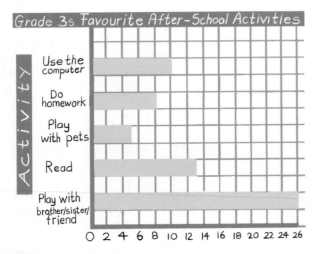

Grade 3s Favourite After-School Activities

Angie found out:
- The favourite after-school activity is playing with brother, sister, or friend.
- Twice as many students like to use the computer as play with pets.

Tell what else you know from Angie's survey.

1. Conduct a survey.
   Ask as many children as you can:

   How many minutes did you spend doing homework last night?
   0 ___   1 – 10 ___   11 – 20 ___
   21 – 30 ___   more than 30 ___

   Minutes Spent Doing Homework

Time in Minutes	Tally	Number of Students
0		
1 – 10		
11 – 20		
21 – 30		
30+		

   a) Copy and complete this chart.
   b) What do you know from your chart?

2. Find out your classmates' favourite after-school activities.
   a) Use the list of activities in *Connect*.
      Include "Other" for children who do something else.
   b) Draw a graph.
   c) How does your graph compare with Angie's?
      How is it the same? Different?

3. Survey your classmates.
   How many wear digital watches?
   How many wear watches with hands?
   a) Record your data. Draw a graph.
   b) What did you find out?
   c) Write 2 questions you can
      answer using your data.
      Answer your questions.
   Show your work.

Reflect

Describe a survey you conducted
and what you found out. What
would you do differently next time?

Numbers Every Day

Mental Math
Add or subtract.

98 + 44   48 – 19

350 + 90   57 – 31

Which strategies did
you use?
Which other strategies
could you have used?

LESSON

1
2

1. Look at these shoes.

a) Choose 2 attributes. Sort the shoes.
Record the sorting.

b) Did you use a chart or a Venn diagram?
Explain your choice.

c) Choose 3 different attributes. Sort the shoes.
Record the sorting.

3

2. a) How many chocolate donuts were sold?

Donuts Sold at the Bake Sale

represents 5 donuts

b) Which type of donut was sold the most? The least?

c) Which type of donut was bought twice as often
as another donut?

d) What else do you know from this graph?

3. **a)** Which circle graph below
      shows the same data
      as this bar graph?
      How do you know?

   b) What is the scale on
      the bar graph?

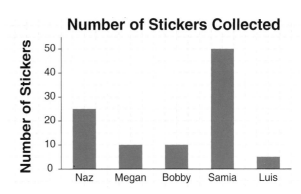

Number of Stickers Collected

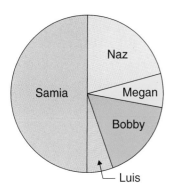
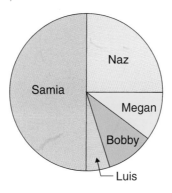
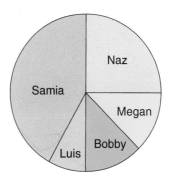

   c) Which child collected the most stickers?
      How many stickers did this child collect?

   d) Can you use the circle graph to answer part c? Explain.

   e) Write a question about the bar graph.
      Answer your question.

4. Choose 6 children from the class.
   a) Measure each child's elbow to fingertip.
   b) Record the results.
   c) Draw a graph.
      Explain your choice of graph.
   d) Write 3 things you know
      from your graph.

U N I T

5 Learning Goals

   ☑ sort and classify objects
      and data
   ☑ collect and organize data
   ☑ draw graphs
   ☑ interpret graphs
   ☑ conduct surveys

Using Data to Answer Questions

What is the favourite lunch of
children in your class?
Survey your classmates to find out.

Work in a small group.
➤ Record the question you will ask.
➤ Ask the question, then record the results.
➤ Graph the data.
➤ Write what you know from your graph.
➤ Show your work.

Check List

Your work should show
☑ the question you asked and possible answers
☑ your data in a chart or table
☑ a graph that is easy to understand, with labels and a title
☑ a clear explanation of what you found out

Reflect on the Unit

How can you sort data? How can you show data?
Explain your thinking.

6

Bake Sale

Measurement

Bake Sale

**COME TO OUR
GIANT BAKE SALE!**

Place: Basil Street
School

Date: Friday
January 26

Time: 1:30–3:00

Learning Goals

- use calendars and clocks
  to measure time
- tell and write time
- use a thermometer to measure
  temperature
- count money, make change, and
  read and write money amounts
- measure the capacity of a
  container in millilitres and litres
- measure the mass of an object
  in grams and kilograms

Basil Street School plans a bake sale to raise money for playground equipment. Each class will bake goodies for the sale.

Price List

Chocolate Chip Cookie	20¢
Cupcake	25¢
Baklava	40¢
Bannock	65¢
Blueberry Muffin	30¢
Popcorn Ball	50¢
Oatmeal Bar	35¢
Fortune Cookie	5¢

Key Words

analog clock

digital clock

elapsed time

thermometer

temperature

degree Celsius

change

capacity

litre

millilitre

mass

kilogram

gram

• At what time will the bake sale start? End?

• Why does the invitation not show the time as a.m. or p.m.?

• Will the sale last more than 1 hour or less than 1 hour?

• Which item costs most?

• Which coins could you use to buy it?

Exploring the Calendar

Tell what you know from looking at this calendar page.

MARCH

S	M	T	W	T	F	S
			1	2	3	4
5	6	7	8	9	10 Report Cards	11
12	13	14	15	16	17	18
←			Spring Break			→
19	20	21 1st day of spring	22	23	24	25
26	27	28	29	30	31	

Explore

Use the calendar your teacher gives you. This chart shows the after-school programs offered in the second term. All programs run until the last week before spring break.

Program	Start-Up Date	How Often Held
Chess for Beginners	Feb. 8	Every week
Arts and Crafts	Jan. 23	Every 2 weeks
Folk Dancing	Jan. 5	Every 3 weeks
Floor Hockey	Jan. 31	Every Tues. & Thurs.

➤ Choose a program you would like to sign up for.
Record all the dates you will go.

➤ Choose a second program.
Make sure it is held on days different from your first program.
Record the dates you will go.

Show *and* Share

Talk with a classmate about your dates.
Which 2 programs could you not
sign up for? Explain.

JANUARY

S	M	T	W	T	F	S
1	2	3	4	5 F.D.	6	7
8	9	10	11	12	13	14

JANUARY	FEBRUARY	MARCH	APRIL

MAY	JUNE	JULY	AUGUST

SEPTEMBER	OCTOBER	NOVEMBER	DECEMBER

Each calendar page shows the days and weeks of one month of the year.

There are 365 days in a year.

Every 4 years, there are 29 days in February.

That year has 366 days.

There are 52 weeks in a year.

There are 12 months in a year.

Zach's puppies were born on April 16th. To find out when they will be 3 months old:

Think:

From April 16th to May 16th is 1 month.
From April 16th to June 16th is 2 months.
From April 16th to July 16th is 3 months.

Zach's puppies will be 3 months old on July 16th.

Numbers Every Day

Mental Math

Find each difference.
Look for a pattern.
Explain the pattern.

$15 - 12 = \square$

$16 - 13 = \square$

$17 - 14 = \square$

$18 - 15 = \square$

$19 - 16 = \square$

Use the calendar in *Connect*.

1. **a)** How many school days are there in February?
    b) How many months have 31 days?
    c) If you love Saturdays, which are your favourite months? Explain.

2. Name the date that is
    a) 6 days after June 7th   **b)** 9 days before September 3rd
    c) 7 weeks after May 4th   **d)** 4 weeks before November 14th
    e) 3 months after January 27th **f)** 5 months before October 30th

3. Suppose you take judo lessons on Mondays every second week.
    The first class is on October 23rd.
    What are the dates of the next 2 classes?

4. Laci's birthday is on August 24th. Julian's is on September 21st.
    How many weeks after Laci's birthday is Julian's?

5. Ulayak and his family are going to their camp in July and August.
    How many days will they be gone? How do you know?

6. Johanna is 2 years and 3 months old.
    How old is Johanna in months?

7. Pick one date. Write clues to help someone guess your date.
    Trade riddles with a classmate.
    Solve your classmate's riddle. Show your work.

Reflect

How would you find how many weeks have passed
since your last birthday?
Use words, pictures, or numbers to explain.

Telling Time

It takes 5 minutes for the minute hand to move from one number to the next number.

5 minutes after 3 o'clock
3:05

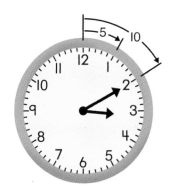

10 minutes after 3 o'clock
3:10

Explore 👥

➤ Use the 9 clock cards your teacher gives you.
Make a set of 9 time cards to match the clock cards.
Each time should end in 5 or 0.
➤ Mix the time cards and the clock cards.
Trade with your partner.
Sort your partner's cards into 9 matching sets.

7:25

6:50

Show *and* Share

Check each other's work.
How did you match the cards?

Math Link

Number Sense

You can multiply by 5 to find the time in minutes.

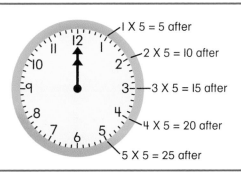

1 X 5 = 5 after
2 X 5 = 10 after
3 X 5 = 15 after
4 X 5 = 20 after
5 X 5 = 25 after

A clock with numbers and hands is an **analog clock**.
A clock face shows the numbers from 1 to 12.
There are 24 hours in 1 day.
Each day, the hour hand moves twice around the clock.
There are 60 minutes in 1 hour.
Each hour, the minute hand moves once around the clock.

This clock shows
20 minutes after 9 o'clock.

You write: 9:20
You say: "Twenty after nine"
or "Twenty past nine"
or "Nine twenty"

Skip count the minutes: 5, 10, 15, 20

This clock shows
55 minutes after 11 o'clock or
5 minutes before 12 o'clock.

You write: 11:55
You say: "Five before 12"
or "Five to twelve"
or "Eleven fifty-five"

Skip count the minutes: 5, 10, 15, 20, 25, 30, 35, 40, 45, 50, 55

A clock with numbers and no hands
is a **digital clock**.

This clock shows 47 minutes after 5 o'clock.

You write: 5:47
You say: "Five forty-seven"

Numbers Every Day

Mental Math

Maya subtracts 43 – 8
in her head like this:
Add 2 to each number.
45 – 10 = 35

Use a similar method
to subtract.

35 – 9 = ☐
53 – 7 = ☐

234

1. Write the time on each analog clock.
Skip count the minutes if you need to.

a)

b)

c)

d)

e)

f)

2. Write each time two ways. The first one is done for you.

a)  10 after 10
10:10

b)

c)

d)

e)

f)

3. Match each analog clock with the digital clock
that shows the same time.

a)

b)

c)

d)

A
`5:05`

B
`9:45`

C
`4:25`

D
`6:50`

4. a) Suppose it is 6:20.
What time will it be in 5 minutes?

b) Suppose it is 9:00.
What time will it be in 10 minutes?

c) Suppose it is 4:55.
What time will it be in 15 minutes?

5. School starts at 9:00.
a) Corrina was 4 minutes late.
Draw a digital clock to show what time she arrived.
b) Sammy was 10 minutes early.
Draw an analog clock to show what time he arrived.
Write the time two ways.
Show your work.

6. Show 10 minutes before 11.
Then write 10 minutes before 11 another way.

7. Kelly began to read at 2 o'clock. She read for 60 minutes.
At what time did Kelly finish reading?

8. Draw a digital clock to show each time.
a) eleven thirty-seven
b) half past two
c) two twenty-one
d) six sixteen
e) quarter to eleven
f) one fifty-three

At Home

Reflect

Which clock do you prefer
to use—analog or digital?
Explain your choice.

Find all the clocks in
your home.
Draw a picture of
each clock at a
different time during
the day. Write each
time in words.

Elapsed Time

➤ Saba sent this invitation to 5 friends.
Help Saba plan the afternoon.
Choose 4 games to play.

➤ Make a chart to show each game
and its start and end times.
Remember to include a time for eating.

➤ Trade charts with another pair
of classmates.
Find how many minutes will be
spent playing each game.

Show *and* Share

Check each other's work.
Talk about the strategies you used
to figure out the time in minutes.

You are invited
to an afternoon
of fun & games

Place: 235 Hickory Hollow Drive
Date: Saturday, February 6
Time: 1:15 pm.- 4:00 pm.

 Food will be served

a.m.—times from midnight to noon
p.m.—times from noon to midnight

The amount of time from the start to the
end of an activity is the **elapsed time**.

Fatima and Clara played checkers from
9:20 a.m. to 10:05 a.m.

To find the elapsed time in minutes,
count on by 5s.

Fatima and Clara played checkers for 45 minutes.

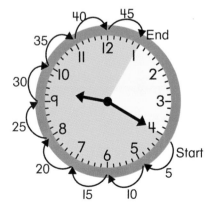

1. Recess starts at 10:10 a.m. and ends at 10:25 a.m. How long is recess?

2. Find each elapsed time.
   a) 9:15 a.m. to 10:10 a.m.
   b) 3:30 p.m. to 4:15 p.m.
   c) 11:50 a.m. to 12:10 p.m.

3. Aaron listened to music for 35 minutes.
   He started at 6:25 p.m.
   At what time did Aaron stop?

4. You have 20 minutes to clean your room.
   You start at 3:45 p.m. You finish at 4:10 p.m.
   Did you clean your room in time? Explain.

5. Suppose it is now 7:50 p.m.
   How many minutes will it be until 8:15 p.m.?
   How do you know?

6. A spider took 30 minutes to spin its web.
   The spider finished spinning at 11:40 a.m.
   At what time did it start?

7. This chart shows Emma's Saturday activities.
   Copy and complete the chart.

	Activity	Start Time	End Time	Elapsed Time
a)	Library visit	9:15 a.m.	9:55 a.m.	
b)	Hockey practice	4:25 p.m.		40 minutes
c)	Help with supper		7:10 p.m.	35 minutes

Numbers Every Day

Number Strategies

Complete each number pattern.

5, ☐, 15, ☐, 25, 30

6, 12, ☐, ☐, 30, ☐

☐, 35, 28, ☐ , ☐ ,7

☐, 45, ☐ , 65, 75, ☐

8. Arlo and Wilfred met at the park at 2:30 p.m.
   Arlo took 20 minutes to get to the park.
   Wilfred took 25 minutes.
   At what time did each boy leave home? How do you know?

9. Look at each analog clock. What time will it be 45 minutes later?

a)  **b)** 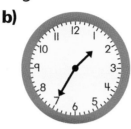 **c)** 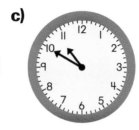 **d)**

10. Here is a schedule of
   activities for the trip
   to the Outdoor
   Nature Centre.

Activity	Time Period
Snowshoeing	1:00 – 1:50
Bird-watching	2:00 – 2:30
Snack time	2:40 – 2:55
Looking for animal tracks	3:00 – 3:55

   a) Why does the chart
   not show a.m. or p.m.?

   b) Which activity takes the most time?
   How much time does it take?

   c) How much time do bird-watching
   and looking for animal tracks take together?

   d) It takes 40 minutes to ride from school
   to the nature centre.
   At what time should the class leave school?

   e) About what time will the class arrive back
   at school after the trip? How do you know?

   f) Make up your own question about the trip.
   Answer your question.
   Show your work.

Reflect

Suppose you know the time an activity begins and ends.
How can you find how long it takes? Explain.

Measuring Temperature

You use a **thermometer** to measure **temperature**.
Temperature is measured in **degrees Celsius** (°C).

The thermometer at the right shows a temperature of 19°C.
You say: 19 degrees Celsius

You will need a thermometer.
Choose 4 different places in or around the school.

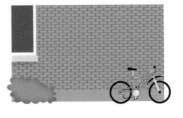 

Measure and record the
temperature in each place.

Here are some ways to record your work.
- Use a chart.
- Colour pictures of thermometers.

Place	Temperature
Sunny window	22°C

Show *and* Share

Talk with your partner about the
temperatures you recorded.
Why are some temperatures the same? Different?

The liquid in a thermometer rises as the temperature goes up, and falls as the temperature goes down.
Here are some benchmark temperatures.

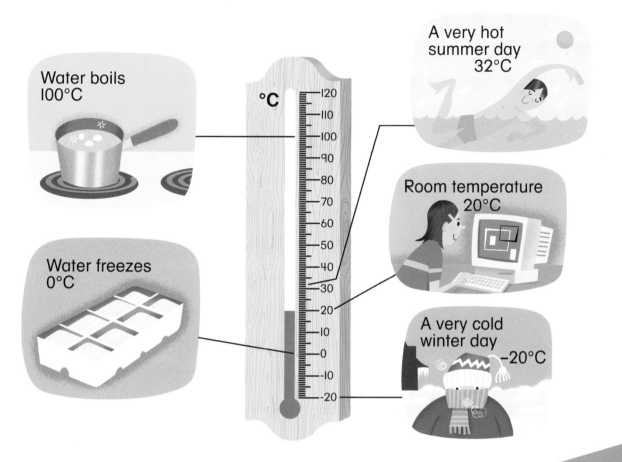

A very hot summer day 32°C

Water boils 100°C

Room temperature 20°C

Water freezes 0°C

A very cold winter day −20°C

Temperatures below zero are written with a minus sign.
You read:
−9°C as "9 degrees Celsius below zero" or as "minus 9 degrees Celsius."

Numbers Every Day

Number Strategies

$4 \times 2 = 8$
$3 \times 2 = 6$

How can you use these results to find 7×2?

Use pictures and words to explain.

1. Write each temperature.

   a) Inuvik in
      September

   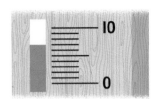

   b) Oshawa in
      August

   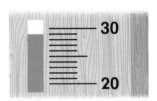

   c) A cup of
      warm milk

   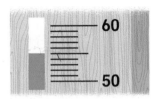

   d) Winnipeg in
      October

   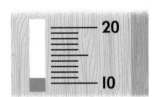

   e) Yellowknife in
      September

   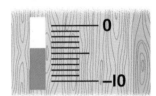

   f) Your body
      temperature

   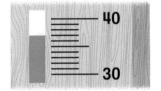

2. Estimate the most likely temperature for each picture.

   a) 15°C –4°C 21°C

   b) –5°C 20°C 80°C

   c) 40°C 0°C 99°C

   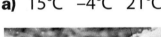

3. Order the temperatures from highest to lowest.

   a) 27°C, –44°C, 13°C

   b) 58°C, –3°C, 3°C

   c) 14°C, 32°C, –45°C

4. Use the graph to answer each question.

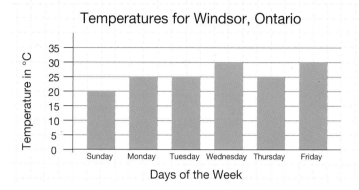

a) What season of the year do you think it is? Give reasons.
b) What was the temperature on Thursday?
c) Which day was hottest? How do you know?
d) How much greater was the temperature on Monday than on Sunday?
e) Which temperature will it most likely be on Saturday: 14°C, 32°C, or −4°C? How do you know?
f) Write your own question about this graph. Answer your question.
Show your work.

5. Draw clothes you would wear to play outside in each temperature.
a) 29°C   b) −12°C   c) 13°C

6. Choose the more likely temperature.
a) It is snowing outside.   −8°C or 20°C
b) My ice cream is melting!   12°C or 27°C
c) I had better wear a jacket today.   7°C or 31°C
d) This hot chocolate is too hot to drink.   10°C or 90°C

Reflect

When do you need to know the temperature?
Explain.

Exploring Money

Here are 6 different coins we have in Canada.

| penny | nickel | dime | quarter | loonie | toonie |

| 1¢ | 5¢ | 10¢ | 25¢ | one dollar | two dollars |

Here are the 5 different bills.

Think of an item you can buy for about five dollars. Twenty dollars. One hundred dollars.

Explore

You will need play money.

➤ Choose one of these bills.

LESSON FOCUS | Explore the relationships among coins and bills.

➤ Have your partner use as many of the coins or bills below as necessary. She must show the amount equal to the bill you chose in as many ways as she can.

➤ Record your work.
➤ Switch roles. Repeat the activity with another bill.

Show *and* Share

Talk with your partner about the strategies you used to show the amounts of money.

Connect

You can skip count to show how some coins and bills are related.

➤ To show how many quarters make one dollar, count on by 25s:

4 quarters make one dollar.

25,   50,   75,   one dollar

➤ To show how many twenty-dollar bills make one hundred dollars, count on by 20s:

5 twenty-dollar bills make one hundred dollars.

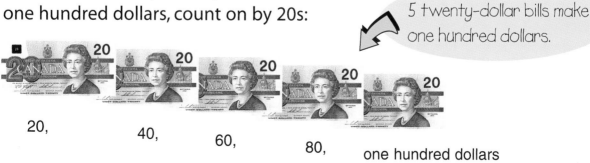

20,   40,   60,   80,   one hundred dollars

1. Copy and complete.
    Use play money and skip counting to help you.

    a) 1 quarter = ☐ nickels   **b)** one dollar = ☐ nickels

    c) one dollar = ☐ dimes   **d)** one dollar = ☐ quarters

    e) 1 toonie = ☐ loonies   **f)** one dollar = ☐ pennies

2. How many ten-dollar bills make one hundred dollars?

3. How many toonies make twenty dollars? Show how you know.

4. How many fifty-dollar bills would you get for a
    one-hundred dollar bill?

5. Suppose you wanted to exchange 8 quarters for loonies.
    How many loonies would you get?

6. You have a five-dollar bill.
    How many quarters should you trade the bill for?
    Draw a picture to show your answer.

7. Geraldine needs change for a ten-dollar bill.
    Her brother gives her 5 toonies.
    Is this a fair trade? Explain.

8. Amar gave his brother 11 dimes
    for a loonie. Who got the better deal?

Numbers Every Day

Mental Math

How can you use the first sum
to find the second sum?

23 + 30 = ☐

23 + 32 = ☐

How can you use the first
difference to find the
second difference?

100 − 5 = ☐

102 − 5 = ☐

Reflect

Suppose you could buy a toy.
What would it cost? What bills and coins
would you use to pay for it?
Use words and pictures to show your work.

Estimating and Counting Money

Explore

You will need a bag of play money.
➤ Look at the bag.
   Estimate how much money is in the bag.
   Record your estimate.
➤ Take the money out of the bag.
   Take turns counting it.
   Record the sum.
   Who had the closest estimate?
➤ Repeat this activity with other bags of money.

Show and Share

Talk about the strategies you used to estimate.
What strategies did you use to count the money?
Is it easier to start with the dollars or the pennies?

Connect

Zena earns money shovelling snow.

➤ Here is how Zena counted the money
   she has earned so far.
   • First she sorted and counted the dollars.

"5,   7,   8, 9 dollars"

- Then she sorted and counted the other coins.

"25,   35, 45, 55,   60, 65, 70, 75 cents"

The decimal point separates the dollars and cents.

Zena has nine dollars and seventy-five cents, or $9.75.

dollar sign   decimal point

➤ Zena's grandpa gave her a quarter. Now Zena has ten dollars.
You can write ten dollars in 2 ways: $10 or $10.00

You can write amounts less than one dollar in 2 ways:

In cents: 25¢
In dollars: $0.25

25 cents

➤ Zena found a nickel and 2 pennies in her jeans pocket.
You can write amounts less than ten cents in 2 ways:

In cents: 7¢
In dollars: $0.07

Practice

Use play money when it helps.
1. Count the money. Write each amount in dollars.

a)

b)

c)

d)

2. Write each amount in question 1 parts c and d another way.

3. Draw pictures to show each amount.
   a) $1.49   **b)** $0.27   **c)** $2.13   **d)** 36¢   **e)** $0.04

4. What coins could you use to buy each drink? Record your answer.
   a) 65¢   **b)** 90¢   **c)** $1.35

5. Show $5.00 using the fewest coins. Draw the coins.

6. Show $1.27 using the fewest coins. Draw the coins.

7. Lizzie emptied her piggy bank and sorted the coins.
   This is what she had: 3 $1 coins, 1 $2 coin,
   9 quarters, 11 dimes, 4 nickels, 17 pennies
   a) Estimate how much money Lizzie had.
   b) Find out exactly how much money she had.
   Show your work.

8. Show 3 different ways to make each amount
   using any coins except pennies.
   a) $6.00   **b)** $3.75   **c)** $5.40

9. Show 3 different ways to make each amount
   using loonies, toonies, and $5.00 bills.
   a) $8.00   **b)** $10.00   **c)** $9.00

10. Mateo has more than one dollar in coins
   in his pocket. But he can't count out
   exactly one dollar. What coins might
   Mateo have? How do you know?

Reflect

Why is it important to know how to count
money? Write about your ideas.

Numbers Every Day

Calculator Skills

Estimate how many
hours you sleep in a
year. Then use a
calculator to find out.
Tell how you did it.

Strategies Toolkit

Explore

Fatini used 8 coins to pay for his hardcover book.
He did not get any change.
What coins did Fatini use?

Work together to solve this problem.

Show *and* Share

Describe the strategy you used to solve the problem.

Connect

Claire emptied her piggy bank.
There were 14 coins altogether.
Claire counted the money. She had $6.48.
What coins did Claire have?

Understand

What do you know?
• There were 14 coins.
• There was $6.48.

Plan

Think of a strategy to help you
solve the problem.
• You can use **guess and check**.
• Use play money.

Strategies

• **Make a table.**
• **Use a model.**
• **Draw a picture.**
• **Solve a simpler problem.**
• **Work backward.**
• **Guess and check.**
• **Make an organized list.**
• **Use a pattern.**

Show $6.48 using any coins.
How many coins did you use?
If you used fewer than 14 coins,
trade some coins of greater value
for some of lesser value.
If you used more than 14 coins, trade some coins
of lesser value for some of greater value.
Keep trading until you have exactly 14 coins.

How could you have solved this problem another way?

Practice

Choose a strategy from the

Strategies

1. Hunter had 10 coins. They totalled $7.62.
   Which coins did he have?

2. Sylvie paid $7.95 for a book about horses.
   She used one bill and 8 coins.
   Which bill and coins did Sylvie use?

3. Kala has $5.30 in coins. Amanda also has $5.30 in coins.
   Kala has more coins than Amanda.
   Which coins could each girl have?

Reflect

Suppose your friend has 4 quarters and you have 10 dimes.
He thinks he has less money because he has fewer coins.
How would you help him understand that both of you
have the same amount of money?
Use pictures, words, or numbers to show your work.

LESSON 8

Making Change

Explore

You will need play money.
Choose a fish you would like to buy.
You pay for it with a $5 bill.
Your partner is the sales clerk.
What does your partner do?

Switch roles.
This time, use a $10 bill to buy a fish.
Show your work.

Show and Share

Talk about strategies you use when you don't
have the exact money to buy a fish.

Tropical Fish Prices

Black Mollie	$1.15
Neon Tetra	$0.89
Angel fish	$6.49
Swordtail	$2.75
Zebra fish	$1.95
Glow-Light Tetra	$2.37

Connect

Suppose you bought this fishbowl with a $10 bill.
The clerk will give you **change**.

Here is one way the clerk can make change for you.
Count on from $7.29 to $10:

$7.29

$7.29... $7.30, $7.40, $7.50, $7.75, $8.00, $10.00

Add up the coins. Your change would be $2.71.

Use play money when it helps.

1. Here are some things for sale at a yard sale.

Draw pictures to show the money you would use to make change.
Write the change in dollars.

a) Simbi buys a comic book with a toonie.

b) Hugo pays for the rollerblades with two $5 bills.

c) Priya buys the hockey stick with 12 quarters.

d) Sally buys the computer game with a $5 bill and 2 toonies.

2. Ramona bought a CD for $9.13.
She paid for it with a $5 bill, 2 toonies, and 1 loonie.
Show how the store clerk might have made change for Ramona.

3. Ollie's lunch cost $4.10. He paid for it with a $5 bill.
Show 3 ways the clerk could have made change
for Ollie.

4. Tad buys a novel that costs $6.37.
He pays with a $10 bill and gets
$2.63 in change.
Did Tad get the correct change?
Explain your thinking.

Reflect

Suppose you bought something for $1.29.
Show how you would count on
to make change from $2.

Numbers Every Day

Number Strategies

How can you use the first
two sums to find the third sum?

$40 + 30 = \square$
$6 + 3 = \square$
$46 + 33 = \square$

Find.

$53 + 21 = \square$
$48 + 32 = \square$
$24 + 52 = \square$

Adding and Subtracting Money

Explore

You will need play money.
Suppose you put on a show for friends.
Here are some props you can buy.
You have $10.00 to spend.
Choose two props to buy.
Find the total cost.
Find how much money you would have left.
Record your work.

Show *and* Share

Talk with a classmate about the strategies
you used to solve the problem.
How did you make sure you were not spending
more than $10.00?

Connect

➤ Here is one way to find the total cost
of the mask and shoes.

• Use play money to show $3.14.

- Use play money to show $5.27.

- Put the 2 groups of money together. Count to find the total.

The total cost of the mask and shoes is $8.41.

➤ Here is one way to find how much money is left from $10.00.
  - Use play money to show $10.00. Take away $8.00.

- You need to take away $0.41. You have only 1 toonie left.
  Trade this toonie for other coins. Then take away $0.41.

There is $1.59 left.

Use play money when it helps.

1. How much do you have altogether?
   a) $0.25 and $0.41
   b) $1.25 and $0.76
   c) $1.49 and $3.26
   d) $4.35 and $2.17

   e) $5.25
      + $1.14

   f) $0.69
      + $0.85

   g) $1.28
      + $2.42

2. Find how much money you will have left.
   a) You have $7.00. You spend $3.28.
   b) You have $4.98. You spend $2.33.
   c) You have $6.50. You spend $5.29.

3. a) Suppose you bought the cap and baseball.

$2.75

$4.99

   How much do they cost in total?
   How much change would you get from $10.00?
   b) What is the difference in prices for the cap and the baseball?

Math Link

Your World

The Royal Canadian Mint in Winnipeg makes Canada's coins and bills. The Royal Canadian Mint in Ottawa makes special coins. When you visit the Mint, you can watch the coins being made.

4. Sebastian has 2 toonies, 3 loonies, 1 quarter, and 4 dimes.
Jitka has 1 toonie, 4 loonies, 4 quarters, and 5 nickels.
Who has more money? How much more?
How do you know?

5. a) Emi had $8.00.
She bought 2 pairs of toe socks on sale.
How much did Emi pay?
How much money did she have left?

b) Sylvia estimates that 4 pairs of toe socks
will cost about $12.00.
Is this a good estimate? Explain.
Show your work.

$2.89

6. Celine had $3.00.
She bought one of the props on page 254.
She has $1.71 left.
Which prop did Celine buy? Explain your thinking.

7. Write a story problem about 2 items you would like to buy.
Solve your problem. Show your work.

Reflect

Suppose you want to buy
2 healthy snacks.
How do you make sure
you have enough money?
Use words, numbers, or
pictures to explain.

At Home

Look through a catalogue or flyer.
Find 2 items that you estimate
would cost less than $10.00.
Check your estimate by finding
the total cost.

Exploring Capacity: The Litre

Ruby carries a drinking bottle when she hikes.
The bottle holds one **litre** of water.
We use the symbol **L** for litres.

Explore

You will need some containers and sand.

➤ Look at the container
that holds one litre.
Choose another container.
Estimate whether it holds
less than one litre,
more than one litre,
or about one litre.
Check your estimate.
Record your work.
Repeat this activity with
other containers.

➤ Choose a large container.
Estimate its capacity in litres.
Record your estimate.
Check your estimate.
Record your work.

I think it holds less than one litre.

I think it holds more than one litre.

Show *and* Share

Discuss the strategies you used to make your estimates.
Can containers of different shapes hold about the same amount?
Do you drink more or less than one litre of liquids in a day?

When you measure how much
a container holds,
you measure its **capacity**.

This carton has a capacity of one litre.
You write: 1 L
The carton holds one litre of juice.
One litre fills about 4 glasses.

Here are some other things
that are measured in litres.

Practice ....

1. Which containers hold less than one litre?

   a)   b)   c)

   d)   e)   f)

2. Choose the better estimate.

   a) 5 L or 210 L   b) 9 L   c) 2 L
      or 1 L   or 26 L

   d) 1 L or 17 L   e) 4 L or 25 L   f) 1 L or 6 L

3. Order these containers from least to greatest capacity.

4. Suppose you make 4 L of lemonade.
About how many glasses can you fill?
Explain how you know.

 5. Each person at a barbecue was served 1 glass of juice.
Fifteen litres of juice were served.
About how many people were at the barbecue?
Explain how you know.

6. Raphie wants to give each of his 20 guests a glass of fruit punch.
How many litres of punch should he make?
How do you know?

7. The doctor told Jia she should drink 8 glasses of water a day.
About how many litres should Jia drink
in one week? Explain.

Reflect

Use words, pictures, or numbers
to explain what *capacity* means.

Exploring Capacity: The Millilitre

This is Chef Alonzo's favourite soup recipe.
She serves it piping hot with sour cream.
Each item in the recipe is measured in litres
or **millilitres**.
We use the symbol **mL** for millilitres.

Blueberry Soup
Water ... 1 L
Blueberries ... 500 mL
Sugar ... 50 mL
Cornstarch ... 15 mL
Cinnamon ... 2 mL
Lemon Juice ... 5 mL

Explore

You will need some containers and water.

➤ Look at the measuring cups marked
in millilitres.
Choose a container.
Use the measuring cups to
estimate the capacity of
the container in millilitres.
Check your estimate.
Record your work.
Repeat this activity with
other containers.

➤ Look at a 1-L container.
Estimate how many
millilitres it holds.
Check your estimate.

Show *and* Share

Compare your estimates with those of others in your group.
Tell what things are measured in millilitres.

....

The millilitre (mL) is a small unit of capacity.

This eyedropper has a capacity of 1 mL.
It holds about 10 drops.

This measuring cup has a capacity of 500 mL.
It holds 500 mL of water.

It takes 2 of these measuring cups
to fill the one-litre container.
500 mL + 500 mL = 1000 mL
One litre is equal to one thousand millilitres.

1 L = 1000 mL

Practice ....

Use measuring cups when they help.
1. Choose the better estimate.

    a) 5 mL or 100 mL   **b)** 15 mL or 250 mL   **c)** 20 mL or 300 mL

    d) 75 mL or 15 mL   **e)** 250 mL or 900 mL   **f)** 10 mL or 500 mL

2. Which unit would you use to measure each capacity: millilitre or litre? Explain your choice.

a)
b)
c)

3. Which measure is closest to 1 L? How do you know?

400 mL   889 mL   799 mL   850 mL

4. Order the capacities of these containers from greatest to least.

5. It was hot working in the sun. Janny drank 400 mL of water in the morning and 500 mL in the afternoon.
How many millilitres of water did Janny drink altogether?
Show your work.

6. Laslo drank one-half of 1 L of water.
How many millilitres of water does Laslo have left?
How do you know?

7. Suppose you estimate that you made about 1 L of lemonade.
How can you check your estimate if you do not have a 1-L container?
Show your work.

Reflect

When do you have to measure something in millilitres?
Use words, pictures, or numbers to explain.

Numbers Every Day

Calculator Skills

Estimate the number of times your heart beats in one minute. Count your pulse for one minute to check. Find out how many times your heart beats in one hour. Tell how you did it.

Exploring Mass: The Kilogram

Some fruits and vegetables
are sold by the **kilogram**.
We use the symbol **kg**
for kilograms.

Explore

You will need items like those in the picture below.
Choose an object.
Estimate whether it is greater than, less than,
or about one kilogram. Check your estimate.
Record your work.

Repeat this activity with other objects.

Numbers Every Day

Number Strategies

Ella made these mistakes on a
test. Tell what she did wrong.
Correct her mistakes.

$$\begin{array}{r} 78 \\ + 34 \\ \hline 1012 \end{array} \qquad \begin{array}{r} 52 \\ - 38 \\ \hline 26 \end{array}$$

Show and Share

Talk about how you estimated.
Which objects were more than 1 kg?
Which were a lot more? How could you tell?

Connect

When you measure how heavy an object is, you measure its **mass**.
The kilogram (kg) is a unit of mass.

This bag of flour
has a mass
of about 1 kg.

This case of iced tea
has a mass
of about 9 kg.

Practice

1. Which objects have a mass of more than 1 kg?

   a)

   b)

   c)

   d)

   e)

   f)

2. Choose the better estimate.

   a) 1 kg
      or 15 kg

   b) 50 kg
      or 5 kg

   c) 6 kg
      or 25 kg

3. Match each item with its estimated mass: 40 kg, 75 kg, 1 kg, 7 kg

a)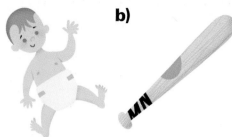
b)
c)
d)

4. Use the prices on page 264 to answer these questions.
  a) How much would you pay for 2 kg of apples?
  b) Will you pay more or less than $10 for 3 kg of potatoes?
    Explain your thinking.
  c) Suppose you bought 1 kg of tomatoes.
    How much change would you get from a $10 bill?

5. Could you lift a 50-kg box of apples?
  Why or why not?

6. Hans wants to buy 15 kg of peanuts
  to feed the blue jays in his backyard.
  Peanuts are sold in bags
  of these sizes.
  Find 3 different ways
  Hans could buy the peanuts.
  Show your work.

7. Yvette said she caught a 500-kg fish in the river
  behind her house. Do you think this is possible?
  Explain your thinking.

Reflect

Do bigger objects always have a greater mass than
smaller objects? Explain your thinking.
Give examples to support your answer.

Exploring Mass: The Gram

Hold a centimetre cube in your hand.
How would you describe its mass?
A centimetre cube has a mass of about one **gram**.
You write: 1 **g**

Explore

You will need items like those in the picture.

➤ Choose an object.
Estimate the mass of
the object in grams.
Check your estimate.
Record your work.
Repeat this activity with
other objects.
Order the objects from
least mass to greatest mass.

➤ Put a 1-kg mass, such as
a 1 kg bag of sugar, on the balance scales.
Estimate how many grams it takes to balance 1 kg.
Check your estimate. Write about what you found.

Show *and* Share

How did you decide which masses
to use to balance an object?

Object	Estimate of Mass	Mass
Nickel	9g	4g
Scissors	150g	225g

The gram is a small unit of mass.
The mass of an object you can hold in the palm of your hand
is usually measured in grams.

A jellybean has a mass of
about 1 g.

A banana has a
mass of about 200 g.

It takes 1000 g to balance 1 kg.

1000 g = 1 kg

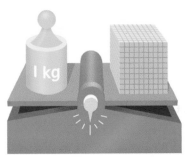

Practice

1. Choose the better estimate.

   a) 1 g or 50 g

   b) 2 g or 100 g

   c) 25 g or 400 g

2. Which unit would you use to measure each mass: gram or kilogram?
   Explain your choice.

   a)

   b)

   c)

   d)

   e)

   f)

3. Choose the better estimate.

a) 2 g or 2 kg

b) 100 g or 100 kg

c) 1 g or 1 kg

4. Which object has the greater mass? How do you know?

a)

 or

b)

 or

c)

5. Bert's cookie recipe calls for 500 g of nuts.
Will two 200-g bags be enough?
Show your work.

6. Janet needs 1 kg of birdseed for her feeder.
The store had only these bags:

Find 2 different ways Janet could buy
the birdseed. Show your work.

Reflect

Suppose you estimate the mass of an object.
How do you know if its mass
will be measured in grams or kilograms?
Use words, pictures, or numbers to explain.

Numbers Every Day

Number Strategies

Guido has 87¢ in his
piggy bank.
What coins might he have?
Give 4 other sets of coins
Guido might have.

Show What You Know

1   **1.** Juan's grandfather came to visit from Mexico on March 15th. He stayed for 4 months. On what date did Juan's grandfather leave?

     2. Cara's dog is 2 years old. How many months is that?

     3. Jason said, "My younger sister will be 1 year old in 3 weeks." How old is his sister now?

2   **4.** Write the time on each analog clock in 2 ways.

     a)    **b)**    **c)**    **d)**

3   **5.** For each clock in question 4:
     a) What time will it be in 20 minutes?
     b) What time was it 15 minutes earlier?

2   **6.** Draw a digital clock to show each time.
     a) seven nineteen   **b)** three forty-seven   **c)** quarter to nine

1 2   **7.** Which unit of time would you use to measure how long it takes to:
     a) learn to swim at summer camp?
     b) hold a baseball tournament?
     c) tie your shoes?
     d) grow 20 cm taller?

4   **8.** Tell what the temperature might be. How do you know?
     a) It's snowing outside.
     b) You need to wear a light jacket to play outside.
     c) Some children are swimming in the lake.

9. Use play money. Draw money to show each amount.
Use the fewest coins and bills possible.

a) $1.89   **b)** $0.47   **c)** $6.03   **d)** $0.99   **e)** 58¢

10. a) Suppose you bought the stickers and paid with 2 toonies.
Draw money to show your change.

b) Suppose you want to buy the balloons and the truck.
Is $3.00 enough to pay for them? Explain.

c) Choose 2 items above. Draw money to show how much they
cost and how much change you would get from $6.00.

11. Which unit would you use to measure
each capacity?

a)

b)

c)

d)

12. Which unit would you use to measure
each mass?

a)

b)

c)

d)

UNIT
6 Learning Goals

☑ use calendars and clocks
to measure time
☑ tell and write time
☑ use a thermometer to
measure temperature
☑ count money, make
change, and read and
write money amounts
☑ measure the capacity
of a container in millilitres
and litres
☑ measure the mass of an
object in grams and
kilograms

Bake Sale

Look at pages 228 and 229.

Part 1

Sadayeh and Denezeh baked bannock for the sale.
Here are the ingredients they used:

- Name 2 ingredients that are sold by mass
  and 2 that are sold by capacity.

- The bannock baked for 30 minutes at 165°C.
  The bannock was put in the oven at 9:50.
  What time was it taken out?

- Ms. Haviland bought 5 blueberry muffins.
  She paid for them with a $5 bill.
  She got this change:

  Did Ms. Haviland get the correct change?
  Explain.

- Amelia bought 3 popcorn balls.
  Draw coins to show 3 different ways
  she could have paid for them.

Part 2

Write a story problem about the bake sale.
Solve your problem.
Show your work.

Part 3

Plan a bake sale at your school.
- Make an invitation.
- Make a list of the items for sale
  and their prices.

Reflect on the Unit

Write about the different things you measured
in this unit.

Motion Geometry

At the Amusement Park

Learning Goals

- work with maps and grids
- explore slides, turns, and flips
- explore lines of symmetry

Key Words

grid

slide, translation

vertical

horizontal

turn, rotation

turn centre

quarter turn

half turn

three-quarter turn

clockwise

counterclockwise

flip, reflection

reflection line

image

line of symmetry

Look at the map of the amusement park.

- What rides do you see?
- How do people move on each ride?

1 Grids and Maps

David Howell plays chess. At 8 years old, he was the youngest person to beat a grand master.

One chess piece is the knight.
The knight can move these ways.

1 right, 2 up or 2 down
1 left, 2 up or 2 down
2 right, 1 up or 1 down
2 left, 1 up or 1 down

The chessboard is a **grid**.

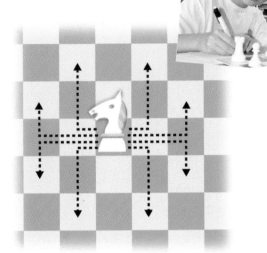

Explore

There is a grid in the playground.
Children stand on the grid.
They move right → or left ← and
up ↑ or down ↓.

Choose two people on the grid. How does
one person move to get to the other?
Write how many squares in each direction.

Repeat for several pairs of people.

Show *and* Share

Share your moves with a classmate.
How can you find the shortest way to move
from one person to another?

A map is drawn on a grid.

↑ Up
↓ Down

Right →
← Left

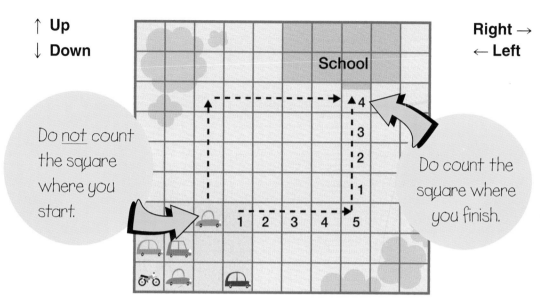

Do **not** count the square where you start.

Do count the square where you finish.

To go from the car to the school, you move:
5 squares right and 4 squares up
or 4 squares up and 5 squares right

Here is another map.
On this map, every building is at an intersection.

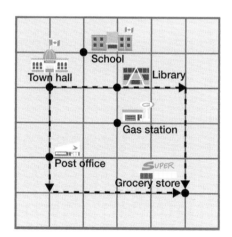

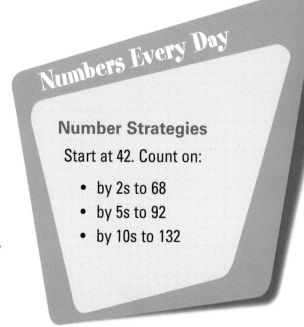

Numbers Every Day

Number Strategies
Start at 42. Count on:

- by 2s to 68
- by 5s to 92
- by 10s to 132

To go from the town hall to the grocery store, you move:
4 squares right and 3 squares down
or 3 squares down and 4 squares right

Practice

1. How do you move to go from:
   a) the bus station to school?
   b) the department store to the bus station?
   c) the toy store to the post office?
   d) the gas station to the bank?

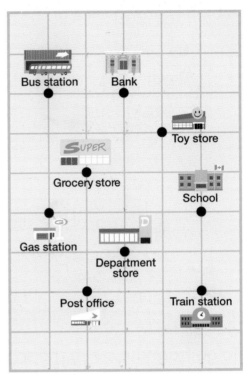

2. Suppose you start at the gas station. You go 2 squares right, 3 squares up, 1 square left, and 2 squares down. Where do you end up? How do you know?

3. You are at the train station. To get there, you went 2 squares down and 4 squares right. Where did you start? How do you know?

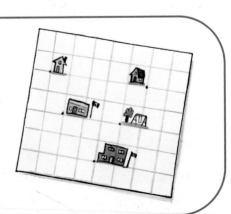

Social Studies

The grids and maps in this lesson are like the maps you made of the place you live.
How do you move on your maps to get from one place to another?
How did you show different places on your maps?

4. You can move right, left, up, or down on the grid below.

You are on:　　　How do you get to:

a) 4×4　　　　5×7?
b) 3×5　　　　2×2?
c) 6×2　　　　3×3?
d) 7×7　　　　4×5?

1	2	3	4	5	6	7	8	9	10
11	12	13	14	15	16	17	18	19	20
21	22	23	24	25	26	27	28	29	30
31	32	33	34	35	36	37	38	39	40
41	42	43	44	45	46	47	48	49	50

Play the game with a classmate.
You choose two number facts.
Your friend tells you how to move from one number to the other.

5. Here is a pattern of squares on a grid. What is the rule to move from one red square to the next?

6. On a 1-cm grid, draw a different pattern of squares. Write the rule for your pattern.

End

Start

Reflect

Mark two points, A and B, on grid paper.
Explain how to get from A to B, and from B to A.

Looking at Slides

As people ride the moving walkway, they stay still while their position changes. How does this picture show a slide?

Explore

Find pairs of blocks that show a slide.
Which pairs of blocks do *not* show a slide?
Record what you found out.

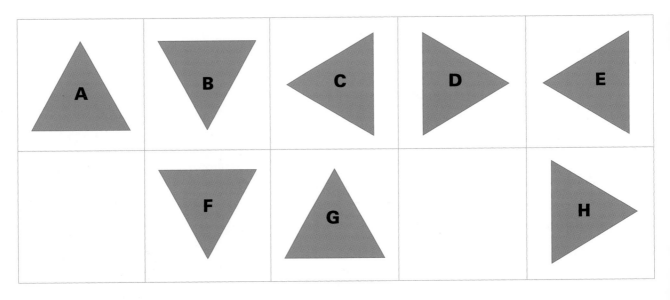

Show *and* Share

Show your partner how you know that 2 blocks show a slide.
Have you found all possible slides? How do you know?
Describe each slide.
How do you know that 2 blocks do *not* show a slide?

A **slide** moves an object along a line.
The object does not turn.
That means, the way it faces does not change.

This picture shows a slide.

This picture does *not* show a slide.

The way the child faces does not change.

The child does not move along a line.

Slides can be in different directions.

A **vertical** slide moves a figure up or down.

A **horizontal** slide moves a figure left or right.

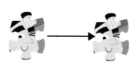

A **diagonal** slide moves a figure on a slant.

A slide is sometimes called a **translation**.

Numbers Every Day

Number Strategies

You say 5. I say 11.
You say 10. I say 21.
You say 15. I say 31.
You say 30. I say 61.

Guess my rule.

You say 35.
What will I say?
I say 101. What did you say?

1. Which pictures show a slide? How do you know?
   Which pictures do *not* show a slide? How do you know?

a)

b)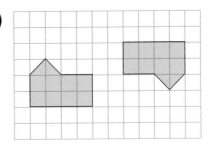

c)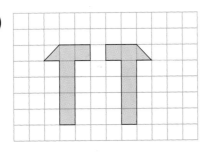

d)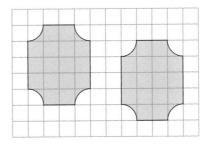

e)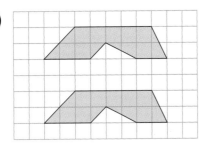

f)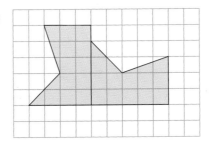

2. Describe the movement in each picture.

a)

b)

c)

3. Look around your classroom.
  a) Describe 3 things that slide.
  b) Describe 3 things that move but do *not* slide.

4. In this board game, Jill may slide her
counter up, down, right, or left.
Jill's counter is on the red square.
It took 2 slides to get there.

On the first slide,
Jill moved the counter 3 squares.

On the second slide,
Jill moved it 2 squares.

On which square could Jill have started?
Could Jill have started somewhere else?
How do you know?

1	2	3	4	5	6
7	8	9	10	11	12
13	14	15	16	17	18
19	20	21	22	23	24
25	26	27	28	29	30
31	32	33	34	35	36

At Home

Reflect

Imagine that a classmate missed
this lesson. Use words and
pictures to explain to her
what a slide is.

Name 3 things that slide.
Name 3 things that move
but do *not* slide.

3

Strategies Toolkit

Explore

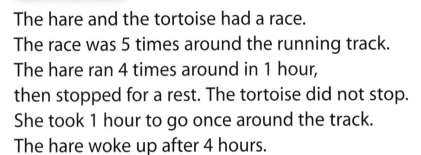

The hare and the tortoise had a race.
The race was 5 times around the running track.
The hare ran 4 times around in 1 hour,
then stopped for a rest. The tortoise did not stop.
She took 1 hour to go once around the track.
The hare woke up after 4 hours.
Who won the race?

Show *and* Share

Explain how you solved the problem.

Connect

A snail is at the bottom of a well. It climbs 2 m
every day, but it slides back 1 m at night.
The well is 6 m deep. How many days does it
take the snail to get out of the well?

Understand

What do you know?
• Each day, the snail climbs
  2 m up the well.
• Each night, the snail slides back 1 m.
• The snail has to climb 6 m to get out.

Plan

Think of a strategy to help you solve
the problem.
• You can **draw a picture.**
• Show where the snail is each day.

Strategies

• **Make a table.**
• **Use a model.**
• **Draw a picture.**
• **Solve a simpler problem.**
• **Work backward.**
• **Guess and check.**
• **Make an organized list.**
• **Use a pattern.**

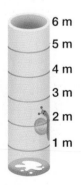

6 m
5 m
4 m
3 m
2 m
1 m

Use grid paper to record how far the snail moves.
Use a different colour for each day.
Count the days when the snail reaches the top of the well.
When does the snail get out of the well?

Write a similar problem.
Have a classmate solve your problem.

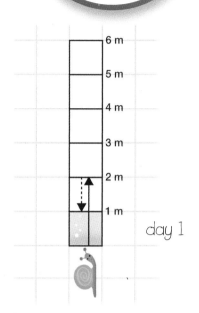

day 1

Practice

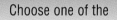

Choose one of the

Strategies

1. Shannon is shorter than Bruce.
   Olivia is shorter than Alex but taller than Bruce.
   Who is the tallest? Shortest?

2. Hannah and Liam are using a compass.
   They move 30 m north, then 30 m west, and then 30 m south.
   What direction do they go to get back to where they started?
   How far must they go?

Reflect

How does drawing a picture help you to solve a problem?

What Is a Turn?

From 2 o'clock to 3 o'clock, the minute hand moves **1 turn.**

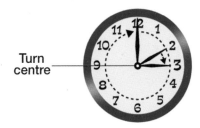

Turn
centre

The centre of the clock is the **turn centre**.

Explore

You will make a pinwheel to show
different turns.

You need 2 pieces of grid paper and glue.
➤ On one piece of grid paper, draw
   4 congruent figures.
   These are the arms of your pinwheel.
   Make them long and thin.
➤ Colour the arms, then cut them out.
➤ Paste the arms on the second piece of
   grid paper to show how a pinwheel's
   arms turn around a centre.

Show *and* Share

Show your pinwheel to a classmate.
Describe the turn from one arm to the next.
Write the words you use.

After 1 turn, a figure is back to where it started.

When the minute hand moves from 12 to 3, it moves a **quarter turn**.

This is a **clockwise** turn.

When the minute hand moves from 12 to 6, it moves a **half turn**.

When the minute hand moves from 12 to 9, it moves a **three-quarter turn**.

When the turn is the opposite way, it is a **counterclockwise turn.**

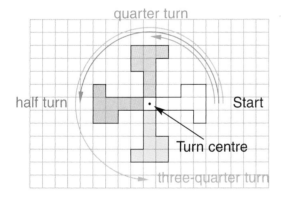

A turn is sometimes called a **rotation**.

Numbers Every Day

Calculator Skills

Multiply.
$1 \times 89, 2 \times 89, 3 \times 89, 4 \times 89$
What pattern do you see in the products?

Use the pattern to find:
$5 \times 89, 6 \times 89, 7 \times 89, 8 \times 89$
When does the pattern stop?

Practice

1. Which picture shows a turn? How do you know?
   Does any picture show a slide? How do you know?

   a)
   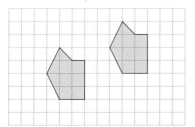

   b)
   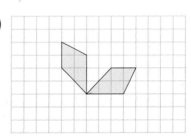

2. Which pictures show a turn? How do you know?
Which pictures do *not* show a turn? Explain.

a)

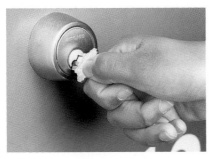

Unlocking a door

b)

Spinning a top

c)

Playing checkers

d)

Tossing a coin

3. Explain how this picture shows a turn.
Try to do this in 2 ways.

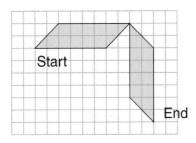

4. **a)** It is 3:00 a.m.
The hour hand makes a quarter turn.
What time is it then? How do you know?
 b) It is 6:30 p.m.
The hour hand makes a half turn.
What time is it then? How do you know?
 c) It is 9:45 a.m.
The hour hand makes a three-quarter turn.
What time is it then? How do you know?

5. Work with a partner.
   Draw 2 congruent figures on grid paper.
   Cut out one of them.
   Place this figure on top of the other.
   Move the top figure to show a quarter, half,
   or three-quarter turn.
   Ask your partner to:
   • Point to the turn centre.
   • Say what fraction of a turn the figures show.
   • Say the direction of the turn.

6. Janetha started to brush her dog at 9 o'clock.
   When she finished, the minute hand
   had made a quarter turn.
   How long was Janetha brushing her dog?

7. Rick turns the minute hand of this clock a
   three-quarter turn counterclockwise.
   He then turns the minute hand a quarter turn
   clockwise.
   What time does the clock show?
   How do you know?

8. What fraction of a turn
   does this picture show?
   Estimate the position
   of the turn centre.

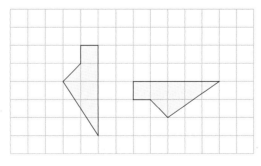

Reflect

Think of 3 things you have turned since you woke up
this morning.
Use words, pictures, or numbers to describe each turn.

LESSON

Exploring Reflections

This is Kan Shu.

This is his image.

Explore

You will need Pattern Blocks, grid paper, and a Mira.

➤ Draw a line on grid paper. Use this as a mirror line.

➤ Place a Pattern Block on one side of the mirror line.

➤ Have your partner place a congruent Pattern Block on the other side of the mirror line so that it is the **image** of your block. Use a Mira to check the image.

➤ Take turns to place other congruent blocks to make matching designs on both sides of the mirror line.

Show *and* Share

Copy your designs onto grid paper.
How are the designs the same?
How are they different?

Each figure and its image show a **reflection**.

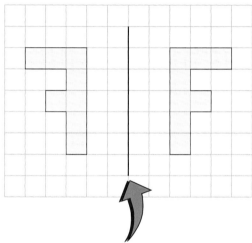
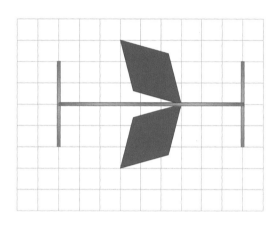

This is the **reflection line** or mirror line.

A figure and its image face opposite ways.

A reflection is sometimes called a **flip**.

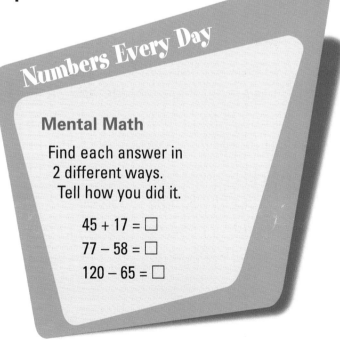

1. Which pictures show a reflection?
   How do you know?
   Where is the mirror line?

   a)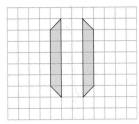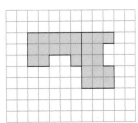

   b)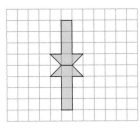

   c)

   d)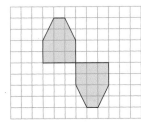

   e) D D

   f) D D

2. In question 1, does any picture show a slide? A turn?
   How do you know?

Math Link

Your World

What does this sign say? Why is it written this way?

3. Which pictures show a reflection? How do you know?

a)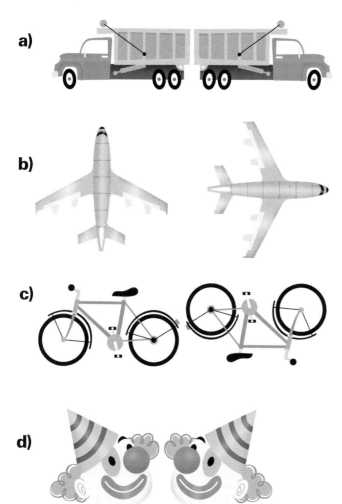

b)

c)

d)

 4. Look at this picture.
It is the image of a figure in a mirror.
Draw the figure.

Reflect

Place 2 congruent Pattern Blocks on grid paper.
How can you tell if they show a slide, a turn, or a
reflection? Use words and pictures to explain.

Lines of Symmetry

Each picture has a **line of symmetry**.

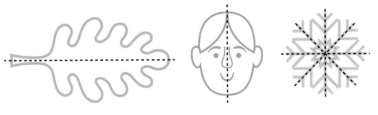

How can you show that each line is a line of symmetry?

Explore

You need a copy of these figures.
Find all the lines of symmetry for each figure.
Share the work.

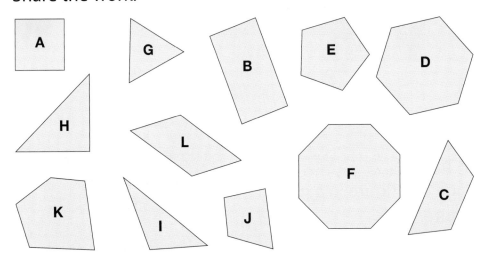

Show *and* Share

Show your group the lines of symmetry you found. Sort the figures.
Which figures have 1 line of symmetry?
More than 1? None?

A line of symmetry divides a figure into 2 congruent parts.

You can fold along the line and the 2 parts match.

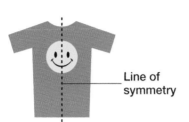

Line of symmetry

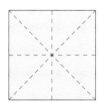

You can use a Mira to check a line of symmetry.

Some figures have more than 1 line of symmetry.

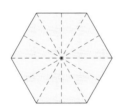

A square has 4 lines of symmetry.

A regular hexagon has 6 lines of symmetry.

Practice

1. Look at the capital letters of the alphabet:

A B C D E F G H I J K L M N
O P Q R S T U V W X Y Z

a) Which letters have 1 line of symmetry? 2 lines of symmetry? More than 2?

b) Which letters have no lines of symmetry? How do you know?

2. Write your name in capital letters.
How many letters have 1 line of symmetry?
Are these letters more than one-half of your name?
Less than one-half?

3. Which flags below have each symmetry?
How do you know?
- a vertical line of symmetry
- a horizontal line of symmetry
- more than 1 line of symmetry
- no lines of symmetry

a) Canada

b) The United States of America

c) Japan

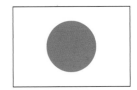

d) France

e) China

f) New Zealand

4. On dot paper, draw a picture that has 2 lines of symmetry.
Tell how you know it has 2 lines of symmetry.

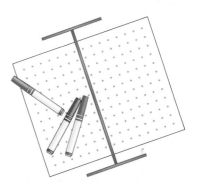

Reflect

Find a picture in a magazine that has 1 line of symmetry.
Cut it out. Paste it in your notebook.
How do you know the picture has 1 line of symmetry?

LESSON

1

1. In the grid below, how do you move to go from

    a) A to B?   **b)** B to D?   **c)** B to G?

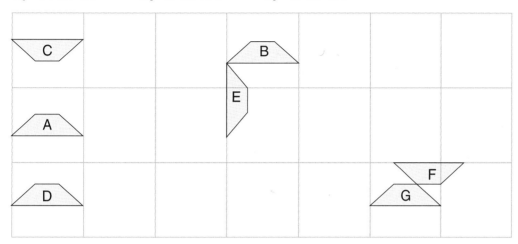

2
4
5

2. In the grid above, which pairs of blocks show

    a) a slide?   **b)** a turn?   **c)** a reflection?
How do you know?

6

3. Use a copy of these figures.
Find the lines of symmetry in each figure.

    a) Name each figure above.

    b) How many lines of symmetry
are there in each figure?

    c) How many sides are there in
each figure?

    d) What patterns do you see in
your answers?

UNIT

7 Learning Goals

☑ work with maps and grids

☑ explore slides, turns,
and flips

☑ explore lines of symmetry

At the Amusement Park

Design a ride for an amusement park.
The ride must move people
in at least 2 *different* ways.

Turns counterclockwise.

Moves up and down.

Think about how you will present your ride to the class.

Will you
– make a drawing?
– make a model?
– write about it?
– talk about it?

How does your ride move people in at least 2 different ways?

Reflect on the Unit

What did you learn about how figures can move?
Use words and pictures to explain.

Are You a Square or a Rectangle?

Part 1

You will need a measuring tape.

➤ Measure your partner's height with her shoes off.

➤ Measure her arm span.

➤ Record these measurements in a table.

Height	Arm Span

➤ Have your partner take the same measurements from you. Is your height greater than, less than, or equal to your arm span?

• If your height is greater than your arm span, you are a tall rectangle.

• If your height is less than your arm span, you are a short rectangle.

• If your height and arm span are within 2 cm, you are a square.

Which best describes you: tall rectangle, short rectangle, or square?

Tall rectangle	Short rectangle	Square

Part 2

You will need grid paper.

➤ Conduct a survey of your classmates.
Have each student record his shape on
a tally chart.
Look at your survey results.

  • Which shape is most common?
    Least common?
  • Are more boys than girls square?
  • Are more girls than boys square?

➤ Graph the data.
Compare your graph with those of other classmates.
How are the graphs similar? Different?

➤ Write your own question about the graph.
Answer your question.
Tell what you found out about the different shapes of
your classmates.
Use pictures, words, or numbers to explain.

Take It Further

Find the shapes of friends and family members.
How do their shapes compare with your classmates' shapes?
Write what you find out.

Exploring

Pizza
Lunch

Learning Goals

- find fractions of a whole, of a length, and of a set
- solve fraction problems
- explore mixed numbers

Fractions

The class is planning a pizza lunch.

Look at the food.

- What are some questions to ask before planning the lunch?

- About how many people could share:
  the pizza?
  the cheese bread?
  the juice?

Key Words

- equal parts
- fractions
- halves
- sixths
- quarters/fourths
- fifths
- eighths
- thirds
- tenths
- mixed number

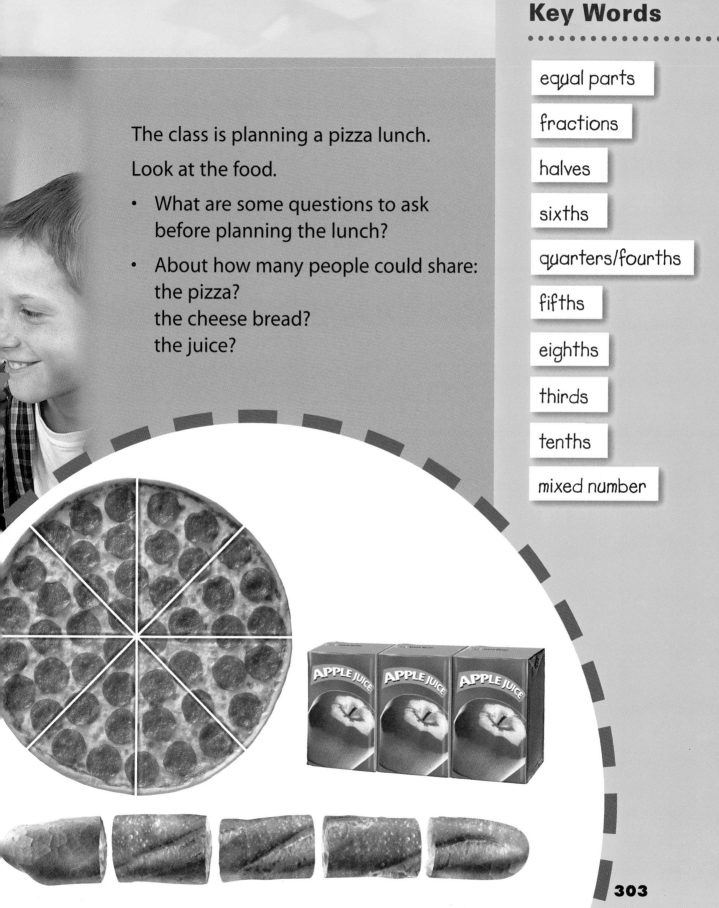

303

Exploring Equal Parts

Think of a time you shared something with a friend.
Did each of you get a fair share?

Fair shares mean **equal parts** for everybody.

Explore •

You will need Pattern Blocks.

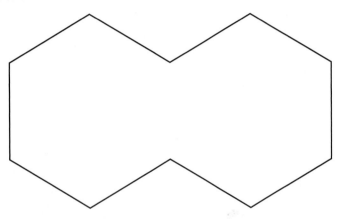

➤ How many ways can you cover
this figure to show equal parts?
Tell about the equal parts each time.
Record your work.

➤ Repeat the activity
with a figure you make
from Pattern Blocks.

Colour of blocks	Number of blocks	Our name for the equal parts
Blue	6	

Show *and* Share

Talk with your partner about the
names you used for the equal parts.
Where have you used some of the names before?

➤ This figure is **1 whole**.

Here are some ways to divide the figure into equal parts.
You can name equal parts with **fractions**.

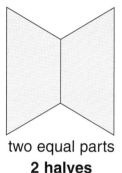

two equal parts
2 halves

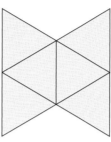

six equal parts
6 sixths

Some of the fraction names you have used as ordinals: thirds, fourths, fifths, . . .

➤ You can show the same fractions in many ways.
Here are some ways to show **fourths** or
quarters of 1 whole.

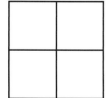 

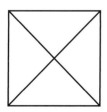

Numbers Every Day

Number Strategies

These facts show a strategy for
multiplying by 5.

$2 \times 10 = 20$ and $4 \times 5 = 20$

Use the same strategy
to multiply.

6×5

8×5

2×5

Practice

1. Use Pattern Blocks to show equal parts of a hexagon 3 different ways.
   a) Draw and name each fraction.
   b) Which fraction is greatest? Least?

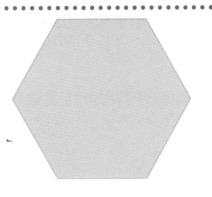

2. Name the equal parts.
   Tell how you know they are equal parts.

   a) 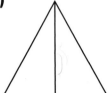 b) 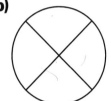 c) 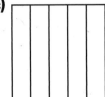 d)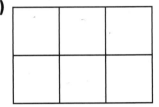

3. Which pictures show equal parts? Tell how you know.

   a) 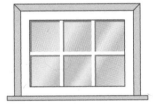 b)

   c) 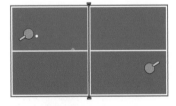 d)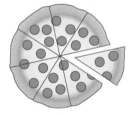

Math Link

Social Studies

Pioneers had to make use of everything they had. Even small scraps of fabric were used to make quilts. Look for fractions in this quilt pattern.

4. Which figures show fourths? How do you know?
What other fractions are there?

a)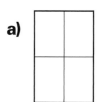

b)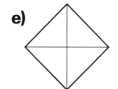

c)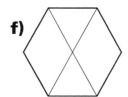

d)

e)

f)

5. a) Draw a figure on grid paper.
Divide your figure to show halves.
b) Draw a figure to show fifths.
c) Draw a figure to show fourths.
How do you know you have equal parts
in each figure?

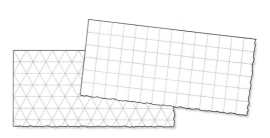

6. Imagine sharing a treat.
Do you get a bigger piece when you share
with many friends or with only a few?
Show why your answer makes sense.

Reflect

Think of a time you needed equal
parts. How did you make sure the
parts were equal?

At Home

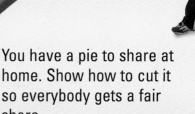

You have a pie to share at
home. Show how to cut it
so everybody gets a fair
share.

2

Exploring Fractions of a Length

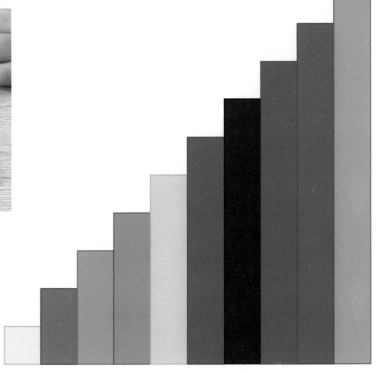

Sami is using different colours of rods to compare lengths.

You can do the same thing using rods or strips of colour paper.

Explore

You will need rods or paper strips.
➤ Start with the orange rod.
   Use the other rods to find different fractions of the orange rod.
   How many ways can you do this?
   Draw pictures and label them to record your work.

➤ Repeat the activity. Start with the blue rod.

Keep these rods or paper strips for Lesson 5.

Show and Share

Show your pictures to another pair of students.
How did you find equal parts?
How can you be sure you found all the possible fractions?

➤ Here is how Carey showed fractions of the dark green rod.

 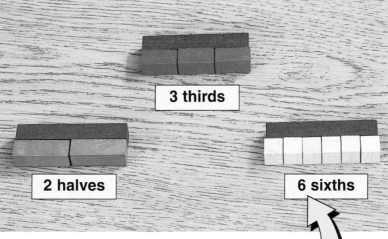

3 thirds

2 halves

6 sixths

Carey knows the white rods are sixths because all of them are equal in length and there are 6 of them.

➤ You can fold a strip of paper to show fractions.

• Fold from end to end to show halves.

2 halves make 1 whole.

• Fold in half again to show fourths or quarters.

4 fourths make 1 whole.

• Fold in half again to show eighths.

8 eighths make 1 whole.

Once you divide the length into equal parts, you can count the parts.

| 3 eighths | 5 eighths |

Use rods or paper strips when they help.

1. Which rod is 1 half of:
   a) the brown rod?　　　　　　　　b) the purple rod?

2. Which rod is 1 third of:
   a) the light green rod?　　b) the dark green rod?

3. Fold a strip of paper into thirds.
   Tell a partner how you did it.
   Colour 1 third of the strip.

4. What fraction of each strip is shaded?
   What fraction is not shaded?

   a)
   b)
   c)
   d)
   e)
   f)

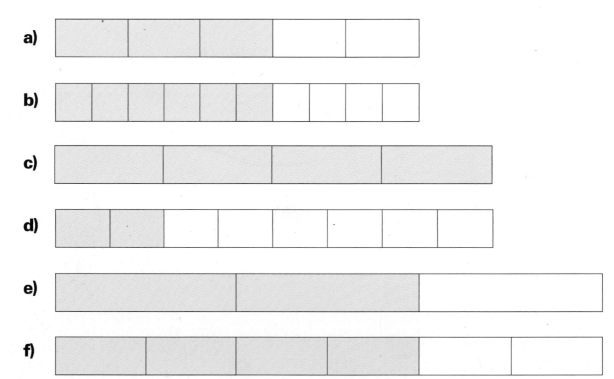

5. Both Jay and Amira had a strip of dried fruit.
Each child folded the strip into equal parts.
Jay had twice as many equal parts as Amira.
Use paper strips to model some possible fractions they used.

6. When is 1 third larger than 1 half?
Make some examples using paper strips or rods.
Use pictures and words to show your ideas.

7. Estimate. What fraction of the race has each
person run? Explain.

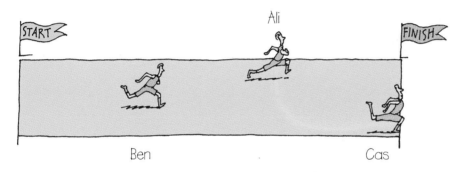

8. At the fair, Kelly played this game.
About how far up the pole did she move the marker?

Numbers Every Day

Mental Math

There are 2 fields.
Each field is divided into
6 equal parts.

How many parts are
there in all?

How many farmers can
have 3 parts each?

Reflect

How is finding a fraction of a length
different from finding a fraction of 1 whole?
How is it the same?

3

Exploring Fractions of a Set

Ten children are ready for art class.

What fraction of the group is girls?

What fraction of the group is wearing a striped shirt?

What other fractions can you use to describe the children?

Explore

You will need 2 colours of counters and a bag.

Put 10 counters of each colour in a bag.

➤ Take out a handful of counters.
➤ Record fractions to describe the set of counters.
➤ Return the counters.
➤ Record your work.

Repeat the activity 5 times.

Show **and** Share

Talk with your partner.

Tell how you knew what fractions to record for each set.

Number of counters pulled out	Fraction of counters that are red	Fraction of counters that are green

To find a fraction of a set, start by counting.

➤ There are 6 stickers.
5 of the 6 stickers are yellow.
5 sixths of the stickers are yellow.

➤ There are 12 spaces in the paint tray.
8 of the 12 spaces have paint.
8 twelfths of the spaces have paint.
4 twelfths of the spaces are empty.

Practice

Use counters when they help.

1. What fraction of each set is red?

   a)

   b)

   c)

   d)

Numbers Every Day

Mental Math

Which number of crackers can you share equally among 4 friends?

12   10   15   24   36

How do you know?

2. Draw your own set of counters.
Name the fractions in the set.

3. What fraction of eggs are left in each carton?
   What fraction of eggs have been used?

   a)    **b)** 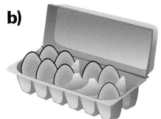   **c)**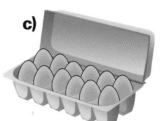

4. Joe has 5 rabbits.
   One-fifth are white.
   The rest are black.
   a) How many rabbits are white?
   b) How many rabbits are black?

5. Jordie has 3 pairs of black shoes and 2 pairs of red shoes.
   What fraction of Jordie's shoes are red?

6. Print your first name.
   a) What fraction of the letters in your first name are vowels?
   b) What fraction of the letters are consonants?
   c) What fraction of the letters have line symmetry?

7. Louella had 2 black caps and 2 red caps.
   a) What fraction of her caps were red?
   b) Louella buys another cap.
   What fraction of her caps might be red now?
   Show your work.

Reflect

How is a fraction of a set different from a fraction of 1 whole?

Finding a Fraction of a Set

Explore ·

You will need counters.
How many ways can you arrange
8 counters to make equal groups?

Draw a picture for each way you find.
Write fractions to describe your pictures.

Repeat this activity with 15 counters.

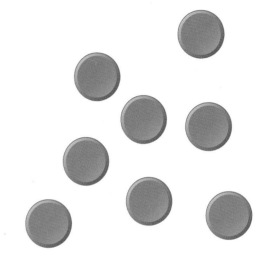

Show *and* Share

Show your pictures to a classmate.
Talk about the strategy you used to make equal groups.
Why can you say that you "divided" the 8 counters
into equal groups?

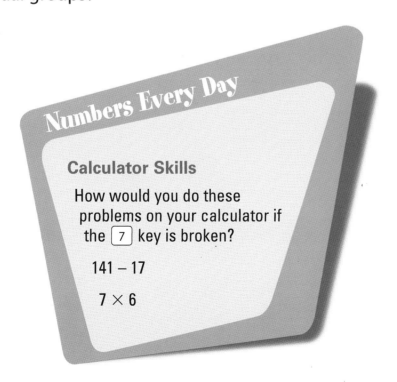

Numbers Every Day

Calculator Skills

How would you do these
problems on your calculator if
the ⟨7⟩ key is broken?

141 – 17

7 × 6

➤ Here are some ways to make equal groups with 12 counters.
Think about sharing the 12 counters.

2 equal groups of 6
Each group is 1 half of 12.

3 equal groups of 4
Each group is 1 third of 12.

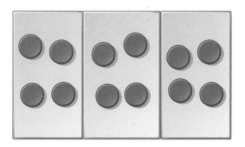

1 half of 12 = 6

1 third of 12 = 4

➤ Jody had 12 dimes.
She gave 1 fourth of them to her brother and kept the rest.
How many dimes did she keep?

Here are 12 dimes in 4 equal groups.
Each group has 3 dimes.
1 fourth of 12 dimes is 3 dimes.
Jody gave 3 dimes to her brother.
She kept 9 dimes.
9 dimes is 3 fourths of 12.

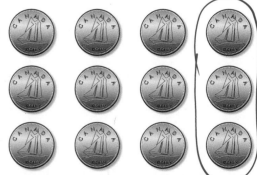

Practice

1. Find equal groups.
   a) 1 half of 8

   b) 1 third of 9

   c) 1 quarter of 12

   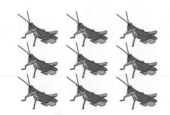

2. Draw a picture to show each fraction.
  a) 1 fifth of 10 beads
  b) 1 fourth of 16 triangles
  c) 1 sixth of 12 stars
  d) 3 tenths of 20 coins

3. Can you divide 12 dimes into 12 equal groups?
Draw a picture to show your answer.

4. Can you divide 12 dimes into 5 equal groups?
Explain your answer.

5. Naj's recipe needs half a dozen eggs.
Draw a picture to show how many eggs Naj needs.

6. Rosa had 15 goldfish.
She gave 1 fifth of them to her friend.
  a) Draw a picture to show how many goldfish Rosa gave away.
  b) How many goldfish did Rosa have left?

7. Draw a picture to show 3 thirds of 18 apples.

8. When is 1 half of a set less than 1 third of a set?
When is it more? Draw a picture to show your ideas.

9. Ranji has to clean the 20 windows in his house.
Each day he cleans 1 fifth of the windows.
How many windows are clean after 3 days?
Draw a picture to show your thinking.

Reflect

Use words, pictures, or numbers.
Explain how all these pictures show 1 third.

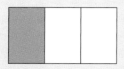

Naming and Writing Fractions

You can use fractions to tell about:
- equal parts of a whole
- equal parts of a length
- equal parts of a set

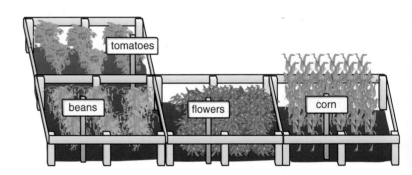

This community garden
is divided into 4 equal parts.
3 fourths of the garden are
for growing food.

The fraction name suggests a **symbol** for writing the fraction.

$$\frac{3}{4}$$

← 3
← of
← 4 equal parts are for growing food.

Explore

You will need grid paper, 10 blank cards, and scissors.
Make a fraction puzzle for your partner.

➤ Draw 5 different figures on grid paper.
  Make each figure with a different number of squares.
  Cut the grid paper to separate the figures.

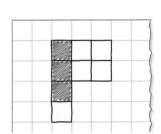

➤ Colour a fraction of the squares on each figure.
➤ On one card, record the fraction
  using words.
➤ On another card, record the fraction
  using a symbol.

LESSON FOCUS | Represent fractions using the fraction symbol.

Show *and* Share

Mix up your figures and cards. Trade with your partner.
Sort your partner's figures and cards into 5 matching sets.
Check each other's work.

Connect

This figure has 7 squares,
so it shows sevenths.

Three of the 7 squares are coloured,
so the fraction is $\frac{3}{7}$.

The **top number** of a fraction tells
how many equal parts are counted.

The **bottom number** of a fraction tells
how many equal parts are in 1 whole.

Math Link

Data Management

You use fractions when you read a circle graph.
This graph shows that about 1 fourth of the
class walks to school.

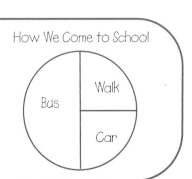

How We Come to School

Practice

1. Write a fraction for each shaded part.

a)

b)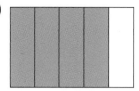

c)

d)

e)

f)

For questions 2 and 3, use the colour rods or paper strips from Lesson 2.

2. a) Find the rod that shows $\frac{1}{3}$ of the dark green rod.

   b) Find the rod that shows $\frac{2}{3}$ of the dark green rod.

3. a) The light green rod is $\frac{1}{3}$ of which rod?

   b) The yellow rod is $\frac{1}{2}$ of which rod?

4. Use fractions to describe each flag.

a)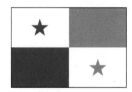

Panama

b)

Nigeria

c)

Ecuador

d)

Papua New Guinea

5. Draw a flag for each description.

a) $\frac{2}{3}$ yellow and $\frac{1}{3}$ blue

b) $\frac{1}{4}$ green, $\frac{1}{4}$ orange, and $\frac{2}{4}$ white

c) $\frac{2}{5}$ white, $\frac{1}{5}$ green, and $\frac{2}{5}$ black

6. Some children take dance classes.
Some take karate classes.

a) What fraction of the children take dance class?

b) What fraction of the children take karate?

c) What fraction of the children take dance and karate?

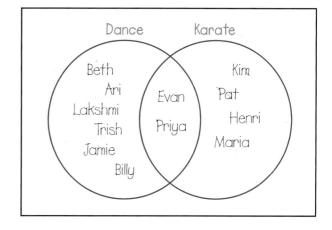

7. Ms. Chung's yard looks like this now.
She has finished $\frac{1}{4}$ of her patio.
Use grid paper.
Draw a picture to show what the whole patio might look like.
How many different ways can you do this?

8. Use counters or draw a picture to show $\frac{2}{3}$ of 18 markers.

Reflect

How would you explain the fraction $\frac{2}{5}$ to a Grade 2 student?

Strategies Toolkit

Explore

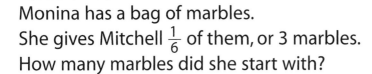

Monina has a bag of marbles.
She gives Mitchell $\frac{1}{6}$ of them, or 3 marbles.
How many marbles did she start with?

Work together to solve this problem.
Use any materials you think will help.

Show *and* Share

What strategy did you use to solve the problem?

Connect

Cass and Kim are sorting figures.
Kim says that $\frac{1}{8}$ of all his triangles are green.
Kim has 3 green triangles.

How many triangles does Kim have?

Understand

What do you know?
- There are 3 green triangles.
- There are more triangles in the whole set.
- Only $\frac{1}{8}$ of them are green.

Plan

Think of a strategy to help you solve the problem.
- You can **work backward**.
- Use triangles or counters.

Strategies

- Make a table.
- Use a model.
- Draw a picture.
- Solve a simpler problem.
- Work backward.
- Guess and check.
- Make an organized list.
- Use a pattern.

Put 3 triangles together.
This group is $\frac{1}{8}$ of the set.

How many groups make $\frac{8}{8}$ of the set?

How many triangles are in $\frac{8}{8}$ of the set?

How many triangles does Kim have?

How could you solve this problem another way?

Practice

Choose one of the

Strategies

1. Maya had 14 markers.
   She gave $\frac{1}{7}$ of them to Robert.
   How many markers does Maya have left?

2. One pie is cut into fourths. Another pie of
   the same size is cut into sixths.
   Which pie has larger slices?

3. Chintan has a bag of marbles. One-third of
   them are blue. Six of the marbles are blue.
   How many marbles does Chintan have?

4. Luigi gave $\frac{1}{5}$ of his stickers to Anna.
   How many stickers could Luigi have started with?

Reflect

Write about a time when you had to find a fraction of a set.
Use words, pictures, or numbers to tell how you did it.

Mixed Numbers

This sandwich tray has 11 quarter-sandwiches.

This is $\frac{11}{4}$ sandwiches.

That makes 2 whole sandwiches and $\frac{3}{4}$ of another sandwich.

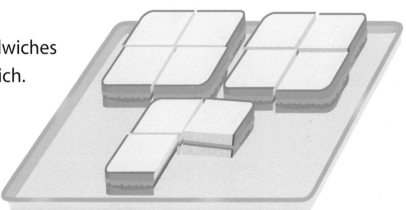

Explore

You will need Pattern Blocks.

➤ Use a blue Pattern Block as 1 whole.
Take a handful of green Pattern Blocks.
Write the green blocks as a fraction of
the blue block.
How many wholes are there?
What fraction is left over?

Record your work.

➤ Repeat this activity 5 times.

Show *and* Share

Share your results with another pair of classmates.
How did you know how many wholes there were?

Connect

You can use whole numbers and fractions to name amounts greater than 1.

When the red trapezoid is 1 whole, the green triangle is $\frac{1}{3}$.

8 green triangles are $\frac{8}{3}$, or 2 and $\frac{2}{3}$.

Here is how I write 2 and $\frac{2}{3}$.

$2\frac{2}{3}$ is a **mixed number**.

Practice

1. Use 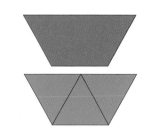 as 1 whole.
   Which mixed number describes each set of green Pattern Blocks?

   Write the number and say the words.

   a)

   b)

   c)

Numbers Every Day

Mental Math

What are the next 4 numbers in each skip-counting pattern? Tell how you know.

6, 8, 10, □, □, □, □

200, 225, 250, □, □, □, □

35, 30, 25, □, □, □, □

2. Describe each picture two different ways.

a)

b)

c)

d)

3. Draw a picture to show each mixed number.

a) $1\frac{2}{3}$ b) $3\frac{3}{4}$ c) $2\frac{1}{3}$ d) $4\frac{1}{2}$

4. At a family dinner, each pie was cut into 6 equal slices.
After dinner, there were $1\frac{5}{6}$ pies left.
How many slices were left?

5. How many different ways can you show $2\frac{1}{4}$?
Show your work.

Reflect

When do you use mixed numbers to show how much
or how many? Use pictures, numbers, or words to explain
your example.

LESSON

1

1. Which picture shows fourths? How do you know?

a)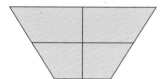

b)

c)

d)

2

2. Fold a paper strip to show sixths.
   a) Colour $\frac{1}{6}$ of the strip.
      Explain the strategy you used.
   b) What fraction is not coloured?

1
2
3
5

3. What fraction does each picture show?

a)

b)

c)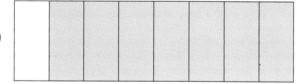

3
4
5

4. Use a set of 16 counters.
   a) What fraction of the set is 4 counters?
   b) What other fractions can you show
      with 16 counters?
      Draw a picture for each one.

7

5. Draw a picture to show $3\frac{3}{4}$ pies.
   How many quarters is this?

U N I T

 Learning Goals

☑ find fractions of a whole,
   of a length, and of a set

☑ solve fraction problems

☑ explore mixed numbers

It's time to prepare the order for the pizza lunch.
There are 10 children who stay for lunch.

Part 1

What fraction do you think each person will eat:
- of a whole pizza?
- of a loaf of cheese bread?
- of a package of juice boxes?

You can organize your work in a chart like this.
In the 3rd column, use numbers and pictures to show
how much food you think will be eaten.
Use counters when they help.

Lunch Order	Food	Fraction Eaten by 1 Child	Amount Eaten by 10 Children
	Pizza		

Part 2

When you order the food, you cannot buy fractions of pizzas!

For 10 people, how many should you order:
• of whole pizzas?
• of whole loaves of bread?
• of juice box packages?
Explain how you know your order is correct.

Part 3

Suppose everyone eats the same amount.
• Will there be food left over?
• What fraction of each item would be left over? Expain how you know.

Part 4

Suppose you could add one other type of food.
• What would it be?
• How much would you need for 10 people?
• How much would be left over?

Check List

Your work should show
☑ correct answers to the questions and how you found them
☑ a clear explanation of your food order and how you know it is correct
☑ your plan for adding another type of food
☑ correct math language used to record and explain your answers

Reflect on the Unit

Write one important thing you learned about fractions. Use words, pictures, or numbers to explain.

UNIT

1

1. How many different 3-digit numbers can you write
   with the digits 5, 9, and 7? Use each digit once.
   Order the digits from least to greatest. Explain how you did it.

2

2. Look at these numbers: 26, 85, 41, 73, 95, 24
   a) Estimate which two numbers have the sum
      that is closest to 100.
   b) Estimate which two numbers have the difference
      that is closest to 50.

3. Find two 3-digit numbers that have a difference of 234.
   Write a story problem for the numbers you chose.

3

4. On dot paper, draw:
   a) 2 different trapezoids   b) 2 different parallelograms
   c) 2 different rhombuses   d) 2 congruent squares
   Tell about the angles in each figure.

4

5. Which of these numbers
   are divisible by 5? By 10?
   How do you know?
   2, 5, 10, 15, 18, 20, 25,
   30, 35, 40, 45, 46
   Copy this Venn diagram.
   Sort the numbers.

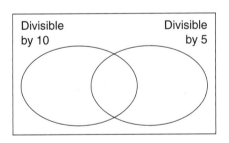

Divisible by 10   Divisible by 5

5

6. Use Attribute Blocks. Choose 3 attributes.
   Draw a Venn diagram.
   Place 2 Attribute Blocks in each space.
   Have a classmate find your attributes,
   then use them to sort other blocks.

7. **a)** What does this circle graph show?
   b) What fraction of the leaves are brown? Red?
   c) How does the number of red leaves
      compare with the number of yellow leaves?
      How do you know?

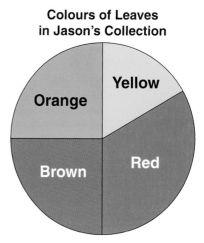

**Colours of Leaves
in Jason's Collection**

8. It took Hanif 20 minutes to do his homework.
   He started at 7:15 p.m.
   What time did Hanif finish? How do you know?

9. Georgia buys a skipping rope that costs $5.79.
   She pays for it with a $10 bill.
   Show 3 ways the clerk can make change for Georgia.

10. In the grid below, how do you move to go from:
   a) F to A?   **b)** C to E?   **c)** D to G?

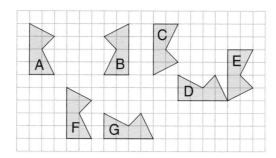

11. In the grid above, which pairs of figures show:
   a) a turn?   **b)** a slide?   **c)** a reflection?

12. Fold a paper strip to show fifths. Colour $\frac{3}{5}$ of the strip.
   What fraction of the strip is not coloured?

13. Use a set of 18 counters.
   What fraction of the set is 9 counters?
   What other fractions can you show with 18 counters?
   Draw a picture of each fraction.

Design a Playground

PLAYGROUND

Learning Goals

- measure lengths
- measure the distance around a figure
- measure the amount of space a figure covers

and Area

Key Words

- centimetre
- length
- width
- height
- metre
- kilometre
- perimeter
- units
- area
- square units

- Which section of the playground covers the most space?

- Which section has the longest distance around?

- Is it farther from the swings to the slides or from the swings to the roundabout? How do you know?

Measuring Length in Centimetres

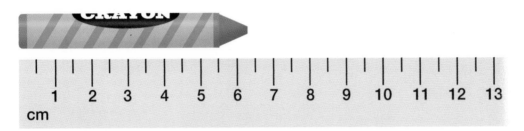

This crayon is between 6 cm and 7 cm long.

It is **longer** than 6 cm but **shorter** than 7 cm.

The length is closer to 6 cm than to 7 cm.

The crayon is about 6 cm long, or 6 cm to the nearest centimetre.

Explore

You will need a metre stick or a 30-cm ruler.

➤ Estimate the lengths of the following parts of your body. Record your estimates.

- your hand
- your thumb
- your arm
- your leg from knee to heel
- your foot
- your nose

➤ Talk about how you will use a ruler to measure.

➤ Measure the lengths of these body parts to the nearest centimetre. Record your measurements.

Here are two ways to record your work.

- Draw and label a picture.
- Make a list.

Share your results with another pair of students.

Suppose you lost your ruler.
How could you use your measurements to find the width of your textbook?

Connect

A **centimetre** (cm) is a unit of **length**.

1 cm

Centimetres can be used to measure how long, how tall, or how wide an object is. Here are some benchmarks to help you think about centimetres.

Your finger is about 1 cm wide.

100 cm

A classroom door is about 100 cm wide.

Think of something that is about 50 cm wide, long, or tall.

Use a metre stick or a ruler when it helps.
For exercises 1 and 2, find each object in your classroom.

1. Measure the length and width to the nearest centimetre.
Record each measurement.

    a) a paper clip   **b)** scissors   **c)** a tabletop

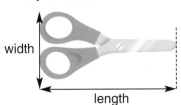
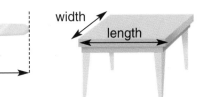

2. Estimate the length.
Then measure it to the nearest centimetre.
Record each estimate and measurement.
How close were each estimate and measurement?

    a) a classmate's shoe   **b)** a bulletin board **c)** a marker pen

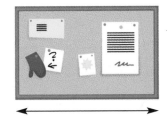

3. Choose an object.
Estimate its height.
Measure its height.
Record your results.

4. Name an object that is about
    a) 10 cm long
    b) 50 cm high

How do you know your answers are correct?

5. Measure a crayon, an eraser, and your shoe.
Which is the longest? The shortest?
Write the measurements in order from longest
to shortest.

6. Find two things so that one thing is
about 10 cm wider than the other.
Write or draw what you found.
Explain your work.

7. Daniel broke his ruler.

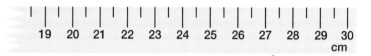

How can Daniel use his broken ruler
to measure the length and width of his desk?

8. A small paper clip is about 3 cm long.
A large paper clip is about 5 cm long.
How many of each paper clip would fit
along a 30-cm ruler?
How do you know?

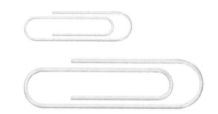

Reflect

Suppose you do not have a ruler.
How can you tell if a pencil is
longer or shorter than 10 cm?
Use words, pictures, or
numbers to explain.

At Home

You know that your finger
is about 1 cm wide. Use
your fingers to measure
some things at home.
Draw pictures to show
what you measured.

Measuring Length in Metres

Explore ·

You will need a metre stick.
Work together to measure.

Hold a Mini-Olympics.
Take turns to try each event 2 times.
Record your results.
Circle your best result for each event.

Event 1: Tube Roll

Roll a cardboard tube.
Measure how far it rolls.

Event 2: Counter Flick

Use your thumb and middle finger to flick a counter.
Measure how far it goes.

Event 3: Cotton Ball Puff

Blow a cotton ball as far as you can in one breath.
Measure how far it goes.

Show and Share

Share how you recorded each length.
How did you write a length when it was more than one metre?
Compare your best results with those of others in your group.
Who came in first? Second? Third?

One **metre** (m) is a length of 100 cm.

$$1 \text{ m} = 100 \text{ cm}$$

A baseball bat is about 1 m long.

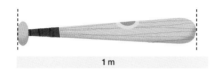

1 m

Lindsay is 3 years old. She is about 1 m tall.

1 m

1 m

A refrigerator is about 150 cm tall. You can write this as 1 m 50 cm.

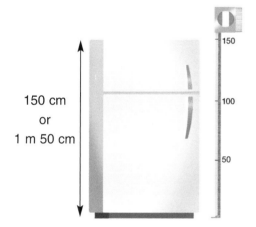

150 cm or 1 m 50 cm

150

100

50

A minivan is about 180 cm wide or 1 m 80 cm.

180 cm or 1 m 80 cm

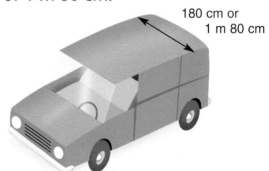

1. Name 2 objects that are about 1 m long.

2. Name 2 objects that are taller than 1 m but shorter than 2 m.

Numbers Every Day

Number Strategies

In each pair, which is greater? Explain your strategies.

$42 \div 6$ or $42 \div 7$

5×1 or 6×1

$5 + 5 + 5$ or 4×5

$3 + 3 + 3 + 3$ or $4 + 4 + 4$

$24 \div 6$ or $24 \div 4$

3. Match each item with its estimate: 1 m, 6 m, 300 m

a) the width of a classroom

b) the height of a skyscraper

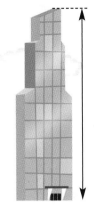

c) the length of a shovel

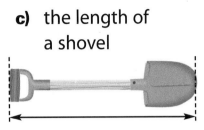

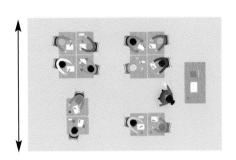

4. Use a measuring tape or metre stick.
Find each item in your classroom.
Record each measurement in metres and centimetres.

a) the length of the teacher's desk

b) the height of the classroom door

c) the width of a window

5. Would you measure each item in centimetres or metres? Explain.

a) the height of a cereal box
b) the length of a hallway
c) the height of a tall tree
d) the length of a goldfish

6. Copy and complete this table.
How could you use skip counting? What patterns do you see?

Metres	1	2	3	4	5	6	7	8	9	10
Centimetres	100									

Data Management

In Unit 5, you drew horizontal and vertical bar graphs.
Exercise 7 shows how you can use a bar graph to order lengths.

7. This bar graph shows the heights of 4 children.
Write each height in metres and centimetres.
Order the children from shortest to tallest.

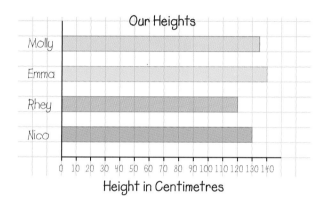

8. Suppose you do not have a metre stick.
How do you know if an object is about 1 m long?

9. A pencil is 18 cm long.
About how many pencils like this
would fit end-to-end along a metre stick?
How do you know?
Explain your work.

Reflect

When would you *not* use metres to measure?
Use words, pictures, or numbers to explain.

The Kilometre

Long distances are measured in **kilometres** (km).

It takes about 15 minutes to walk 1 km.

It takes about 10 minutes to rollerblade 1 km.

Is the distance from your home to school less than 1 km, more than 1 km, or about 1 km? How do you know?

Explore

About how many times do you think you would have to walk around the playground to travel 1 km? Decide on a strategy to find out. Write about your strategy.

Show *and* Share

Share your strategy with another group. Which is the better strategy? Draw a picture to show your strategy. How would you present your strategy to the class?

Numbers Every Day

Mental Math

Add or subtract. Explain your strategies.

$27 + 25 = \square$
$55 + 49 = \square$
$100 - 3 = \square$
$35 - 18 = \square$
$18 + 15 + 2 = \square$

LESSON FOCUS | Understand when the kilometre is used to measure distance.

A chain of 800 children stretches about 1 km.

1000 metre sticks laid end-to-end would stretch 1 km.

1000 m = 1 km

Practice

1. Which distances would be measured in kilometres?

a) from the classroom
to the library

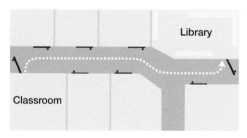

b) from Yukon to
New Brunswick

c) from the school's front
door to the street

d) from your home to
the next town

2. a) Describe two distances you would measure in kilometres.

b) When would it *not* make sense to use kilometres? Explain.

3. Match each item with its estimate: 25 cm, 10 m, 10 km

a) the distance travelled in a car

b) the length of a school bus

c) the distance travelled in 1 minute by a caterpillar

4. Suppose a corner store is 500 m from your home. Would you walk 1 km if you walked to the store and back home? How do you know? Show your work.

Reflect

Outside school, where have you seen distances in kilometres? Use words, pictures, or numbers to explain.

At Home

Talk to your family about how far it is to travel from your home to a relative's home.

Measuring Perimeter in Centimetres

Ellen is gluing coloured wool around this picture frame. The distance around the frame is its **perimeter**.

Ellen measures the perimeter of the frame. The perimeter is 24 cm.

5 cm

7 cm   7 cm

5 cm

Explore

You will need a 30-cm ruler.
➤ In your classroom, find some things whose perimeter you can measure.
➤ Estimate each perimeter. Measure each perimeter. Record your results.
➤ Here are two ways to record your work.

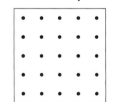

Round to the nearest centimetre when you need to.

• Make a table.

Object	Estimated Perimeter in cm	Approximate Perimeter in cm

• Draw a picture.

For the geoboard perimeter
Estimate: 16 cm
Measure: 20 cm

Show and Share

Share your strategies for estimating with another pair of classmates.
Show how you measured a perimeter.
Which was the longest perimeter? The shortest perimeter?

➤ To find the perimeter of a figure on 1-cm grid paper,
count the units along the outside of the figure.

The perimeter is 10 cm.   The perimeter is 14 cm.

➤ To find the perimeter of this figure, use a ruler to measure each side.
Then add these lengths.

5 cm

2 cm   2 cm

3 cm

3 cm + 2 cm + 5 cm + 2 cm = 12 cm
The perimeter is 12 cm.

This figure is a trapezoid.

Practice

Use a ruler when it helps.

1. Find the perimeter of each figure on 1-cm grid paper.

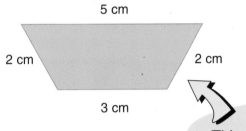

a)   b)   c)

2. Measure the perimeter of each figure.

a)

b)

c)

3. Use your answers from exercise 2.
Write the perimeters in order from greatest to least.

4. Use 1-cm grid paper. Draw a figure with each perimeter.
a) 8 cm   **b)** 12 cm   **c)** 10 cm   **d)** 18 cm

5. Choose 3 different books.
Estimate, then measure the perimeter of the cover of each book.
Write the perimeters in order from least to greatest.

6. How many different rectangles can you draw with a
perimeter of 16 cm?
Use 1-cm grid paper. Draw on the grid lines.
How do you know when you have drawn all the rectangles?

7. Trace your shoe on paper.
Find a way to measure the perimeter of your tracing.
Explain your method.

8. Find two books where the perimeter
of one is about 10 cm shorter
than the perimeter of the other.
Record your results.

Numbers Every Day

Calculator Skills

Estimate how many hours
you spend at school in
a year.

Then use a calculator
to find out. Explain
your thinking.

Reflect

Suppose an ant travelled along the
perimeter of your pencil case. Use words,
pictures, or numbers to explain how you
find the distance the ant travelled.

Measuring Perimeter in Metres

Amina wants to build a fence
around her garden.
She used metres to measure
its perimeter.
What is the perimeter of the garden?

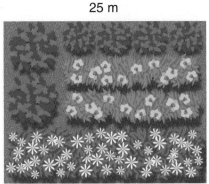

25 m

20 m   20 m

25 m

Explore

You will need metre sticks or measuring tapes.
Choose a region of the school, such as
- the classroom
- the gym
- the principal's office
- the library
- a hallway
- a storeroom

Plan how to find its perimeter.
Find its perimeter.
Record your results.

Show *and* Share

Share your plan with another group.
Show the group how you found the perimeter.
How did you record your results?
- Did you draw a picture?
- How did you label the picture?

Measure each side
of the region to
the nearest metre.

One group found the perimeter of the floor of a storeroom.
Here is the picture.

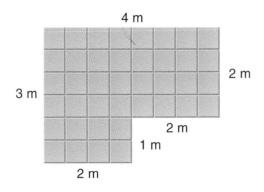

4 m

3 m

2 m

2 m

1 m

2 m

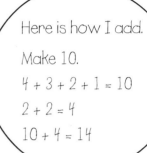

Here is how I add.

Make 10.

4 + 3 + 2 + 1 = 10

2 + 2 = 4

10 + 4 = 14

Perimeter = 4 m + 3 m + 2 m + 1 m + 2 m + 2 m
= 14 m

The perimeter of the storeroom floor is 14 m.

Practice

1. Find the perimeter of each figure.

a)

15 m

10 m

10 m

15 m

b)

25 m

25 m

25 m

25 m

25 m

c)

12 m

6 m

12 m

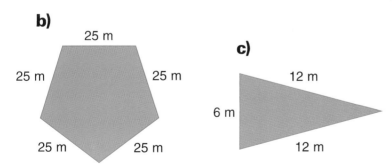

Numbers Every Day

Number Strategies

Find the missing numbers
in each pattern.
Explain your thinking.

28, 35, 42, 49, ☐, ☐, ☐

120, ☐, 100, 90, ☐, ☐

20, ☐, ☐, 32, 36, ☐

2. Use your answers from exercise 1.
Order the perimeters from least to greatest.

3. Find the perimeter of each figure.
The length of each square on the grid represents 1 m.

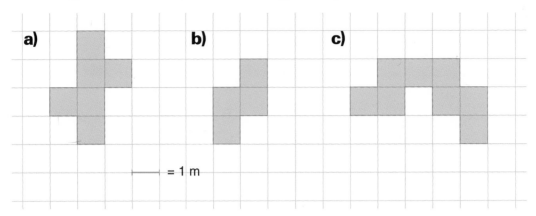

a)

b)

c)

├── = 1 m

4. Which garden plot needs the most fencing to enclose it?
How do you know?

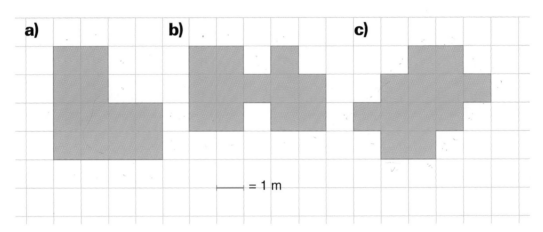

a)

b)

c)

├── = 1 m

5. Liam bought 20 m of fencing to enclose his rectangular garden.
How long and how wide could his garden be?
Draw a picture to show your answer.
How many different ways can you do this?

Reflect

How do you decide when to use centimetres or metres to measure perimeter? Use words, pictures, or numbers to explain.

Covering Figures

Louis counts how many
blue Pattern Blocks it takes
to cover this star.

Explore

You will need Pattern Blocks.

Estimate how many blue Pattern Blocks cover each figure.

Cover each figure to check your estimate.

Order the figures by the number of blocks that cover them.

Show your work.

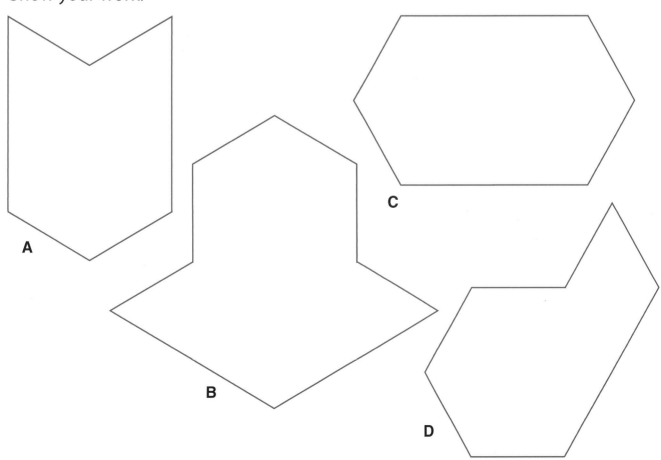

A

B

C

D

LESSON FOCUS | Count congruent non-standard units to measure area.

351

Show *and* Share

Share how you ordered the figures.
How close were your estimates to the actual numbers
of blocks?

Connect ··

The number of units needed to cover a figure is the **area** of the figure.
The units must be the same size.
You can find the area of a figure by counting how many units cover it.

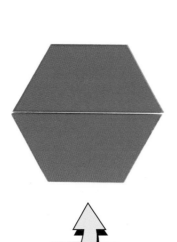

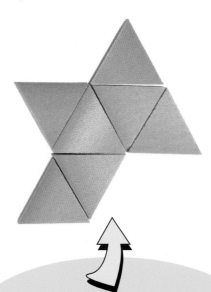

The unit is 1 red Pattern Block.
The area is 2 red Pattern Blocks.

The unit is 1 green Pattern Block.
The area is 7 green Pattern Blocks.

Math Link

Number Sense

In Unit 8, you used Pattern Blocks to find how many equal parts are in one
whole. You counted equal parts and used fractions to name them.

You now use Pattern Blocks to measure the area of a figure.
This time, the equal parts are units of area.

1. Make each figure with Pattern Blocks.
   Use 1 green Pattern Block as the unit.
   Find the area of each figure.

   a)

   b)
   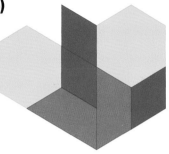

   c)

2. Make your own figure with Pattern Blocks.
   Draw the figure on triangular grid paper.
   Have a classmate find the area of the figure.
   She can choose the units.

3. Use red and yellow Pattern Blocks.
   a) Make a design with area 12 green triangles.
   b) Make a design with area between
      10 and 15 green triangles.
   c) Make a design with area
      6 blue rhombuses.
   d) Make a design with area
      9 blue rhombuses.

   Colour triangular grid paper to show
   your designs.

Numbers Every Day

Number Strategies

You say 6. I say 3.
You say 10. I say 5.
You say 30. I say 15.
Guess my rule.

You say 50. What will I say?
I say 10. What did you say?

353

4. The area of a figure is 6 green Pattern Blocks.
Draw the figure on triangular grid paper.
How many different figures can you make?
Explain how you made the different figures.

5. Use Pattern Blocks to find the area of this fish.
The unit is 1 blue Pattern Block.

6. Suppose the unit for area is 1 green Pattern Block.
How can you find the area of the fish above without
using green Pattern Blocks? Explain.

7. Use tangram pieces.

Find the area of each figure in small triangles.
a) the medium triangle   **b)** the square
c) the parallelogram   **d)** the large triangle

Reflect

Suppose you know how many blue Pattern Blocks cover
a figure. How can you find how many green Pattern Blocks
cover the same figure?
Use words, pictures, or numbers to explain.

7 Measuring Area in Square Units

Explore

You will need construction paper squares of these colours and sizes:

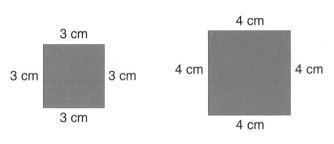

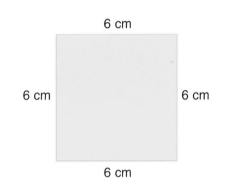

➤ Choose a classroom surface.
Estimate its area in red squares.
Measure the area.
Measure the same area in green squares, then in yellow squares.
Record your work.

➤ Repeat the activity for another classroom surface.

It took 40 red squares to cover this book. It'll take less than 40 green squares.

Show and Share

Share how you estimated, with another pair of classmates.
Show how you recorded each estimate and area.
What did you do when the squares did not cover the surface completely?

It takes 60 small squares
to cover this bulletin board.

It takes 15 large squares
to cover this bulletin board.

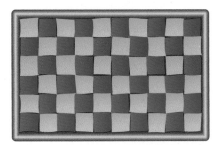

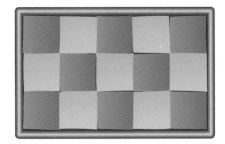

The area of this bulletin board
is 60 small **square units**.

The area of this bulletin board
is 15 large square units.

When you cover a surface with small squares,
the number of square units is greater than when
you cover the surface with larger squares.

Practice •

1. Find the area of each floor. Write your answer in square units.

a)

b)

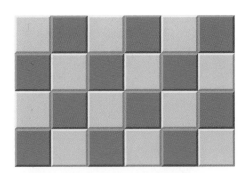

c)

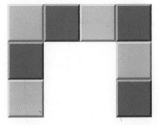

d)

2. Use your answers from exercise 1.
Order the areas from least to greatest.

3. Suppose you wanted to find the areas of the following surfaces.
Would you use small squares or large squares each time?
Explain.

a) the classroom floor

b) the lid of a shoebox

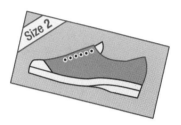

c) the cover of a book

d) the playground

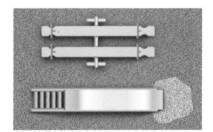

4. Jan said the area of the tabletop is 8 square units.
Madhu said the area is 50 square units.
Who is correct?
Can both Jan and Madhu be correct?
Draw pictures to explain.

Reflect

You have used different figures
to measure area.
Which figure is easiest?
Use words and pictures to explain.

Numbers Every Day

Mental Math

Subtract.
$$150 - 2 = \square$$

What strategy did you use?

Find.
$$150 - 1 = \square$$
$$150 - 3 = \square$$
$$300 - 1 = \square$$
$$300 - 2 = \square$$
$$300 - 3 = \square$$

Using Grids to Find Area

Explore

· ·

You will need grid paper.

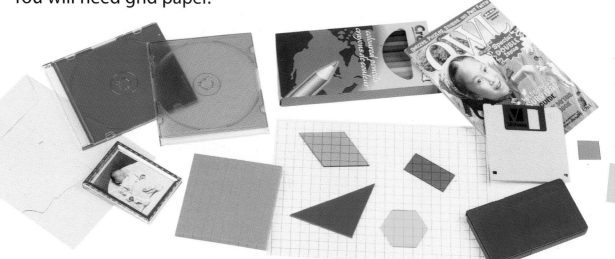

Choose 4 objects.
Trace each object onto grid paper.
Estimate the area of each tracing.
Find each area.
Record your results.

2 half squares make
1 whole square.

Show *and* Share

Show a classmate your tracings and their areas.
Share how you recorded each estimate and area.
How did you use the area of one object
to estimate the area of the next?
Which object had the greatest area? The least area?
How do you know?

Here is one way to find the area of a figure on a grid.

➤ Count the whole squares.
Put an X on each square
to keep track of the count.

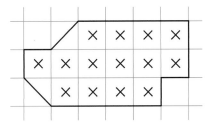

14 whole squares

➤ Next, count the half squares.
Put a dot on each half square
to keep track of the count.

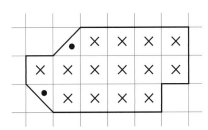

2 half squares = 1 whole square

➤ Find the total number of squares: 14 + 1 = 15
The area of the figure is 15 square units.

Practice

1. Find each area.
Write your answers in square units.

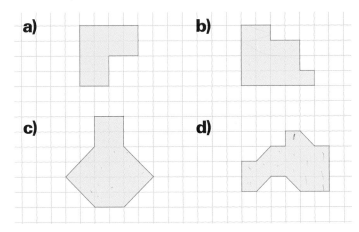

a)

b)

c)

d)

2. Use a geoboard and elastic bands.
Make a figure with each area:
a) 20 square units   b) 14 square units
c) 18 square units   d) 16 square units
Record your work on grid paper.

Numbers Every Day

Number Strategies

For this figure, are the
pieces fair shares?
Explain your thinking.

3. Use grid paper.
   Draw 3 different figures.
   Each figure should have an area of 24 square units.

4. Joe made his name in block letters.
   What is the area of each letter in his name?
   Order the letters from least to greatest area.

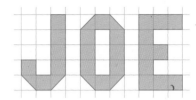

5. Write your name in block letters on grid paper.
   What is the area of each letter of your name?
   Order the letters from greatest to least area.

6. Here is a map of Ms. Sipple's backyard.
   Find the area of each section of the yard.
   Order the sections from least to greatest area.

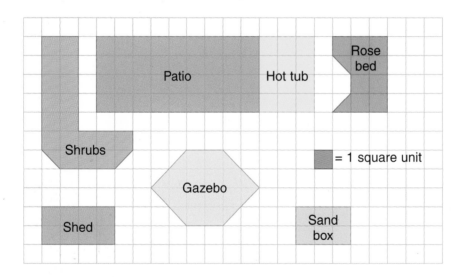

7. Use grid paper.
   Draw all the rectangles that have an area of
   18 square units.
   How do you know you have drawn all possible rectangles?

Reflect

Use words, pictures, or numbers to tell 3 things
you know about area.

Comparing Area and Perimeter

What is the perimeter of this rectangle?
What is its area?
How do you know?

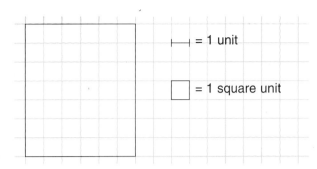

 = 1 unit

= 1 square unit

Explore

You need a geoboard, geobands, and dot paper.

➤ Make 5 different figures.
The sides of a figure must be vertical or horizontal.

You may do this: You may *not* do this:

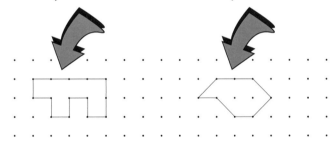

➤ Draw each figure on dot paper.
➤ Record the area and perimeter of each figure.
➤ Write what you notice about the areas and perimeters.

Show *and* Share

Show a classmate your figures and measurements.
Share what you found out about areas and perimeters.

Different figures may have the same area.

Area: 6 square units
Perimeter: 10 units

Area: 6 square units
Perimeter: 14 units

Different figures may have the same perimeter.

Perimeter: 12 units
Area: 6 square units

Perimeter: 12 units
Area: 8 square units

Practice

1. Find the perimeter (in units) and the area (in square units) of each figure.

a)

b)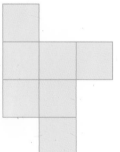

c)

2. Use a geoboard.
   Make 3 different figures with area 4 square units.
   Draw your figures on grid paper or dot paper.
   Write the perimeter and area of each figure.

Numbers Every Day

Calculator Skills

The ⑤ key is broken on Julia's calculator.

How could she display 50 on her calculator?

How could she calculate 8 × 5?

3. Find the perimeter (in units) and the area (in square units) of each rectangle.

a)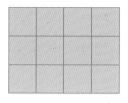

b)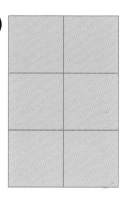

c)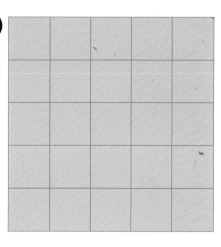

4. Use grid paper.
Draw a square that has sides 2 units long.
Write its area and perimeter.
Draw a square that has sides 4 units long.
Write its area and perimeter.
How do the two areas compare?
How do the two perimeters compare?

5. Use a geoboard.
Make a figure with the same area as this rectangle, but with a greater perimeter.
Make another figure with the same perimeter, but with a smaller area.
Draw your figures on grid paper or dot paper.

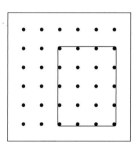

Reflect

Use words, pictures, or numbers to show how 2 figures can have the same area but different perimeters.

Strategies Toolkit

Explore

Zoe bought 4 large squares of plywood to make the floor of a pen for her rabbits. She arranges the squares so that whole sides are touching. Find the shape of the pen that needs the least amount of fencing.

Show *and* Share

Explain how you solved the problem.

Connect

Brad has 12 large squares of plywood to make the floor of a pen for his dog.
Brad wants to make a rectangular pen with the least amount of fencing.
What are the length and width of the pen Brad should make?

Strategies

- **Make a table.**
- **Use a model.**
- **Draw a picture.**
- **Solve a simpler problem.**
- **Work backward.**
- **Guess and check.**
- **Make an organized list.**
- **Use a pattern.**

What do you know?
- The pen will be made with 12 squares.
- The pen must have the shortest possible fence.

Think of a strategy to help you solve the problem.
- You can **use a model**.
- Use Colour Tiles.

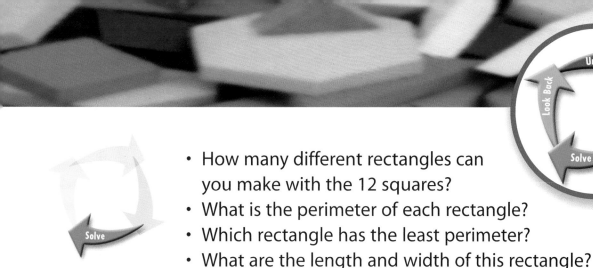

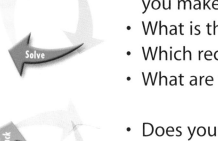

- How many different rectangles can you make with the 12 squares?
- What is the perimeter of each rectangle?
- Which rectangle has the least perimeter?
- What are the length and width of this rectangle?

- Does your pen have the least amount of fencing? How do you know?
- How could you solve the problem a different way?

Practice

Choose one of the **Strategies**

1. Suppose Zoe bought only 3 squares of plywood for the floor of her rabbit pen. How many different shapes could she make the pen? How much fencing would each shape take?

2. Calvin needs exactly 10 m of fencing to fit around his rectangular garden. What might Calvin's garden look like?

3. Raji's garden has the shape of a rectangle. Its area is 15 square units and its perimeter is 16 units. Draw Raji's garden.

Reflect

Use words, pictures, or numbers to explain how you can use a model to solve a problem.

LESSON

1 2

1. Use a ruler. Find
   a) an object longer than 20 cm
   b) an object shorter than 10 cm
   c) an object longer than 1 m
   Measure each object and record its length.

1

2. Which objects are 4 cm long? How do you know?

   a)

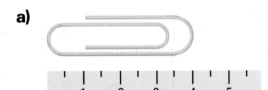

   b)

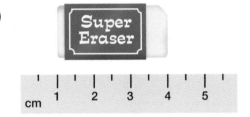

   c)

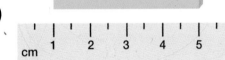

3. Find someone whose arm is about 5 cm shorter than yours. Explain how you did it.

4

4. Draw 2 different figures on 1-cm grid paper. Each figure should have a perimeter of 24 cm.

5

5. How much fencing would you need to enclose this play area?

6 7

6. Mrs. Patel's patio has an area of 16 square units. Use a geoboard. Show what you think her patio looks like. Draw the patio on grid paper or dot paper.

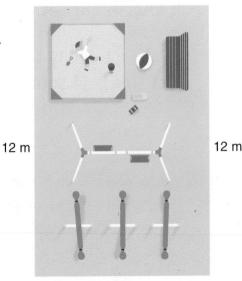

8 m

12 m   12 m

8 m

7. Here is a map of a farm.

a) Find the perimeter (in units) of the pasture, corral, barn, house, and toolshed.
Which perimeter is greatest? Least?

b) Find the area (in square units) of each part of the farm.
Which area is greatest? Least?

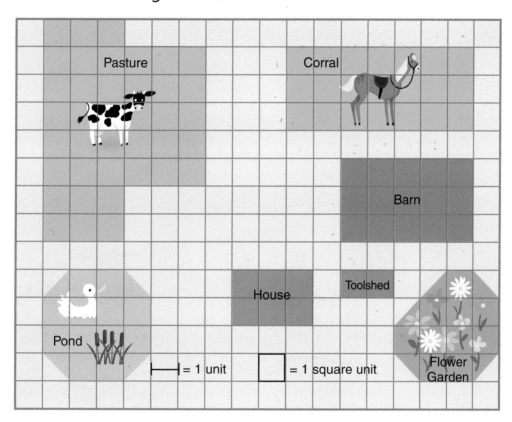

├──┤ = 1 unit   □ = 1 square unit

8. Use 1-cm grid paper.

a) How many different rectangles can you make with a perimeter of 24 cm? Draw each one.

b) Find the area of each rectangle.

c) How do you know you have found all the rectangles?

U N I T

9 Learning Goals

☑ measure lengths
☑ measure the distance around a figure
☑ measure the amount of space a figure covers

Design a Playground

The Little Owl Daycare Centre needs a new playground.
Design the playground.
Find how much fencing it needs.

Here are the guidelines:

- The playground has the shape of a rectangle.
- It is enclosed by a fence.
- It has sections for 4 or 5 pieces of equipment.
- The sections are far enough apart to make sure the children are safe.

- ➤ Use grid paper to draw a plan for your playground.
- ➤ Make a table to go with your plan. The table should show the area and the perimeter of each section.
- ➤ Tell how many units of fencing will be needed to enclose your playground.
- ➤ Explain your plan.

Reflect on the Unit

What is the difference between the perimeter and the area of a figure?
Use words, pictures, or numbers to explain.

Indoor Recess!

Learning Goals

- identify, extend, and create patterns
- describe patterns and pattern rules
- show patterns in tables and on grids

and Geometry

Key Words

pattern rule

growing pattern

repeating pattern

core

- What patterns can you see in this picture?
- How would you describe the patterns?
- What patterns can you see in your classroom?

371

Exploring Number Patterns

The numbers in the coloured squares form a pattern.

1	2	3	4	5	6	7	8	9	10
11	12	13	14	15	16	17	18	19	20
21	22	23	24	25	26	27	28	29	30

What are the next three numbers in the pattern?
How do you know?

Explore

➤ Look at these number patterns:
2, 4, 6, 8, 10, …
1, 2, 1, 3, 1, 4, 1, 5, …
90, 86, 82, 78, 74, …
1, 2, 4, 7, 11, 16, …

Describe each pattern.
Write the next three numbers in each pattern.
Record your work.

➤ Write three number patterns of your own.

Show *and* Share

Trade patterns with a classmate.
Write the next three numbers in each of your classmate's patterns.
Check each other's work.
Share how you found the next three numbers in each pattern.

Connect ●

A **pattern rule** tells how to build a pattern.
You may be able to state a pattern rule more than one way.

➤ Here is a number pattern.
1, 3, 5, 7, 9, 11, …

One pattern rule is:

Start at 1. Add 2 each time.

1   3   5   7   9   11 …
    +2   +2   +2   +2   +2

The numbers start at 1 and go up by 2 each time.

 Another pattern rule is:

The odd numbers starting at 1.

1	2	3	4	5	6	7	8	9	10
11	12	13	14	15	16	17	18	19	20

These are odd numbers.

The next three numbers in the pattern are 13, 15, 17.

➤ Here is another number pattern.
33, 30, 27, 24, 21, 18, 15, …

This pattern rule is:

Start at 33. Subtract 3 each time.

The next three numbers in the pattern are 12, 9, 6.

➤ Here is a different number pattern.
2, 3, 5, 8, 12, 17, …

This pattern rule is:

Start at 2. Add 1. The number you add goes up by 1 each time.

The next three numbers in this pattern are 23, 30, 38.

The numbers start at 33 and go down by 3 each time.

The numbers start at 2 and go up by 1 more each time.

1. Copy each pattern. Write the pattern rule.
   Fill in the missing numbers.
   a) 13, 18, 23, 28, 33, □, □, □   **b)** 22, 19, 16, 13, 10, □, □, □

2. Copy each pattern. Write the pattern rule.
   Fill in the missing numbers.
   a) 5, 6, 8, 11, 15, □, □, □   **b)** 1, 1, 2, 1, 1, 3, 1, 1, 4, □, □

3. Copy and complete each pattern.
   a) 41, 45, 49, □, □, 61, 65, 69   **b)** □, 83, 77, 71, 65, 59, 53, 47, □

4. Write the first six numbers in each pattern.
   a) Even numbers, starting at 2   **b)** Start at 1. Add 3 each time.
   c) Start at 50. Subtract 7 each time.

5. **a)** Choose a start number between 1 and 10.
   Use the pattern rule: Multiply by 2 each time.
   Write the first five numbers in the pattern.

   b) Choose a different start number between 1 and 10.
   Choose a number between 3 and 6 to multiply by.
   Write the first five numbers in the pattern.

6. Write three different patterns that begin with 2, 4, ….
   Write a pattern rule for each pattern.
   Show your work.

Numbers Every Day

Number Strategies

Write the base-ten name
for each number.

63

89

26

31

Reflect

Choose one number pattern in *Practice*.
Describe how to find the pattern rule.
Use words and numbers to explain.

Number Patterns in Tables

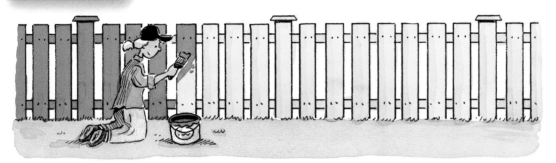

Explore

Sabina is painting her fence.
She can paint 3 sections every hour.

➤ How many sections will be painted after 2 hours? 3 hours?
4 hours? 5 hours?
➤ The fence has 21 sections.
How long will it take Sabina to paint it?

Show your work in a table.

Time in Hours	Sections Painted
1	3
2	
3	
4	

Show and Share

Compare your results
with those of another pair
of classmates.
How do you know if your results
are correct?

Numbers Every Day

Mental Math

Add.

21 + 45
35 + 99
17 + 79
52 + 18
19 + 27

Which strategies
did you use?

Greg's faucet is leaking.
Each hour, 2 L of water are lost.
How much water is lost after 3 hours? 7 hours?
How long is it before 22 L are lost?

➤ You can make a table to show the number pattern in the litres of water lost.

The pattern rule is:

Add 2 each hour.

From the table, 6 L of water are lost after 3 hours.

Time in hours	Litres of water lost
1	2
2	4
3	6

➤ Continue the pattern.
Keep adding 2.

Time in Hours	Litres of Water Lost
1	2
2	4
3	6
4	8
5	10
6	12
7	14
8	16
9	18
10	20
11	22

After 7 hours, 14 L are lost.

It takes 11 hours to lose 22 L.

Practice

1. There is a pattern in each table.
   Copy and complete each table. Write the pattern rule.

a)

Time in Weeks	Amount of Money in the Bank ($)
1	6
2	12
3	
4	24
	30
6	

b)

Row	Number of Seedlings
1	1
2	2
3	4
	8
5	16
6	

2. Jennifer made this pattern with stars.
The pattern continues.

Row	Number of Stars
1	
2	
3	
4	

Copy and complete the table for
Jennifer's pattern.
How many stars will be in Row 7?

3. The table shows how much food
and water George's dogs need
for different numbers of days.
Copy the table.
Find the missing numbers.

Days	Food (kg)	Water (L)
1	3	4
2	6	8
3	9	12
4		16
5	15	20
6	18	24
7	21	
10		

4. This is a special pattern machine.
One number goes in.
A different number comes out.
The table shows some results.
 a) What is the pattern rule?
 b) Number 6 goes in.
  What number comes out?
 c) Number 12 comes out.
  What number went in?
Show your work.

In	2	3	4	5
Out	6	7	8	9

Reflect

How does a table help to solve a problem with
number patterns? Use words and numbers to explain.

Exploring Growing Patterns

Here is a **growing pattern**.

Frame 1   Frame 2   Frame 3   Frame 4

What is the next frame in this pattern?

Explore ....

You will need Pattern Blocks.
➤ Choose one of these Pattern Blocks:

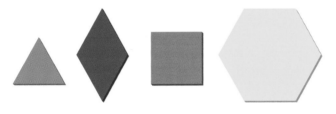

➤ Use your block to show
  the first five frames of a growing pattern.
➤ Repeat this activity with one of
  the other three blocks.

Show *and* Share

Compare your growing patterns with those
of another pair of classmates.
Count the Pattern Blocks in each frame.
What patterns do you see?

➤ Here is one way to create a growing pattern.

Frame 1

Frame 2

Frame 3

Frame 4

Frame 5

Count the number of trapezoids in each frame.
You can show this growing pattern in a table:

Frame	Trapezoids in the Frame
1	1
2	3
3	5
4	7
5	9

The table shows the pattern in the number of trapezoids in a frame.
1, 3, 5, 7, 9, …

 The pattern rule is:

Start at 1. Add 2 each time.

1. Use Pattern Blocks.
   Make the next three frames
   in each growing pattern.
   Make a table to record each growing pattern.

   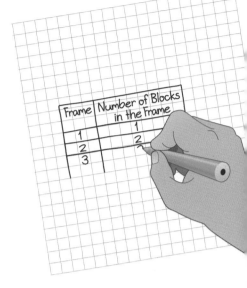

   a)

   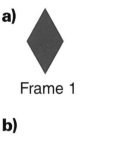

   Frame 1   Frame 2   Frame 3

   b)

   Frame 1   Frame 2   Frame 3

   c)

   Frame 1   Frame 2   Frame 3

2. Look at each pattern in question 1.
   Write the pattern rule for the number of Pattern Blocks in a frame.

3. Use Colour Tiles or congruent squares.
   Make the next three frames in each growing pattern.
   How are these patterns the same? Different?

   a)

   Frame 1   Frame 2   Frame 3

   b)

   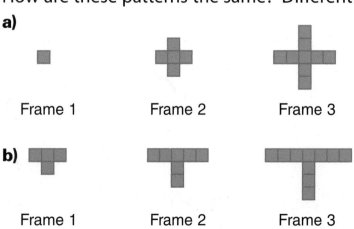

   Frame 1   Frame 2   Frame 3

4. Use Colour Tiles or congruent squares.
Make a growing pattern.
Trade patterns with a classmate.
Continue your classmate's pattern for three more frames.
Check each other's work.

5. a) Use Colour Tiles or grid paper.
Draw the next three frames in this growing pattern.

Frame 1   Frame 2   Frame 3

b) What is the pattern rule for the number of Colour Tiles in a frame?

c) Make a table to show the pattern.

6. a) Make a table to show this pattern.

Frame 1   Frame 2   Frame 3

b) How many of each Pattern Block would be in Frame 5?
How do you know? Show your work.

7. Use Pattern Blocks or Colour Tiles to make a growing pattern.
Draw the first four frames of your pattern.
Write about your pattern.

Reflect

How does a table help to show a growing pattern?
Use words, numbers, or pictures to explain.

Strategies Toolkit

Explore

Joe is building this tower.
He has lots of toothpicks,
but only 30 marshmallows.
How many levels of the tower can he build?

Work together to solve this problem.
Use any materials you think will help.

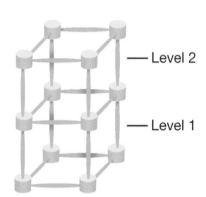

— Level 2

— Level 1

Show *and* Share

Tell about the strategy you used to solve this problem.

Connect

Jaleel is stacking Pattern Blocks.
Each level has the same blocks.
She has 23 triangles and 15 trapezoids.
How many levels can she make?
Will she have any blocks left over?

Strategies

- **Make a table.**
- **Use a model.**
- **Draw a picture.**
- **Solve a simpler problem.**
- **Work backward.**
- **Guess and check.**
- **Make an organized list.**
- **Use a pattern.**

Understand

What do you know?
- There are 3 triangles and 1 trapezoid in each level.
- There are 23 triangles and 15 trapezoids.

Plan

Think of a strategy to help you solve the problem.
- You can **use a pattern**.

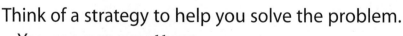

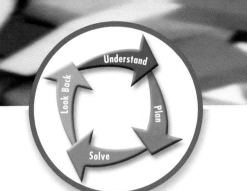

- Make a table.

Level	Total Number of Triangles	Total Number of Trapezoids
1	3	1
2	6	2
3		

Use a pattern to extend the table.
Record the total number of each block
used at each level.

How many levels can you build
before you run out of blocks?

Check your work.
How could you solve this problem another way?

Practice

Choose one of the

Strategies

1. Hakim builds a tower with hexagons and squares.
   There are 5 levels in the tower.
   Each level has 2 hexagons and 3 squares.
   How many squares and hexagons are in his tower?

2. Look at this table.
   The pattern in the table continues.
   How many triangles are in Level 1?

Level	Total Number of Triangles
7	49
6	42
5	35

Reflect

How can you use a pattern to help you solve a problem?
Use words, numbers, or pictures to explain.

Patterns with Two Attributes Changing

In Unit 5, you sorted objects.
Here are some of the attributes you sorted by.

Size	Shape	Colour	Thickness	Position
big	circle	blue	thin	
small	triangle	yellow	thick	quarter turn

What other attributes can you think of?

 **Explore**

You will need Attribute Blocks.

➤ Make a pattern in which two attributes change.
   Have your partner tell which attributes changed.
   Then have your partner continue the pattern.
   Draw a picture to show your pattern.
➤ Switch roles.
   Repeat this activity for a different pattern.

Show *and* Share

Show your patterns to another pair of classmates.
How do you know that two attributes change
in each pattern?

Here are some **repeating patterns** in which two attributes change.

➤ In this pattern, shape and colour change.

The **core** of a repeating pattern is the smallest part that repeats.

The core of this pattern is:

The pattern rule is:

Large red circle, large blue triangle

➤ In this pattern, size and thickness change.

The core of this pattern is:

The pattern rule is:

Small thin yellow square, large thick yellow square

➤ In this pattern, colour and position change.

The core of this pattern is:

The pattern rule is:

Large red triangle, 2 large blue triangles turned a $\frac{1}{2}$ turn

385

Practice

1. Which attributes change in each pattern?
   Identify the core of each pattern.

   a)

   b)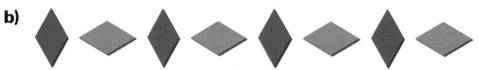

   c)

2. Which set continues the pattern?

   a)

   b)

3. Draw the next four objects in each pattern.

   a)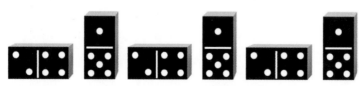

   b)

386

4. Write the pattern rule for each pattern in question 3.

5. Draw the missing objects in each pattern.

a)

b)

6. Use Attribute Blocks or Pattern Blocks.
Choose two different blocks.
Get six of each block.
   a) Make a pattern in which two attributes change.
   Draw pictures to record the pattern.
   b) Use the same blocks.
   Make a different pattern in which two attributes change.
   Record the pattern.
   Write about the patterns you made.

7. Write a pattern rule where two attributes change.
Trade rules with a classmate.
Draw your classmate's pattern.
Check each other's work.

Reflect

Choose one of the patterns you made.
Use words and pictures to show how
two attributes change in your pattern.

Numbers Every Day

Number Strategies

Divide.

$$24 \div 4$$
$$35 \div 5$$
$$12 \div 2$$

Which strategies did
you use?

Patterns with Three Attributes Changing

Explore

You will need Attribute Blocks.

➤ Choose one Attribute Block.
Use it to start a pattern in which
three attributes change.
➤ Have your partner choose an
Attribute Block to add
to the pattern.
➤ Take turns adding blocks
until you have three cores
of your pattern.
➤ Draw pictures to record your work.
➤ Repeat this activity.
Create a different pattern in which
three attributes change.

Show *and* Share

Look at the patterns you created.
How did you decide which block
to add at each step?

Exchange your patterns with those
of another pair of classmates.
Choose one of the patterns.
Tell how you know three attributes
change.

Numbers Every Day

Number Strategies

One book costs $4.99.
Estimate.

About how much do:
2 books cost?
4 books cost?
6 books cost?

Here are some repeating patterns in which three attributes change.

➤ In this pattern, colour, size, and position change.

The core of this pattern is:

The pattern rule is:

 Short red crayon, long blue crayon, long yellow crayon, short red crayon turned a $\frac{1}{4}$ turn clockwise

➤ In this pattern, size, shape, and thickness change.

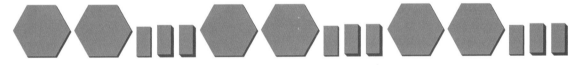

The core of this pattern is: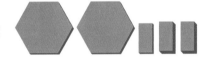

The pattern rule is:

Two large thin red hexagons, one small thin red rectangle, two small thick red rectangles

---

Math Link

Social Studies

Inuit use patterns on kamiks (boots) to show gender. Females' kamiks have horizontal bands. Males' kamiks have vertical bands.

1. Which attributes change in each pattern?

   a)

   b)

   c)

2. Draw the next three objects in each pattern.

   a)

   b)

3. What is the core of each pattern in question 2?

4. Take four each of three different Attribute Blocks.
   How many different patterns can you make with these blocks?
   Record your patterns.
   Write about your patterns.

Reflect

When you look at a pattern, how can you tell how many
attributes change? Use words and pictures to explain.

Patterns on Grids

Some patterns can be made on a grid.

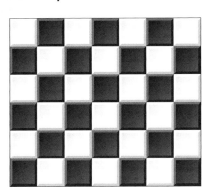

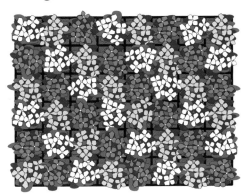

Explore

You will need Colour Tiles, or different colour congruent squares,
2-cm grid paper, and coloured pencils.

➤ Use the tiles or squares to make a pattern on a grid.
➤ Write about the different patterns you see.
➤ Use grid paper to record your work.
➤ Look across rows, down columns, and along diagonals.
  Circle the different patterns you see.

Show and Share

Compare your patterns with those of another pair of classmates.
How are the patterns the same? Different?
How could you extend your patterns?

Here is a pattern on a grid.

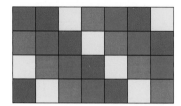

➤ The colours in the first row are:
green, blue, yellow, red, green, blue, yellow
The other rows have the colours in the same order,
but each row starts with a different colour.

➤ The colours in the first column are:
green, red, yellow, blue
The other columns have the colours in the same order,
but each column starts with a different colour.

➤ There are four colours in the pattern.
To extend the pattern across,
add four more squares to each row.
Follow the pattern:
green, blue, yellow, red

➤ To extend the pattern down,
add four more squares to each column.
Follow the pattern:
green, red, yellow, blue

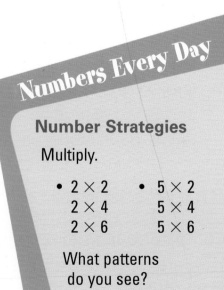

Numbers Every Day

Number Strategies

Multiply.

- 2 × 2
  2 × 4
  2 × 6
- 5 × 2
  5 × 4
  5 × 6

What patterns
do you see?

You will need 1-cm and 2-cm grid paper.

1. Use any number of these Pattern Blocks.

Use a piece of paper.
Make a pattern on the paper.
Record your pattern on grid paper.

2. Use 1-cm grid paper.
Make a grid with 5 rows and 5 columns.
Fill in the grid using the letters
of your first name in order.
Compare your pattern with that of a classmate.
How are the patterns the same? Different?

3. Use 2-cm grid paper.
Use these symbols to make a pattern on the grid.

Write about the patterns you see.
Trade patterns with a classmate.
Extend your classmate's pattern.

4. a) Use 2-cm grid paper.
Draw pictures to create your own pattern on a grid.
b) Circle all the patterns you see.
c) In which rows are the patterns the same?
In which columns are the patterns the same?
d) Write about your pattern. .

5. Sunni collected fallen leaves.
She used them to make
a pattern on a grid.

a) What patterns do you see?

b) In which rows are the patterns
the same?

c) In which columns are the
patterns the same?

d) Suppose Sunni extended the pattern.
In which row would you see the same pattern
as in the 7th row? How do you know?

6. Brian planted a garden.
He planted the flowers in a pattern.
When 10 roses are planted,
how many daisies
will be planted?
How do you know?

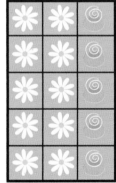

At Home

Reflect

How is a pattern on a grid the
same as a pattern in a line?
How is it different? Use words
and pictures to explain.

On a calendar page, write the
weather every day for a month.
Is there a pattern in the weather?
Write about what you see.

Patterns on a Computer

Work with a partner.
Use *AppleWorks*.

Follow these steps to create a pattern on a computer.

1. Open a new document. Click:

   Drawing

2. If a grid appears on the screen, go to Step 3.

   If not, click: | Options |

   Click: | Show Graphics Grid |

3. Check that the ruler units are centimetres.

   Click: | Format |

   Click: | Rulers ▸ |, then click: | Ruler Settings... |

   Choose these settings:

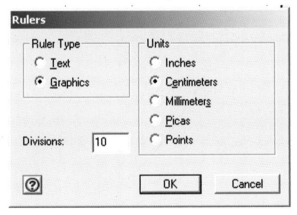

   Click: | OK |

4. Use these tools to draw:

5. To **draw a figure**, select the Tool you want.
The cursor will look like this: +

➤ Click and hold down the mouse button.
Drag the cursor until the figure is the size and shape you want.
Release the mouse button.

➤ If you are making a square or a circle,
hold down the Shift key while you click and drag.

➤ To make a regular polygon, select the Regular Polygon Tool.

Click: Edit , then click: Polygon Sides...

Key in the number of sides you want, then click: OK

6. To **move a figure**, put the cursor inside the figure.
Click and hold down the mouse button.
Drag your figure to where you want it. Release the mouse button.

7. To **colour a figure**, click the figure.

Click the Fill formatting button:

Click the Color palette button:

Then select a colour.

8. To **flip or turn a figure**, click the figure.

   Click: Arrange , then click: `Free Rotate          Shft+Ctrl+R`

   The cursor will look like this: ✕
   Put the cursor on one of the black dots on the edge of
   the figure.
   Click, hold down the mouse button, and drag the figure
   until it is in the position you want.

9. To **copy a figure**, click the figure.

   Click: Edit , then click: `Copy            Ctrl+C`

   Click: Edit , then click: `Paste           Ctrl+V`

   The copy shows on top of the figure.
   Click and drag the copy to where you want it.

10. Use Steps 5 to 9 to create a pattern.

11. Save your pattern.

    Click: File , then click: `Save As...        Shft+Ctrl+S`

    Name your file. Then click: `Save`

12. Print your pattern.

    Click: File , then click: `Print...          Ctrl+P`

    Click: `OK`

Reflect

On a copy of your pattern, write about your pattern.
Write about the attributes that change.

LESSON

1

1. Look at this number pattern: 18, 25, 32, 39, 46, …
 a) Write the pattern rule.
 b) Write the next three numbers in the pattern.
 c) Choose a different start number.
   Write a different pattern that grows the same way.

2

2. The table shows how many people can ride a roller coaster and how many tickets will be collected for different numbers of cars.

Number of Cars	Number of People	Number of Tickets
1	4	12
2	8	24
3	12	36
4	16	48
5		

 a) Describe the patterns you see in the table.
 b) How many tickets do you need to go on this ride?
 c) How many people can ride in 6 cars? Explain.
 d) Suppose the roller coaster has 8 cars.
   The ride was full. How many tickets were collected?

3

3. Look at this pattern.

Frame 1   Frame 2   Frame 3

This pattern continues.
How many squares and how many rhombuses will be in Frame 6?

5 6

4. Write each pattern rule.
Draw the missing objects in each pattern.

a)

b)

6

5. Make a pattern in which three attributes change.
Write your pattern rule.

7

6. Suppose you make a pattern with wildflowers in a garden.
Use B for buttercup. Use R for wild rose. Use L for lily.

a) Use 1-cm grid paper.
Make a pattern on a grid for the garden.

b) Describe all the patterns in the garden.

c) How can you extend your pattern?

UNIT

10 Learning Goals

☑ identify, extend, and
create patterns

☑ describe patterns and
pattern rules

☑ show patterns in tables
and on grids

Indoor Recess!

Part 1

Make a repeating pattern.

Have at least 2 attributes that change.

Record your pattern, then write about it.

Part 2

Make a growing pattern.

Draw your pattern.

Write about your pattern.

Tell how to extend your pattern.

Part 3

Design an activity for children
when recess is indoors.
Use a pattern on a grid in your activity.
Include:
- a list of materials needed
- instructions on how to complete
  the activity
- a sketch of the pattern on a grid
- a description of the pattern

Check List

Your work should show
- ☑ a picture of each pattern
  and how you made it
- ☑ how you extended your
  growing pattern
- ☑ the activity you designed
  with clear instructions
- ☑ appropriate language to
  describe the patterns
  and activity

Reflect on the Unit

Think about the patterns you made in this unit.
Choose your favourite.
Write about the pattern.
Tell what kind of pattern it is and how you made it.

UNIT 11 Probability

Games Day

Guess the Coin Toss

Learning Goals

- do experiments and predict results
- predict if something will happen
- solve probability problems
- use probability words

Key Words

· ·

impossible

possible

certain

likely

unlikely

equally likely

probability

experiment

fair

outcome

SPIN YOUR LUCK!

Look at the picture.

What are the chances that:

· it will rain?
· heads will show on the coin toss?
· 6 will show when the number cube is rolled?
· the pointer on the spinner will land on green?

Exploring Possible and Impossible

This event could never happen.
It is **impossible**.

Your cat will grow wings and fly.

This event could happen.
It is **possible**.

You will read a book today.

This event will definitely happen.
It is **certain**.

The sun will rise tomorrow.

Explore

You will need a copy of this Venn diagram.

➤ Sort these events.
- A A rock dropped into water will sink.
- B You will be at school and at home at the same time.
- C A bird will fly over your school today.
- D An ice cube will be cold.
- E A real goldfish will sing.

➤ Write down 3 different events.
  Sort these events in the Venn diagram.

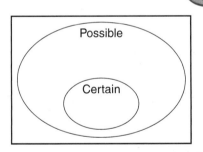

Possible

Certain

Show *and* Share

Share your results with another pair of classmates.
Where did you put events that are impossible?

Numbers Every Day

Mental Math
Add or subtract.

$9 + 8$

$7 + 5$

$13 - 4$

$18 - 6$

Which strategies did you use?

Many events are possible.

If an event probably will happen, it is **likely**.

If an event probably will not happen, it is **unlikely**.

Two events with the same chance of happening are **equally likely**.

You will talk to someone tomorrow.

You will go for a balloon ride today.

Heads and tails are equally likely.

Practice •

1. Tell if each event is impossible, unlikely, likely, equally likely or certain.
   a) You will play golf tomorrow.
   b) The sun will set in the east tonight.
   c) You will go to school on Wednesday.
   d) The driver of the next car that drives by will be female.

2. Write down 2 events that are equally likely. Explain.

3. This spinner has 4 congruent parts.
   Suppose you spin the pointer.
   a) How likely is the pointer to land on each colour?
   b) Is the pointer likely to land on yellow?
   Explain your answer.

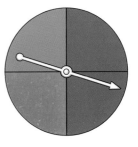

Reflect

Suppose you heard on the radio that it is likely to rain today.
Does that mean that it *will* rain? Explain.

Conducting Experiments

Explore

You will need a number cube.

➤ Suppose you roll the number cube 30 times.
How many times do you think
each number will come up?
Record your prediction.

➤ Roll the number cube 30 times.
Record the result of each roll
on a tally chart.

Number	Tally
1	
2	
3	
4	
5	
6	

➤ How do your results compare
with your prediction?

Show and Share

Compare your results with those of your classmates.
How do the tallies for each number compare?

Emi put these counters in a bag.

Emi will take out a counter 40 times.
She predicted each colour would be picked
about 10 times.

Without looking, Emi took 1 counter
from the bag.
She recorded the colour, then put the counter
back in the bag.
Emi did this 40 times.

Her results are in the tally chart.

Colour	Tally	Total
Red	ⵌ ⵌ	10
Blue	ⵌ IIII	9
Yellow	ⵌ ⵌ I	11
Green	ⵌ ⵌ	10

The totals for the colours are close.

There are 20 counters in the bag.
There are 5 counters of each colour.
So, each colour has an equal chance of being picked.

Taking a counter from a bag is an **experiment**.

When this experiment is repeated many times, each colour
will likely be drawn about the same number of times.

1. **a)** A number cube is to be rolled 40 times.
        About how many times is 5 likely to show?
        About how many times is an even number likely to show?
    b) Roll a number cube 40 times. Record the results.
    c) How do your results compare with your prediction?

2. **a)** A number cube is to be rolled 10 times.
        About how many times is 7 likely to show?
    b) Do you have to roll the number cube 10 times to find out?
        Explain.

3. **a)** Roll a number cube until you get a 6.
        Keep a tally of how many rolls it takes.
    b) Roll a number cube until you get a 4.
        Keep a tally of how many rolls it takes.
    c) Roll a number cube until you get an odd number.
        Keep a tally of how many rolls it takes.
    d) Compare your results for parts a, b, and c.
        How are they similar? Different?
    e) Do you think your results would be the
        same if you tried each part again? Explain.

4. This paper bag contains 6 marbles.
    Each marble is a different colour.
    Suppose you take 1 marble
    from the bag without looking.
    a) How likely is it you will pick
        a green marble?
    b) How likely is it you will pick
        a pink marble?
    c) How is picking a marble from the bag
        like rolling a number cube?
    Show your work.

5. Roll a number cube until you get a 3.
   a) Keep a tally of how many rolls it takes.
   b) Which word describes how likely it is that a 3 will come up on the next roll? certain, likely, unlikely, impossible Explain.

6. Design a spinner.
   Make it so that in 90 spins, the pointer will likely land on:
   • red 30 times,
   • yellow 30 times, and
   • black 30 times.
   Test your spinner.

7. This spinner has 5 congruent parts.
   Suppose you spin the pointer 50 times.
   a) How many times is each letter likely to come up?
      How do you know?
   b) Use a copy of this spinner.
      Use a paper clip for a pointer.
      Spin the pointer 50 times.
      Record your results.
   c) How do your results compare with your prediction? Explain.

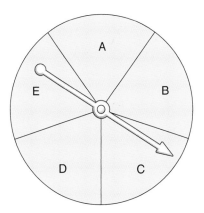

Reflect

Suppose you roll a number cube 50 times. What is likely to happen?

Numbers Every Day

Number Strategies
Divide.

$42 \div 7$ $24 \div 6$
$35 \div 5$ $28 \div 7$

Which strategies did you use?

3 Exploring Probability

Explore

You will need a paper bag and counters.
Put 1 yellow, 2 blue, 2 green,
and 7 red counters in a bag.

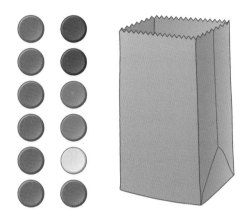

➤ Suppose you took out 1 counter,
without looking.
Is each event below impossible, unlikely,
likely, or certain? Explain.
Which events are equally likely? Explain.

A The counter is blue.
B The counter is green.
C The counter is red.
D The counter is yellow.
E The counter is orange.

➤ Without looking, take 1 counter
from the bag.
Record the colour in a tally chart.
Replace the counter and shake the bag.
Do this 50 times.
How do your results compare with
what you predicted would happen?

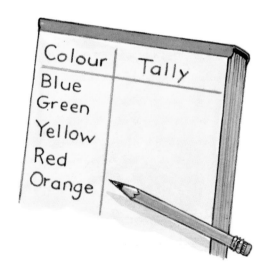

Colour	Tally
Blue	
Green	
Yellow	
Red	
Orange	

Show and Share

Share your results with another pair of classmates.
How do your results compare with theirs?

This spinner has 9 congruent parts.

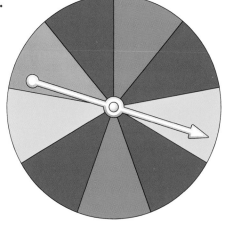

- There are more ⬤ parts than any other colour.
  The pointer is likely to land on ⬤.
- There are the same number of
  ⬤ and ⬤ parts.
  The pointer is equally likely to land on
  ⬤ or ⬤.
- There is only one ⬤ part.
  The pointer is unlikely to land on ⬤.
- Since there are no ⬤ parts,
  it is impossible for the pointer to land on ⬤.

Anita and Vivek spun the pointer 40 times.
Here is their tally chart.
The pointer landed on ⬤ more
than on any other colour.
The pointer landed on ⬤ and ⬤
about the same number of times.
The pointer landed on ⬤ only a few times.

Colour	Tally
Blue	卌 卌 卌 IIII
Green	卌 卌
Yellow	卌 III
Orange	III
Red	

Probability *tells how likely it is something will happen.*

The spinner has 9 congruent parts.

- 4 of 9 parts are ⬤.
  The probability of landing on ⬤ is 4 in 9.
- 2 of 9 parts are ⬤ and 2 of 9 parts are ⬤.
  The probability of landing on ⬤ is 2 in 9.
  The probability of landing on ⬤ is also 2 in 9.
- 1 of 9 parts is ⬤.
  The probability of landing on ⬤ is 1 in 9.

1. The pointer on each spinner is spun.
    How likely is the pointer to land on each colour:
    red, blue, green, orange, yellow?
    Use the words impossible, unlikely, equally likely, likely, or certain.

    a)   **b)**   **c)**

    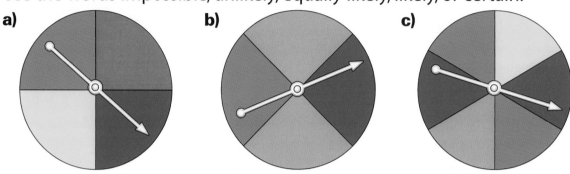

2. Look at the spinners in question 1.
    For each spinner, find the probability of the pointer landing
    on each colour.

3. Suppose you put these counters in a bag.

    You take 1 counter from the bag without looking.
    a) What is the probability
        you will pick a green counter?
        A red counter?
    b) What is the probability
        you will pick a yellow counter?

4. You will need a spinner like this one.

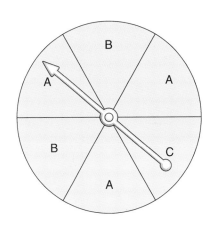

    a) Suppose you spin the pointer.
What is the probability it will land
on each letter?

    b) Spin the pointer 40 times.
Record the results in a tally chart.

    c) How do your results in part b compare
with your answer to part a?

5. Make 2 different spinners with ⬤, ⬤, and ⬤.
Make each spinner so that when the pointer is spun:
- the probability of landing on ⬤ and the
probability of landing on ⬤ are equal, and
- the probability of landing on ⬤ is greater than
landing on ⬤ or ⬤.

Explain your work.

6. Make a spinner with 2 colours.
Make it so that when the pointer is spun,
the probability of landing on black is zero.

7. You will need coloured counters and a paper bag.
Put counters in the bag so the probability of getting
red is 4 in 10.

How many counters of each colour did you put
in the bag? Explain.

At Home

Reflect

The probability of an event is
5 in 7.
How likely is that event to occur?
Use words, numbers,
or pictures to explain.

Describe an event that is
unlikely to happen at home
today. Describe another
event that is certain.

Strategies Toolkit

Explore

Arlo did an experiment.
He used a spinner with green,
yellow, red, and blue parts.
Here are his results.

What might Arlo's spinner look like?

Colour	Tally
Green	||||| |||||
Yellow	||||| ||||| ||||| ||||| ||||| |||||
Red	||||| |||||
Blue	||||| |||||

Show and Share

Describe the strategy you used to solve this problem.

Connect

Jolanta did a spinner
experiment.
Here are her results.
What might her spinner
look like?

Colour	Tally
Green	||||| ||||| ||||| |||||
Yellow	||||| |||||

Strategies

- **Make a table.**
- **Use a model.**
- **Draw a picture.**
- **Solve a simpler problem.**
- **Work backward.**
- **Guess and check.**
- **Make an organized list.**
- **Use a pattern.**

Understand

What do you know?
- The spinner has 2 colours:
  green and yellow.
- The pointer landed on green 20 times
  and yellow 10 times.

Plan

Think of a strategy to help you solve the problem.
- You could **work backward**.
- Use the results to draw the spinner.

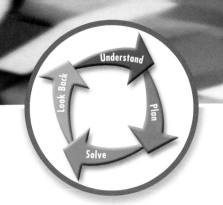

Understand

Look Back

Solve

Plan

Solve

Look Back

How are the numbers in the tally chart related?

How many congruent parts of the spinner are yellow? How many are green?

Draw the spinner.

How many different spinners can you draw?

Practice

Choose one of the

Strategies

1. Sketch the spinner that likely gave each set of data.

a)

Black	ЖЖ ЖЖ
Red	ЖЖ ЖЖ
Orange	ЖЖ ЖЖ
Green	ЖЖ ЖЖ

b)

1	ЖЖ ЖЖ ЖЖ ЖЖ
2	ЖЖ ЖЖ
3	ЖЖ ЖЖ

2. The numbers 1, 2, 3, and 4 were written on the faces of a solid.
The solid was rolled 40 times.
The results are in the tally chart.
Name the solid you think was used.
Explain your choice.

1	ЖЖ ЖЖ I
2	ЖЖ IIII
3	ЖЖ IIII
4	ЖЖ ЖЖ I

Reflect

How does working backward help to solve a problem?
Use words and numbers to explain.

Fair and Unfair Games

Explore ....  Game

You will need a paper bag and
15 congruent cards, numbered 1 to 15.

Numbers in a Bag

How to Play
- Take turns to pick a number card
  without looking.
- Player A gets a point if the number
  is even.
  Player B gets a point if the number
  is odd.
- After each turn, put the card back and shake the bag.
- The first player to get 10 points wins.

➤ Does each player have an equal chance of winning? Explain.
➤ Play the game.
  Record the results of each turn in a tally chart.
  Compare your results with your prediction.

Show *and* Share

Share your results with
another pair of classmates.
How can you tell if
each player has an equal
chance of winning?

Math Link

Fractions

This spinner has
6 congruent parts.
Each part is a
different colour.
Each part is $\frac{1}{6}$ of the whole.
So, it is a fair spinner.

A game is **fair** if all players have
an equal chance of winning.
To tell if a game is fair,
find the probability of each **outcome**.

The Spinner Game  Game

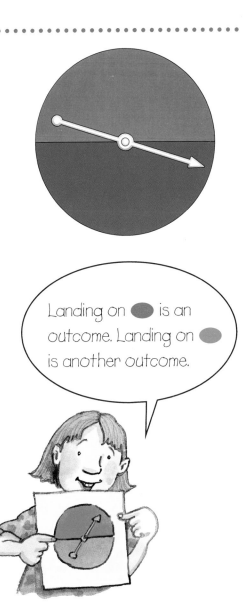

How to Play
- Take turns to spin the pointer.
- If the pointer lands on ●,
  Player A gets a point.
  If the pointer lands on ●,
  Player B gets a point.
- The first player to get 10 points wins.

➤ This spinner has 2 congruent parts.
  The probability of landing on ●
  is 1 in 2.
  The probability of landing on ●
  is also 1 in 2.
  The probabilities are equal.
  So, this is a fair game.

Landing on ● is an outcome. Landing on ● is another outcome.

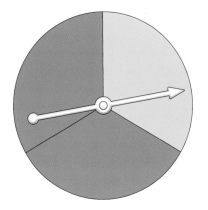

➤ Suppose you used this spinner
  to play The Spinner Game.
  This spinner has 3 congruent parts.
  The probability of landing on ● is 2 in 3.
  The probability of landing on ● is 1 in 3.

  The probabilities are different.
  So, this game is unfair.

Practice

For questions 1 to 3:

Read the rules for the game. Answer these questions:

• Is the game fair?
• How do you know?

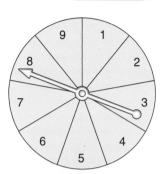

1. The pointer is spun.
Player A gets a point if the pointer lands on an even number.
Player B gets a point if the pointer lands on an odd number.

2. The pointer is spun.
Player A gets a point if the pointer lands on ●.
Player B gets a point if the pointer lands on ●.

3. A number cube is rolled.
Player A gets a point if 1 or 2 shows.
Player B gets a point if 3, 4, 5, or 6 shows.

4. Suppose you are playing a game.
Is rolling a number cube
a fair way to decide who goes first?
Explain.

Reflect

What makes a game fair?
Use words, pictures, or numbers
to explain.

Numbers Every Day

Number Strategies

A notebook costs 99¢.
You have $10.
About how many
notebooks can
you buy?

LESSON

1

1. a) How likely is it to rain today? Explain.

  b) How likely are you to grow 1 cm in height in 1 day?

2

2. a) The pointer on this spinner is to be spun 40 times. About how many times will the pointer land on each letter?

  b) Use a spinner like this. Spin the pointer 40 times. Record the results.

  c) How do your results compare with your prediction?

3

3. A marble is picked from this bag. What is the probability you pick:

  a) a green marble?

  b) a yellow marble?

  c) a blue marble?

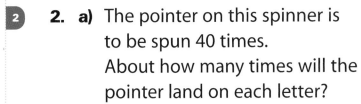

5

4. You will need a number cube and counters.

  ➤ Take turns to roll the number cube.

  ➤ Player 1 takes a counter if an odd number shows.

  ➤ Player 2 takes a counter if an even number shows.

  ➤ Play until one player has 10 counters.

  Is this a fair game? Explain.

UNIT

11 Learning Goals

☑ do experiments and predict results

☑ predict if something will happen

☑ solve probability problems

☑ use probability words

Games Day

Design a fair game for Games Day.
You may use number cubes and counters.
You may make a game board and a spinner.

Write the rules for your game.
Play your game with a classmate.
Write about your game.
How do you know the game is fair?

Your work should show
- ✓ your design for a fair game
- ✓ a record of what happens when you play the game
- ✓ how you know your game is fair
- ✓ a clear explanation of the rules

Reflect on the Unit

Write one important thing you learned about probability.
Use words, pictures, or numbers to explain.

How Do Your Feet Measure Up?

You will need a ruler, 1-cm grid paper, string, scissors, and measuring tape.

Part 1

Take off one shoe.

Trace your foot on grid paper.

- How long is your footprint from the tip of your big toe to your heel?
- How wide is your footprint across the narrowest part? The widest part?
- How could you find the area of your footprint?
  Try out your ideas.

Record your results. Show your work.

Part 2

➤ How would you find the perimeter of your foot?
  Try out your ideas. Write about what you did.

➤ Find a classmate whose footprint has about the same area as yours.
  Are the footprints congruent? Explain.
  How do the perimeters compare? Explain.

Part 3

➤ Look at all the shoes your classmates took off.
  Choose 2 attributes. Choose 6 shoes.
  Sort the shoes. Record your sorting.
➤ Choose 3 attributes. Choose 6 different shoes.
  Sort the shoes. Record your sorting.

Part 4

Put all the shoes in a bag.
Suppose you pick a shoe without looking.
How likely are you to pick a shoe the same
colour as your shoe?
Do an experiment to find out:
➤ Pick a shoe. Record its colour.
  Return the shoe to the bag.
➤ Repeat this activity the same number
  of times as there are shoes in the bag.
➤ Draw a graph to show your results.
How can you use your graph to find the
likelihood of picking a shoe the same
colour as your shoe? Explain.

 ## Display Your Work

Make a poster to show all you found out
about feet and shoes.

Take It Further

Is it likely that the tallest person in your class
wears the largest shoes?
Write down your prediction.
Find out if your prediction is true.
Write about what you found out.

UNIT

1

1. Start at 350. Count on by 25s to 1000.
Write each number you count.
What patterns do you see in the ones digits?
The tens digits? The hundreds digits?

2. Round each number to the nearest hundred.
    a) 490   **b)** 752   **c)** 361   **d)** 640

2

3. 9, 5, and ☐? are the numbers in a set of related facts.
    a) What could the missing number be?
        Write the related facts.
    b) What is another possible missing number?
        Write the related facts for this number.

4. Five hundred sixty-seven children
are at a track and field meet.
- 163 are track competitors.
- 139 are field competitors.
- The rest are in the stands.

How many children are in the stands?

3

5. a) Which solids below are prisms? How do you know?
    b) Which solids below are pyramids? How do you know?

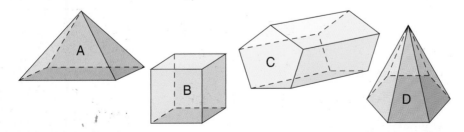

6. Name each solid above.
For each solid, count the number of faces, edges, and vertices.

7. Use a copy of this picture.

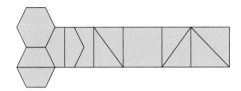

Name each figure.
Which figures are congruent? How do you know?

8. Write the related multiplication and division facts
for each set of numbers.

a) 3, 3, 9   **b)** 5, 7, 35   **c)** 6, 1, 6   **d)** 8, 2, 16

9. What might the missing numbers be?
How many answers can you find?

a) $\square \times \square = 24$ **b)** $\square \div \square = 3$

10. Ali bought stickers for his collection.
He bought 4 strips of 5 stickers.
He also bought 6 strips of 3 stickers.
How many stickers did Ali buy? How do you know?

11. Madison surveyed two grade 3 classes
to find the children's favourite school subject.
Here are her results.

a) How many students did Madison survey?
b) How many students prefer language arts?
Do not prefer language arts?
How are the two answers related?
c) Draw a bar graph.
d) Draw a pictograph.
e) Which graph shows the data better?
Explain.

Children's Favourite School Subjects

Subject	Number
ART	11
LANGUAGE ARTS	16
MATH	12
SCIENCE	5
SOCIAL STUDIES	9

12. Which unit would you use to measure each capacity?

a)    b)    c)    d)

13. Which unit would you use to measure each mass?

a)    b)    c)    d)

14. Use a copy of the figures below.
   a) Name each figure. Draw its lines of symmetry.
   b) How many lines of symmetry are in each figure?

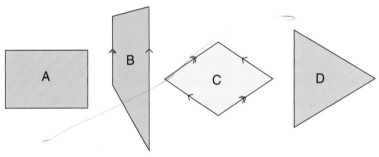

15. Draw a picture to show $2\frac{3}{8}$ pies. How many eighths is this?

16. Would you measure each item in centimetres, metres, or kilometres? Explain.
   a) the height of the CN Tower
   b) the length of a squirrel
   c) the distance from Halifax to Vancouver

17. Use grid paper.

   a) Draw all the rectangles that have an area of 24 square units. How do you know you have drawn all of them?

   b) Find the perimeter of each rectangle.

10

18. Copy each pattern. Write each pattern rule. Fill in the missing numbers or objects.

   a) 6, 7, 9, 12, 16, ☐, ☐, ☐

   b) ○ ● ☐ ■ ○ ● ☐ ■ ○ ☐ ☐ ☐ ○ ● ☐ ■

19. Sketch a pattern in which 3 attributes change. Write your pattern rule.

20. The table shows the length of Jack's beanstalk and the number of magic beans it sprouted each day. The pattern continues.

   a) Copy and complete the table.

   b) Extend the table for 3 more rows.

   c) How long will the beanstalk be on Day 10? How many beans will it sprout? How do you know?

Day	Length of Beanstalk (cm)	Number of Magic Beans
1	7	3
2	14	
3	21	9
4		12
5	35	15

11

21. You will need a number cube and counters.  **Game**

   ➤ Take turns to roll the number cube.

   ➤ On each turn, the player takes the number of counters that shows on the number cube.

   ➤ Keep playing until one player has 25 counters.

Is this a fair game? Explain your thinking.

Illustrated Glossary

Addition fact: $3 + 4 = 7$ is an addition fact. The sum is 7. See also **Related facts**.

Analog clock: A clock that shows time by hands moving around a dial.

Angle: Two sides of a figure, or lines, meet to form an angle.

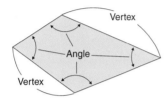

Area: The number of congruent units that cover a figure.

The unit is 1 green block. The area of the yellow block is 6 green blocks.

Array: A set of objects arranged in equal rows.

Attribute: A way to describe a figure or solid; for example, number of sides, number of vertices.

Axis (plural: axes): A number line along the edge of a graph. We label each axis to tell what data it displays.

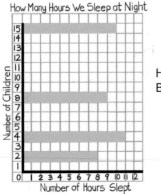

Horizontal Bar Graph

Bar graph: Shows data using bars on a grid. The graph in axis is a horizontal bar graph. The graph below is a vertical bar graph.

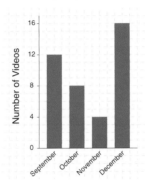

Base: The face that names a solid. See **Prism**.

Base Ten Blocks: Blocks used to model whole numbers. Here is one way to model 158:

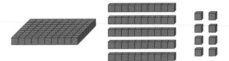

Base-ten name: See **Place value**.

Capacity: A measure of how much a container holds. We measure capacity in litres or millilitres.

Centimetre: A unit to measure length, width, and height. We write one centimetre as 1 cm.

Certain: Will definitely happen.

Circle graph: Shows data using a circle divided into parts.

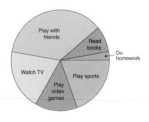

Clockwise / Counterclockwise: The hands on a clock turn in a clockwise direction. The opposite direction is called counterclockwise.

Counterclockwise

Clockwise

Compare: To look at how items are alike as well as different.

Cone: A solid with a circular base, a curved surface, and a vertex.

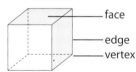

Congruent: Figures, or solids, that have the same size and shape.

Core: See **Repeating pattern**.

Cube: A solid with 6 faces that are congruent squares. Two faces meet at an edge.

Cylinder: A solid with 2 congruent circular bases joined by a curved surface.

Data: Facts or information collected to learn about people or things.

Degrees Celsius: Temperature is measured in degrees Celsius (ºC).

Diagonal: Means "on a slant."

Difference: The result of a subtraction. The difference of 9 and 5 is 4; or $9 - 5 = 4$.

Digit: See **Place value**.

Digital clock: A clock with numbers and no hands.

Divide: To separate into equal parts.

Divisible: A number is divisible by 5 if that number of counters can be divided into 5 equal groups.

15 can be divided into 3 groups of 5. We say: 15 is divisible by 5.

Division sentence: $6 \div 3 = 2$ is a division sentence.
We say: 6 divided by 3 equals 2.

Doubles: 1. The addition of 2 numbers that are the same. Doubles have an even sum. **2.** Rolling two of the same number when using number cubes.

Edge: See **Cube**.

Elapsed time: The amount of time from the start to the end of an activity. The elapsed time between when you eat lunch and when you leave school is about 3 hours.

Equally likely: Events are equally likely when they have the same chance of happening.

Estimate: Close to an amount or value, but not exact.

Experiment: Conduct an activity to gather data.

Face: See **Cube**.

Factor: See **Multiplication sentence**.

Fair: Not favouring one outcome more than another. A game is fair if all players have an equal chance to win.

Figure: A geometric drawing or diagram.

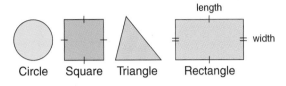

Circle   Square   Triangle   Rectangle

Flip (or reflection): Reflects a figure in a line to create a congruent image.

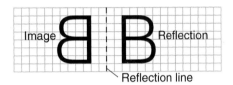

Fractions: Congruent parts of a figure are named with fractions. Common fractions: one-half ($\frac{1}{2}$), one-third ($\frac{1}{3}$), one-quarter ($\frac{1}{4}$), one-fifth ($\frac{1}{5}$), one-sixth ($\frac{1}{6}$), one-eighth ($\frac{1}{8}$), and one-tenth ($\frac{1}{10}$).

Gram: A unit to measure the mass of an object. We write one gram as 1 g.

Grid: A system of equally spaced vertical and horizontal lines that divide a flat surface into rows and columns for easy reference. A map is drawn on a grid.

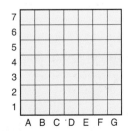

Growing pattern: A pattern that grows in number.

Height: The measurement from top to bottom.

Horizontal: To the left or right.

Image: See **Flip**.

Impossible: Could never happen.

Key: See **Pictograph**.

Kilogram: A unit to measure the mass of an object. We write one kilogram as 1 kg.

Kilometre: A unit to measure long distances. We write one kilometre as 1 km.

Length: The measurement from end to end; how long something is. See **Figure**.

Likely: Probably will happen.

Line of symmetry: Divides a figure into 2 congruent parts. Some figures have more than 1 line of symmetry.

A square has 4 lines of symmety.

Litre: A unit to measure the capacity of a container. We write one litre as 1 L.

Mass: Measures how much matter is in an object. We measure mass in grams and kilograms.

Metre: A unit to measure length, width, and height. We write one metre as 1 m.

Millilitre: A unit to measure the capacity of a container. We write one millilitre as 1 mL.

Mixed number: Has a whole number part and a fraction part. $2\frac{1}{3}$ is a mixed number.

Multiplication sentence: $2 \times 3 = 6$ is a multiplication sentence.

$$2 \times 3 = 6$$

The numbers we multiply are **factors**.

The answer is the **product**.

We say: 2 times 3 equals 6.

Near doubles: The result of adding a number to the next counting number. For example, $7 + 8 = 15$.

Net: A cutout that can be folded to make a model.

Number line: Has evenly spaced numbers marked in order.

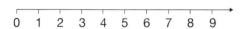

Order: To place in sequence according to some rule.

Ordinal number: A number that shows order or position: 2nd, 4th, 25th.

Outcome: One result of an event or an experiment. Tossing a coin has 2 possible outcomes: heads or tails.

Parallel lines: Two lines that are always the same distance apart and never meet.

Parallelogram: A figure with 4 sides, where 2 pairs of opposite sides are parallel.

Pattern rule: Tells about a pattern or tells how to make a pattern.
1, 4, 7, 10, 13, 16, …
The pattern rule for this pattern is: Start at 1. Add 3 each time.

Perimeter: The distance around a figure. We can find perimeter by measuring and adding side lengths. The perimeter of this rectangle is:
$2 \text{ cm} + 4 \text{ cm} + 2 \text{ cm} + 4 \text{ cm} = 12 \text{ cm}$

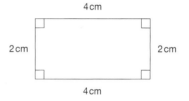

Pictograph: Uses pictures or symbols to show data.

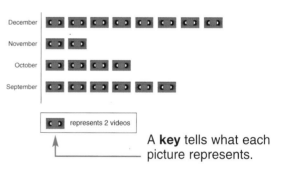

A **key** tells what each picture represents.

Place value: The value of each digit in a number depends on its place in the number.

Hundreds	Tens	Ones
4	9	7

The value of this digit is 4 hundreds, or 400.

The value of this digit is 9 tens, or 90.

The value of this digit is 7 ones, or 7.

The base-ten name is 4 hundreds 9 tens 7 ones.

Polygon: A closed figure with three or more straight sides. We name a polygon by the number of its sides. For example, a five-sided polygon is a pentagon.

Possible: Could happen. Possible events can be likely, equally likely, or unlikely.

Prism: A solid with 2 bases. The shape of the bases gives the name to the prism.

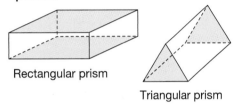

Rectangular prism

Triangular prism

Probability: How likely it is something will happen.

Product: See **Multiplication sentence**.

Pyramid: A solid with 1 base and triangular faces. The shape of the base gives the name to the pyramid.

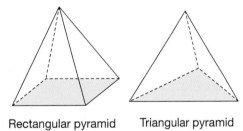

Rectangular pyramid   Triangular pyramid

Quarter hour: One-fourth of an hour, or 15 minutes.

Rectangular prism: See **Prism**.

Reflection line: See **Flip**.

Regular figure: Has all sides equal and all angles equal. A square is a regular figure.

Related facts: Addition and subtraction have related facts.
4 + 3 = 7 is related to 7 − 3 = 4.
Multiplication and division have related facts.
5 x 2 = 10 is related to 10 ÷ 5 = 2.

Repeating pattern: A pattern with a core that repeats. The smallest part that repeats is the core.

core

Rhombus: A parallelogram with 4 equal sides.

Right angle: Two sides of a figure, or lines, that make a square corner at the vertex form a right angle.

90°

Rotation: See **Turn**.

Round: Replace a number by an approximate value of the number.

Scale: The number of items each square on a bar graph represents.

Slide (or translation): A slide moves a figure along a line. The figure does not turn. This picture shows a slide.

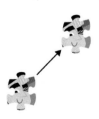

Sphere: A solid shaped like a ball.

Square unit: Area is measured in square units.

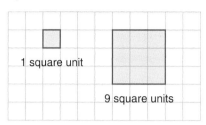

Standard form: Numbers written using digits: 37, 904.

Subtraction facts: 11 − 7 = 4 and 11 − 4 = 7 are subtraction facts. See also **Related facts**.

Sum: The result of an addition. The sum of 2 and 3 is 5; or 2 + 3 = 5.

Survey: Used to collect data. You can survey your classmates by asking them which is their favourite sport.

Tally chart: A chart on which a count is kept.

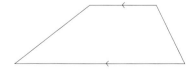

Thermometer: Used to measure temperature in degrees Celsius.

Trapezoid: A figure with 4 sides, where 2 sides are parallel.

Triangular prism: See **Prism**.

Turn (or rotation): A turn moves a figure around a turn centre. After 1 turn, the figure is back to where it started.

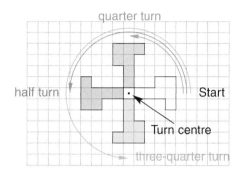

Turn centre: See **Turn**.

Unit: A standard amount used for measuring.

Unlikely: Probably will not happen.

Venn diagram: A diagram that is used to sort items.

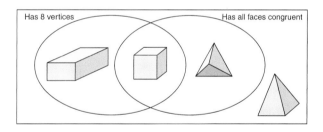

Vertex (plural: vertices): 1. A point where 2 sides of a figure meet.
2. A point where 2 or more edges of a solid meet.

Vertical: Straight up and down.

Width: The distance across something; how wide it is. See **Figure**.

Index

Acknowledgments

The publisher wishes to thank the following sources for photographs, illustrations, and other materials used in this book. Care has been taken to determine and locate ownership of copyright material in this text. We will gladly receive information enabling us to rectify any errors or omissions in credits.

Photography

Cover Image David Nunuk/firstlight.ca; p. 2 Ian Crysler; p. 3 Ian Crysler; p. 8 (top) Ray Boudreau; p. 8 (bottom) Ian Crysler; p. 15 Ian Crysler; p. 16 Ian Crysler; p.19 Ian Crysler; p. 22 Ian Crysler; p. 27 Ian Crysler; p. 35 Ian Crysler; p. 44 Ian Crysler; p. 45 Ian Crysler; p. 46 Photodisc Collection/Photodisc Blue; p. 53 (left) Robin Sachs/PhotoEdit Inc.; p. 53 (right) Martin Rogers/Photographer's Choice; p. 54 Ian Crysler; p. 56 Ian Crysler; p. 64 Ray Boudreau; p. 65 Ian Crysler; p. 66 Ian Crysler; p. 68 Ian Crysler; p. 77 Corel Collection; p. 80 David Young-Wolff/PhotoEdit Inc.; p. 81 Ian Crysler; p. 93 Ray Boudreau; p. 94 Ian Crysler; p. 97 Rene Johnston/Canapress; p. 100 Ian Crysler; p. 107 Ian Crysler; p. 119 (top) Tate Gallery, London/Art Resource, N.Y.; p. 119 (bottom) Ian Crysler; p. 124 (top left) Corel Collection; p. 124 (top right) Ian Crysler; p. 124 (bottom) Ian Crysler; p. 128 Ian Crysler; p. 135 (top) J. David Andrews/Masterfile; p. 135 (bottom) Ian Crysler; p. 137 Ray Boudreau; p. 142 Ian Crysler; p. 143 Ian Crysler; p. 144 Mary Kate Denny/PhotoEdit Inc.; p. 146 Ian Crysler; p. 149 Ian Crysler; p. 152 Ian Crysler; p. 155 Ray Boudreau; p. 168 Ian Crysler; p. 172 Shaun Best/Canapress; p. 174 Ian Crysler; p. 181 Ian Crysler; p. 183 SW Productions/Photodisc; p. 187 Rudi Von Briel/PhotoEdit Inc.; p. 190 (top) Photodisc Collection/Grade School; p. 190 (bottom) Eyewire/Photodic Collection ; p. 191 (top) David Madison/Stone; p. 191 (bottom) Nicola Sutton/Life File; p. 192 Ian Crysler; p. 195 Ray Boudreau; p. 201 Larry Dale Gordon/Image Bank; p. 207 Ian Crysler; p. 208 Ian Crysler; p. 215 (left) Jim McGuire/Index Stock; p. 215 (right) Pat Powers and Cherryl Schafer/Photodisc; p. 218 Ian Crysler;

p. 220 Ray Boudreau; p. 221 Don Smetzer/Stone; p. 226 (top left) Corbis/Royalty-free; p. 226 (top right) Corel Collection; p. 226 (centre) Corel Collection; p. 226 (bottom left) Corel Collection; p. 226 (bottom right) Lawrence M. Sawyer/Photodisc Green; p. 227 Ian Crysler; p. 228 Ian Crysler;

p. 236 Ian Crysler; p. 237 Ian Crysler; p. 238 James Gritz/Photodisc; p. 242 (left) PhotoLink/Photodisc Green; p. 242 (centre) foodpix; p. 242 (right) Karl Weatherly/Photodisc; p. 245 Ian Crysler; p. 247 Ian Crysler; p. 256 Ken Gigliotti/Canapress; p. 257 Ray Boudreau; p. 258 Ian Crysler; p. 261 Ian Crysler; p. 264 Ian Crysler; p. 267 Ian Crysler; p. 273 Ian Crysler; p. 276 Used by permission of *Chess Monthly* magazine, published by The London Chess Centre, London UK; p. 280 Comstock; p. 283 Ray Boudreau; p. 286 Ray Boudreau; p. 288 Ray Boudreau; p. 290 Ray Boudreau; p. 292 Russell Illig/Photodisc Green; p. 294 Ray Boudreau; p. 298 Ray Boudreau; p. 300 Ian Crysler; p. 301 Ian Crysler; p. 302 Ray Boudreau; p. 304 Ray Boudreau; p. 307 Ray Boudreau; p. 308 Ray Boudreau; p. 309 Ray Boudreau; p. 312 Ray Boudreau; p. 322 Ray Boudreau; p. 334 Ray Boudreau; p. 337 Ray Boudreau; p. 338 Ray Boudreau; p. 342 (left) Michael Newman/PhotoEdit Inc.; p. 342 (right) David Young-Wolff/PhotoEdit Inc.; p. 343 Ray Boudreau; p. 344 Ian Crysler; p. 345 Ray Boudreau; p. 348 Ray Boudreau; p. 351 Ray Boudreau; p. 355 Ray Boudreau; p. 358 Ray Boudreau; p. 361 Ian Crysler; p. 368 Ray Boudreau; p. 369 (left) Lawrence Migdale/Stone; p. 369 (right) Michael Newman/PhotoEdit Inc.; p. 378 Ian Crysler; p. 388 Ian Crysler; p. 389 Galen Rowell/Corbis/Magma Photo.com; p. 391 Ian Crysler; p. 394 Ian Crysler; p. 395 GeoStock; p. 400 Ian Crysler; p. 406 Ian Crysler; p. 413 Ray Boudreau; p. 416 Ian Crysler; p. 420 Ian Crysler; p. 421 (left) Don Smetzer/PhotoEdit Inc.; p. 421 (right) Bill Aron/PhotoEdit Inc.; p. 422 Ian Crysler; p. 423 Ian Crysler

Illustrations

Amid Studios
Jackie Besteman
Linda Hendry
Brian Hughes
André Labrie
Paul McCusker
Mike Opsahl
Dusan Petricic
Michel Rabagliati
Bill Slavin
Neil Stewart
Craig Terlson